Current Issues in Accounting

Philip Allan textbooks in Business Studies

Consulting Editors:

BRYAN CARSBERG
Professor of Accounting, University of Manchester

W DUNCAN REEKIE
Lecturer in Business Policy, University of Edinburgh

RAYMOND THOMAS
Professor of Business Administration, University of Bath

Current Issues in Accounting

Editors:

BRYAN CARSBERG and TONY HOPE

University of Manchester

Philip Allan

First published 1977 by

PHILIP ALLAN PUBLISHERS LIMITED
MARKET PLACE
DEDDINGTON
OXFORD OX5 4SE

0 86003 503 4 (hardback)
0 86003 603 0 (paperback)

Set by Preface Limited, Salisbury
Printed in Great Britain by The Camelot Press Limited, Southampton.

Contents

Preface

We first saw the need for a book such as this when we were working jointly on the development of the introductory course in accounting at the University of Manchester. Traditionally, introductory courses in accounting had concentrated on the basic techniques of financial accounting, leading to the preparation of profit and loss accounts and balance sheets, and perhaps also on the fundamentals of managerial accounting. Many texts on these subjects were available to provide a framework for courses. However, we wished to depart from traditional patterns in a number of ways. We wished to introduce students to a wide range of topics which they would study later at a more advanced level. We wished to present the analytical principles of financial decision taking in a way which would demonstrate the common basis for financial and managerial accounting and provide a structure within which to evaluate the strengths and weaknesses of traditional techniques. We wished to show some of the extent to which other social sciences — particularly economics and behavioural sciences — could contribute to the development of accounting; and we wished to provide an introduction to some research problems of topical importance. We hoped that such an approach would enable students to gain insight, at an early stage of their studies, to the significance of accounting in modern society whilst preparing themselves effectively for more advanced work. We found a shortage of background reading available to help with these wider objectives and designed this book to provide the material which we thought to be required. We believe that many other courses have similar needs.

The book comprises seventeen chapters each of which is self-contained. Consequently, the chapters may be used in any sequence and selectively and the book has the flexibility to be used with various alternative syllabi. Each chapter has been written by an expert on the topic concerned but the writing is at an elementary level, assuming no advanced background knowledge. The book is primarily intended to be used to supplement a basic text in first and second year courses at degree level and in foundation studies for professional students. However, its precise role will vary according to the structure of the course concerned and it may well be suitable for use by final-year undergraduates and postgraduates reading for degrees in general business studies. We hope also that the book will be of interest to professional accountants and business managers who wish to obtain a view of some important modern developments in accounting.

The chapters of the book may be classified into three main groups, leaving unclassified three chapters of a more general nature. The first chapter provides a historical introduction to the subject and is included because of our belief that the rationale of current practices may be understood only in a historical context. The second chapter gives a survey of the present organisation of the accounting profession. It will help students to understand some of the organisational background to modern developments. Next follows the first of the three main groups of chapters. It comprises four chapters dealing with topics which have been the subject of rapid development and often controversy recently: the drive to achieve standardisation of financial accounting practice, the accounting implications of the United Kingdom's membership of the European Economic Community, the treatment of inflation in accounting reports and methods of conducting audits by which independent accountants report on whether published accounts disclose a 'true and fair' view.

The second group of chapters examines a traditional subject, the preparation of accounts for publication, in a modern framework. It adopts a 'user-oriented' approach, examining information requirements from four different viewpoints, those of: the shareholders, whose needs have most often been the focus of attention in the past; the representatives of employees, whose interests have recently come to the forefront of debate; society at large, in recognition of the social responsibilities of organisations; and the government, as a taxing authority. The fifth chapter in this group considers the special factors which affect the accounts of nationalised industries, responsible today for the management of such a large proportion of national resources.

The third group of chapters explores the contributions made to accounting by five closely related disciplines: economics, a fundamental subject the contribution of which has been recognised only recently in accounting; finance, which might be regarded as part of accounting according to some definitions but which has a distinct methodology; operational research, which brings mathematical methods to bear on the analysis of financial decisions; behavioural science, which recognises the importance of human behaviour to the design of accounting systems; and computer science, which has transformed the information handling capacities of accounting systems. The book concludes with a chapter which discusses the nature of research in accounting and examines some subjects which seem likely to represent the main challenges to research capabilities for the next few years.

We should like to thank our colleagues in the preparation of this book. They include the recent Technical Director of the Institute of Chartered Accountants in England and Wales and members of nine different university departments; five, apart from ourselves, are at the University of Manchester. We are grateful for their ready agreement to participate in the venture and for helping us to meet a tight timetable for publication, in spite of many competing pressures on their time. In this and other ways they eased our job as editors. We should also like to thank Debbie Jameson and Colette White for the efficiency with which they carried out the secretarial work.

University of Manchester   Bryan Carsberg
                                                     Tony Hope

1
Historical background to accounting

JOHN FREEAR
Senior Lecturer in Accounting, University of Kent

Introduction

The intention of this chapter is to set the historical background to this book. An historical perspective will be used to consider the evolution of accountancy, and the extent to which it has conditioned, or been conditioned by, its environment. The word 'accountancy' will be taken to mean the work of public practitioners — 'the accountancy profession' — and the word 'accounting' will be used to describe the subject to be studied. It will become clear that accounting encompasses more, much more, than 'double-entry' or any other form of 'book-keeping', although the terms are often regarded as synonymous. Within the subject of accounting, 'financial' accounting is often distinguished from 'management' accounting. Financial accounting is usually taken to mean the reporting of the affairs of the organisation to interested parties outside the organisation, whereas management accounting deals with the provision of reports about the organisation to its managers. Although the distinction can be helpful, there is a real danger of its obscuring the common foundations of both branches and the extent to which they are related.

Accounting is, in the first place, the recording of data about economic events, expressed mostly, but not exclusively, in numerical form. No one is likely to go to the trouble and expense of recording such data unless, thereby, some purpose is to be served or some need is to be met. Secondly, accounting consists of communicating the data for use. What constitutes 'useful data' (here described as 'information') is, ideally, to be arranged between the producer of the data and the potential user of the information. Considerable difficulties may arise in negotiating the information element in the data, particularly if there are many potential users of information. Different users may have different information needs, which may also change over time. One solution to this problem is to arrange separate information sets to meet separate information needs; this would be desirable, but cumbersome and expensive. Another solution is to arrange a single 'compromise' set of data which will, hopefully, meet most of the needs of most users. This is, broadly, what modern company annual accounts seek to do, although it is arguable that they satisfy no one's needs. A third solution is to 'transmit' all available data and leave the user to select his own information, but there is a danger that information is 'lost' in all the data and is, as a result, poorly communicated.

Why is information needed? It is needed primarily for decision purposes, that is, to assist the user in making a decision. This definition is compatible with the three-fold division of accounting into policy decisions, control of policy decisions and the reporting of the results of policy decisions. The prime reason for reporting results is to enable the recipient to take a decison. For example, one might imagine that a shareholder likes to receive the annual accounts of 'his' company in order to decide whether to continue, increase, diminish or relinquish his holding; or, where this is possible, to seek to influence its affairs more directly. The process of control requires that decisions must be taken to correct any departures from the decided policy. Policy decisions are the more major, strategic decisions about future courses of action. The outcome of past decisions may be useful as a guide to future decisions, but if the decision concerns new and untried courses of action, there may be little or no available information.

In this chapter, it will not be possible to do more than

outline the more important developments in the history of accounting. The emphasis will be almost exclusively on industrial and commercial organisations in Britain. The rest of the chapter is in five sections: the first deals with accounting before the Industrial Revolution; the second discusses the place of double-entry book-keeping in accounting history; the third reviews, very briefly, 'internal' accounting particularly over the last hundred years; the last two sections concentrate on 'external' accounting from the Industrial Revolution onwards. It is hoped that the Notes and References section at the end of the chapter will enable the reader to supplement the discussion in this chapter.

Accounting before the Industrial Revolution

The heading of this section implies rather a long time span ending about the start of the Industrial Revolution in Britain. It is probably true that the reliability and availability of historical evidence is in inverse proportion to its distance in time from the present. No detailed study of 'ancient accounting' can be carried out here. It may be observed, however, that documented accounting practices appear to be in accord with the basic ideas of meeting the informational needs of users, given the constraints of the high cost of recording materials and the high degree of popular illiteracy. In Britain, most accounting during the first 1500 years AD was concerned with secular and religious estates. The main emphasis was on the control and accountability of stewards and agents, and a system, commonly known as the 'charge and discharge' system was developed to effect this control. The 'charge' was the balance, in the hands of the steward, at the start of the period plus sums of money and other property which ought to have been received during the year; the 'discharge' was any sums properly spent by the steward, property or other goods properly disposed of, and the balance at the end of the period. The sum of the charges equalled the sum of the discharges. The steward's accounts were subject to audit by the owner or his representative. Often, quite elaborate 'internal' accounts were maintained by stewards, both for internal control purposes and also so that proper account could be rendered to the owner. So far, the parallels with 'modern' accounting are considerable; but accounts were kept more for the protection of the steward — to show that he had performed his tasks as required — than for the purposes of indicating changes in net wealth. 'No clear distinction was made between capital and revenue expenditures, the cost of the horse being recorded in much the same way as the cost of the hay it consumed. Expenses might be allocated to various activities in detail, to show the results of each, but overall profit and loss was normally of little interest. Sometimes an account narrative was interrupted to make room for estimates of what might have been earned if a different course of action had been taken.'[1]

Without forgetting the link between medieval stewardship and modern notions of stewardship relating to managers of large public corporations, we must now move away from estate accounting towards trade or commerce. What follows is hard to fit into even an approximate time scale; it might, however, be said to describe the most common forms of 'business' organisation before the joint stock company with limited liability. Table 1, which summarises the following discussion, has many inadequacies: it oversimplifies the relationships and it says nothing about how successfully user needs were met. It is best seen as expressing the likely information requirements of owners of businesses, and how these were met.

Under the most simple conditions a trader in sole, direct control of his business could probably manage without written records. The scale of his operations would be such that he would work among his possessions and stock-in-trade and so be able to maintain a continual check on them. His main preoccupation would be to make a gross profit (the difference between the buying price and the selling price of his stock) of a size sufficient, according to past experience, to cover any overheads (unlikely to be a significant amount) and to preserve his accustomed lifestyle. If he (or, on his death, his heirs) wished to estimate his wealth, a list or 'inventory' could be drawn up of all his possessions. If he wanted to check any net increase in his wealth, he could compare the current inventory (or stocktaking) with the last inventory. The inventory need not be exclusively in money terms, and would frequently encompass all his material possessions, not just his trading

Table 1

Form of organisation	Information needs of users	Information needs supplied by
Direct sole control by owner	Knowledge of: (1) physical quantities of assets owned; (2) prices paid for assets to be traded as a guide to selling price by the addition of a gross profit margin.	Physical inspection; memory; records in the form of infrequent inventory lists.
Indirect sole control by owner (some direct control by stewards or managers)	Knowledge of: (1) as above; (2) as above; (3) physical quantities of assets in hands of stewards or managers.	Physical inspection; memory; records in the form of inventory lists divided between inventory in the hands of stewards or managers and inventory in the hands of the owners; some form of *accountability* of stewards or managers to owners.
Direct joint control by more than one owner (Partnership, joint venture)	Knowledge of: (1) as above; (2) as above; (3) above — not applicable; (4) proportion of business owned by each owner, and any changes.	Physical inspection; memory; records in the form of inventory lists and of transactions between owners and organisation; *recognition of separate existence of organisation*; irregular final accounting, e.g. on death or ownership changes.
Indirect joint control by more than one owner (some direct control by stewards or managers)	Knowledge of: (1) as above; (2) as above; (3) physical quantities of assets in hands of stewards or managers. (4) proportion of business owned by each owner, and any changes.	Physical inspection; memory; inventory records; transaction records; 'stewardship' records and periodic or irregular accountability checks; inventories and final accounting irregularly, e.g. on death or ownership changes.

assets. Thus, it would be no easy matter to calculate a 'net profit' — not that he would have any need for such a calculation.

As soon as the trader begins to buy or sell goods without giving or receiving immediate payment, the need for a more formal recording method becomes urgent. Debts payable or receivable are negative or positive items of wealth and must feature in his assessment of his wealth in the same way as bolts of cloth. If he has given credit, that is, handed over goods without receiving immediate payment, evidence of the debt to him must be recorded in some way. Otherwise, the intangible nature of the debt would make it difficult for him to prove his claim in a legal action to recover the debt.

Suppose now that the trader's business expands so that he can no longer keep personal direct control over all aspects of it. He will probably introduce 'stewards' or 'managers' to act on his behalf. His control over his possessions must now be conducted, partly at least, through his control of his stewards. It is no longer sufficient for him occasionally to take an inventory of what the stewards have; he must also know what they ought to have. The parallels with steward-ship in landed estates are clear; but the 'trading steward' is perhaps less easy to control, because he is more involved in selling goods for cash and might therefore be able to avoid accounting for some of the sale proceeds, unless the market is tightly controlled.

A further development of our sole trader's business career might be that he takes his steward into partnership. The questions to be resolved are the proportions of the business to be owned by each of them. Notice that the business is now separated from the personal affairs of the partners, and the relationships between the partners and between each of them and the business will have to be agreed upon, and any transactions affecting the relationships will have to be recorded in a way which is satisfactory to both partners. Every now and then, the current state of the business will be assessed by inventory and subsidiary records and the amounts due to or from the business from or to each partner will be estimated. Such an accounting will take place on the death or retirement or admission of a partner and at such other times as the partners decide. If the partnership is seen as a temporary one, for example, the financing of a trading voyage as a joint venture, the partnership will be terminated when all the proceeds of the venture have been disposed of. Further extensions of the partnership organisation include the employment of stewards or managers by the partners, and the taking into partnership of 'dormant' partners who supply finance but not time and expertise. Another extension is that of 'joint stock' companies, which will shortly be discussed.

Throughout this section, the emphasis has been on the control of movements of physical resources, of stewards and managers, and on the relationships among joint owners. What of policy decisions? An obvious, and possibly common, policy decision is to continue to operate the same business in the same way, with the result that control is dominant. If alternative policies are considered — if only to be rejected — then they have to be evaluated. This might be done 'intuitively', although experience and knowledge do much to educate the intuition, or the decision might be taken more explicitly on the basis of estimates and calculations. These might well draw on the accounting records, but to some extent they will be conjectural. In any event, they tend not to enter into the formal records of the organisation. The chances of their survival are thus reduced, making it hard for the historian to assess their prevalence or importance. A surviving example of the degree of sophistication which might be reached in decision calculations can be seen in the series, 1610 to 1620, of farm accounts kept by Robert Loder of Harwell, Berkshire. Each year he grappled with the problem of whether to grow more wheat or more barley, using records of past results and quantifying what would have happened if he had adopted a different cropping policy, to help him to decide on future policy.[2]

Double-entry book-keeping

The information needs of the organisations so far considered could be met without the use of double-entry book-keeping yet Table B of the 1856 Companies Act, which had statutory force unless a company drew up its own regulations, required that the books of the company had to be kept on a double-entry basis. We may wonder why a particular system of recording was given official recognition. It is not possible, here, to embark on a full description of the system.[3] The system recognises and records the movements and changes of resources and indebtedness by recording each movement or change twice. For example a debtor pays to a trader the money he owes; the double-entry system would record this as both a reduction in his indebtedness and an increase in the trader's cash balance. To ensure that this duality of all entries is preserved, accounts are deliberately created to provide a 'home' for the second entry. The internal arithmetical accuracy of the records can be confirmed by checking that the sum of the first entries equals the sum of the second entries; but this check does not discover that a wrong figure has been entered twice, correctly, into the system, nor does it discover an entry made in the correct way but in the wrong account. The first published text on double-entry book-keeping was by Luca Pacioli in 1494. It is clear from his work and from other evidence, that he was recording, refining and generalising mercantile practices which had developed over the previous two or three centuries. Essentially, double-entry is a very adaptable, versatile and flexible classifying system which does not determine the nature of the data with which it has to deal. In this sense it is neutral, and has little influence on profit calculations and asset valuations other than to ensure that there is consistency between the two.[4] The complexity of the system necessitated some form of training in its use. This, no doubt, was a cause of the large number of texts, particularly in the eighteenth and nineteenth centuries, which expounded, often in the form of long lists or rules, the working of the system. The need for training in its use, however rudimentary that training might be, could be said to have had two effects. First, some people were, perhaps, diverted from attempting to master the complex system towards other, simpler, systems.[5] Second, those who did persevere successfully were then able to operate the system efficiently with all the advantages previously mentioned, so that other, less sophisticated systems, probably suffered by comparison. What effect those factors had on the extent to which double-entry was used in practice is far from clear from the evidence that is available.

To pick up a point referred to earlier: the production of balance sheets and profit and loss accounts does not depend upon the use of the double-entry system. Indeed, many of the writers up to the nineteenth century regarded the balance sheet and profit and loss account as a byproduct of the system, not a central feature. Often it was recommended that a balance sheet need only be prepared when the ledger's pages were full.[6] Account balances which were to be carried to the new ledger (e.g. cash, debtors) were entered directly in the balance sheet; account balances which did not need to be carried to the new ledger (e.g. household expenditure) were transferred to the profit and loss account, only the balance of which was entered in the balance sheet. In this way, the system produced, mechanically, balance sheets and profit and loss accounts. For these purposes, a physical inventory was not needed, because the account balances recorded, at original transaction cost, the assets and liabilities of the organisation. For the purposes of control and accuracy checks, this 'mechanical' system worked: but the profit and loss account balance came to be regarded, in the nineteenth century, both as an indicator of the organisation's performance and as a limit to the amount of cash (dividend) which might be paid to owners; and the balance sheet came to be seen as a measure of the organisation's worth. Perhaps because double-entry was one of the few reliable weapons in the accountant's armoury, its output, in the form of balance sheet and profit and loss account, was not regarded as critically as it should have been. Little attention was paid to what information was needed by shareholders and on what theoretical basis this information should be produced and communicated. Although we might, therefore, accept that double-entry is essentially neutral, its practitioners came to use its mechanical production of sets of accounts as a substitute for a more fundamental reappraisal of the purpose of those accounts. In this sense, at least, the influence of double-entry book-keeping on company accounting in the nineteenth and twentieth centuries has been appreciable. Some writers, particularly Sombart, have expressed the view that double-entry book-keeping was essential to the 'flowering of the spirit of capitalism'. Other writers, such as Yamey, have refuted this view, and the debate seems to be continuing.[7]

Accounting within the organisation from the Industrial Revolution onwards[8]

Until the advent of 'absentee' owners of large joint stock companies, the emphasis of accounting was on information for internal control and decision. Reporting to 'outside' users was to be found mainly in the affairs of landed estates and governments. More is known of the external reporting practices of companies than about their internal records and systems, mainly because of statutory disclosure requirements and because the whole point of this facet of accounting is to communicate externally, on a selective basis, internal data. In considering internal accounting, great reliance has to be placed upon the public utterances of practitioners in the form of textbooks, lectures and articles. These, however, only appeared in any numbers in the last quarter of the nineteenth century; a major work was by E. Garcke (an engineer) and J. M. Fells (an accountant) entitled *Factory Accounts*, first published in 1887, which is a good, if regrettably rare, example of cooperation between the two disciplines. Before this, we are left to assume that the double-entry system, or other systems of recording, supplied control and decision information, which satisfied the needs of managers of companies in analogous ways to those described in pre-industrial Britain.

We shall see that a major difficulty confronting those responsible for external reporting was the treatment of fixed assets; this problem showed itself internally as a problem of how to deal with costs which could not readily be identified with a single product or process and/or which were seen not to vary according to production volume. These costs are commonly known as 'overheads'. Elaborate systems could be, and were, devised to ascertain and to allocate direct and variable costs to products or processes, but overheads were a different matter. One way of dealing with them was to allow a big enough 'profit margin' between the price and the identifiable costs of a product to cover overheads and leave enough distributable profit. In the depression of the late nineteenth century, managers began to appreciate the need for information about the cost structures of their organisations, for product pricing purposes. This led to overheads being allocated, perhaps as a percentage addition to labour costs, or some other arbitrary way. Thus, total costs were spread over total production so that prices could be calculated which allowed an adequate overall profit. Some writers observed that arbitrary allocations of overheads could distort pricing and profits, and could produce strange results if the company were not achieving normal productive activity levels. Suppose, for example, that an addition of 150% to the direct labour costs of a product was regarded as sufficient to recover the overheads, at normal activity levels. If the activity levels fell by one half, because fewer units were being sold, an addition of 300% to direct labour would be needed to recover the overheads. The consequent substantial product price rise would not necessarily be a natural entrepreneurial response to falling demand. The recognition of this problem had two aspects. First, it led to a reconsideration of the nature of costs for decision-making purposes; a distinction was increasingly made between costs which were affected by a decision and those which were not. From this developed ideas of 'marginal costing' and the 'contribution margin' approach which are themselves related to economic ideas of cost. Second, the idea of 'normal' activity levels caused attention to be directed towards the positive control of costs rather than just the passive ascertainment of costs; the efficiency of production could be measured, and steps taken to improve it. From these ideas stemmed the 'scientific management' school of thought and what later became known as 'standard costing' — the comparison of actual outcomes with predetermined standards. All these developments shifted the emphasis towards control and decisions and away from merely recording and reporting, important though these are in the business organisation. That internal accounting might have reacted more than external accounting to the needs of users may be attributed to several factors: first, the users are much less remote than external users and, in any case, are often in a position to dictate requirements; second, their needs are less diverse than the range of potential users of external accounts; and third, the internal accounting function has had to work more closely with other functions which involved other disciplines such as economics (particularly in the areas of costs for decisions, and in finance) and, more recently, behavioural science,

computing and management science. Contact with such
disciplines might have induced an awareness of some of the
limitations of accounting practice.

Accounting from the Industrial Revolution to 1900

The increasing use of large-scale, more capital intensive
methods of production required more financing and a
greater permanence of organisational form. The typical
industrial organisation in the late eighteenth and early nineteenth centuries was the partnership. Under the 1719
Bubble Act, repealed in 1825, partnerships were limited to
six partners; joint stock companies could only be created by
Royal Charter, Letters Patent or private Act of Parliament,
often known as parliamentary companies. These
companies, usually with limited liability, were the main
vehicle for the creation (in 1830) and extension of the
railway system. By means of incorporation and limited
liability, absentee investors could be persuaded to buy a proportion of the company (in the form of shares) in the
knowledge that, if the company failed, their liability to meet
its debts would be limited to their nominal shareholding in
the company.

Provided that they had paid in full for their shares they
could 'only' lose the money they had contributed for the
shares. The rest of their personal wealth, if any, could not be
touched by unsatisfied creditors of the company. The regulation of parliamentary companies, particularly as regards
record keeping, regular accounting and audit, was
strengthened by the Company Clauses Consolidation Act,
1845 for all parliamentary companies subsequently created.
This Act was amended in 1863 and 1869. The Joint Stock
Companies Act, 1844 allowed the generality of organisations to achieve corporate status by registration with the
Board of Trade. The Act required regular balancing of the
books, the production of a 'full and fair' annual balance
sheet, signed by the directors and audited by one or more
shareholders, who had wide powers of inspection and
inquiry and who could employ 'accountants' as assistants.
The main audit emphasis was on checking the solvency of
the company and the honesty of the directors. There was no
guidance as to the basis of asset valuation or as to the

specific form in which the balance sheet was to be presented, or indeed as to how auditors were to decide whether or not the balance sheet was 'full and fair'. No profit and loss statement was required. These, and other, deficiencies in the Act led to its abuse; for example, directors were able to file, with the Registrar of Companies, statements which revealed little about the company's affairs and, indeed, it was possible to file identical balance sheets year after year. The Registrar was given no powers to deal with such abuses.

The 1844 Act was a brave attempt at the regulation of corporate accountability, but it could be argued that its promoters tried to go too far too quickly. Many of the provisions about the regulation of accounting and auditing were important and far-sighted, but could not, at the time, be put into effect. There was no organised accounting profession to whom the shareholder-auditors could turn for professional services of guaranteed minimal quality; nor had there been any consistent or coordinated attempt to settle on a body of conventions — let alone an underlying theoretical structure — for the regulation of such matters. Chatfield[9] points out that the very absence of these factors at once made the attempt at legal regulation necessary and rendered it inadequate. Following the granting of limited liability to all registered companies, by the 1855 Act and the consolidating Joint Stock Companies Act 1856, the accounting and auditing regulations of the 1844 Act were replaced by 'model' regulations (Table B, 1856 Act) which could be, but did not have to be, adopted by registered companies. The model balance sheet in table B is reproduced here as table 2. Thus, the legislators, instead of providing for more rigorous enforcement of the 1844 accounting and auditing regulations, removed them from the statutory requirements. These were continued, in voluntary form, as Table A of the Joint Stock Companies Consolidation Act, 1862, which remained in force until 1908.

Although shareholders' liability could, from 1855, be limited, it was still substantial. Shareholders entrusted their money to directors who, if the permissive regulations of the 1856 Act were adopted, had to produce an annual balance sheet for audit by representative shareholders. The position of creditors had, however, been weakened by the introduction of limited liability. In the event of the failure of the

Table 2   Form of balance sheet referred to in Table B.

Dr.   BALANCE SHEET of the

CAPITAL AND LIABILITIES.

		£ s. d. £ s. d.

I. Capital   Showing:

1.   The total Amount received from the
     Shareholders; showing also:
     (a) The number of Shares
     (b) The Amount paid per Share
     (c) If any Arrears of Calls, the
         Nature of the Arrear, and
         the Names of the Defaulters.
         Any Arrears due from any Di-
         rector or Officer of the Com-
         pany to be separately stated.
     (d) The Particulars of any forfeited
         Shares.

II. Debts and   Showing:
Liabilities of   2.   The Amount of Loans on Mortgage or
the Company   Debenture Bonds.
                  3.   The Amount of Debts owing by the
                       Company, distinguishing—
                       (a) Debts for which Acceptances
                           have been given.
                       (b) Debts to Tradesmen for Supplies
                           of Stock in Trade or other
                           Articles.
                       (c) Debts for Law Expenses.
                       (d) Debts for Interest on Debentures
                           or other Loans.
                       (e) Unclaimed Dividends.
                       (f) Debts not enumerated above.

VI. Reserve   Showing:
Fund   The Amount set aside from Profits to
                        meet Contingencies.

VII. Profit   Showing:
and Loss   The disposable Balance for Payment
                        of Dividend, &c.

Contingent   Claims against the Company not ac-
Liabilities   knowledged as Debts.
                        Monies for which the Company is
                            contingently liable.

PROPERTY AND ASSETS.

£ s. d. £ s. d.

III. Property
held by the   4.
Company

Showing:
Immovable Property, distinguishing:
   (a) Freehold Land
   (b)   ,,   Buildings
   (c) Leasehold   ,,

           5.

Movable Property, distinguishing
   (d) Stock in Trade
   (e) Plant

The Cost to be stated with De-
ductions for Deterioration in
Value as charged to the Reserve
Fund or Profit and Loss.

IV. Debts
owing to the   6.
Company

Showing:
Debts considered good for which the
   Company hold Bills or other Se-
   curities.

           7.

Debts considered good for which the
   Company hold no security.

           8.

Debts considered doubtful and bad.

Any Debt due from a Director
or other Officer of the Company
to be separately stated.

V. Cash and
Investments   9.

Showing:
The Nature of Investment and Rate of
   Interest.

          10.

The Amount of Cash, where lodged,
   and if bearing Interest.

company, no longer could they look to the personal fortune
of the shareholders, beyond that represented by their shareholding in the company, for the satisfaction of their claims.
Some creditor protection was offered by the compulsory
addition of the warning word 'limited' to the company's
name, and by an examination of the company's balance
sheet, if it was available. Now that creditors could only look
to the capital of the company for the satisfaction of their
claims, this capital had not to be eroded by excessive
payments of dividends to shareholders. The 1862 Act ruled
that dividends were not to be paid other than out of profits.
Although the 1856 and 1862 Acts went into some detail
about the items to be taken into account in arriving at a
'profit' figure, nothing was set down about the basis of asset
valuation, on which the profit figure depended. There is a
clear implication in Article 71 of the 1856 Act that assets
were to be maintained at recorded, historic transaction cost:
'where any item of expenditure which may in fairness be
distributed over several years has been incurred in any one
year the whole amount of such items shall be stated, with
the addition of the reasons why only a portion of such
expenditure is charged against the income of the year'. This
treatment of 'fixed assets' has a modern ring, and is to be
contrasted with the haphazard practice of fixed asset
accounting which seemed to have obtained in many
companies in the nineteenth century.[10] The importance of
the 'profit' concept — and the related concept of asset
valuation — thus became important from two points of
view: shareholders, who were assumed to be concerned
primarily with cash dividends, recognised that their
dividends would be constrained by profits; creditors were
concerned that dividends were only paid out of profits,
otherwise the capital of the company would shrink, and
with it the security for their claims. As there were no clear
guidelines as to the calculation of profit and the valuation
of assets, other than those to do with dividends and capital
maintenance, it was perhaps natural for the growing
profession of accountancy to believe that the historic transaction costs, which were already used, mechanically, by the
double-entry system to produce a set of accounts, were
adequate for these purposes. Of course, there were difficulties, which were to a large extent the result of dividing a

company's existence into arbitrary time periods of one year for the purposes of accountability. For example, profits would be distorted if the whole cost of an item of equipment were charged against the profits of one year, when it would also be instrumental in earning revenues in later years. Profits would also be distorted, at least for comparative purposes, if repairs to equipment were charged against profits in one case or added to the cost of the asset (capitalised) in another. Costs and revenues were to be matched both to the relevant year and to each other. As a result, the profit figure moved further away from a 'cash' basis towards what is now known as an 'accruals' basis.

There is some disagreement among accounting historians about the development of the doctrine of 'conservatism' in accounting.[11] In essence, the doctrine requires that it is better to understate asset values and profits than to overstate them, because understatement has fewer unpleasant consequences (such as shareholders receiving a lower dividend than otherwise) compared with overstatement (the risk of paying dividends out of capital). There seems to be little doubt that this doctrine came more into prominence from the 1870's onwards, when the newly organised accountancy profession was faced with increasing numbers of business failures. Examples of the application of this doctrine are the valuation of stock-in-trade at the lower of cost or market value, and the recognition, by prior provision, of anticipated losses, but not recognising gains until they have been realised. It is also clear from the available evidence, that some nineteenth century accountancy practices were far from conservative. In the early days of the railways, for example, locomotives were often not depreciated, nor were repairs always charged against profits, so that profits were overstated (in comparison with more modern accounting practice) and excessive dividends paid.

By the end of the nineteenth century, profits seemed to be calculated broadly along modern lines: an accruals basis rather than a cash basis was adopted; fixed assets were usually depreciated over their useful lives and attempts were made to distinguish between capital and revenue items; stock-in-trade was valued at the lower of cost or market value; and anticipated losses were provided for, but not anticipated gains. However, disclosure requirements then were less stringent than now and this, among other effects, enabled directors to build up 'secret reserves' against un-happier times by excessively rapid depreciation policies, excessive provisions against losses and liabilities, and charging 'capital' items to 'revenue'. Most of these practices could be said to derive from the statutory requirement of 1862 that dividends must not be paid other than out of profits.

Accounting from 1900 onwards

The year 1900 saw the next major piece of accounting legislation: the introduction of compulsory annual auditing of companies along the lines of Table B, 1856 and Table A 1862 — which, as there had to be something to audit, meant the compulsory production of annual accounts. Before 1900, there had been some unsuccessful attempts to reintroduce the permissive accounting and auditing regulations of 1856 and 1862 as statutory require-ments, but most of the legal activity related to case law inter-pretations of the meaning of profits, depreciation, dividends and assets.[12]

The 1900 Companies Act was followed by the 1907 Act (consolidated in 1908), which required a public company to file annual audited balance sheets with the Registrar of Companies, and in so doing picked up the theme of the 1844 Act. Certain items had to be disclosed in the balance sheet, and the Act required the auditor to go 'behind' ledger balances in checking the annual accounts; the auditors' independence was strengthened by a requirement that two weeks' notice had to be given to shareholders and auditors of an intention to change auditors. The Companies Acts of 1928 and 1929 added substantially to the list of compulsory accounting and auditing regulations: an income statement (profit and loss account) had, for the first time, to be sub-mitted to shareholders, although auditors were not required to report on it, nor need it be filed with the Registrar; assets had to be divided between fixed and current (see table 2), and the basis of valuation indicated; loans to directors and officers had to be declared; and there were new regulations concerning the issue of new shares. It was not until the

Companies Acts of 1947 and 1948 (Consolidated) that the audit of public companies had to be conducted by professionally qualified auditors. The 1948 Act revised the form of audit report to contain statements as to whether or not the auditor believed that proper books of account had been kept, that he had obtained all the information needed for his audit, that the balance sheet and profit and loss account were in accordance with the books and that a 'true and fair view' of the affairs of the company was displayed by the published accounts. The Act also specified the annual presentation of balance sheets and profit and loss accounts; the Eighth Schedule listed items of information to be disclosed; consolidated accounts had to be produced for holding companies. The 1967 Act added to the disclosure requirements, particularly regarding significant fixed asset changes, share capital changes, directors' emoluments, directors' interests in the shares and debentures of the company, and the turnover and profitability of each significant class of business conducted by the company.

The compulsory disclosure and audit requirements from 1900 onwards, as briefly described above, represent something of a departure from the old entrenched ideas about company affairs: 'resistance to the introduction of compulsory publication of accounts was symptomatic of the old entrepreneurial attitude — shared by many directors, especially of old-established 'family' firms which had been converted to companies — that a businessman's accounts were his private concern, that outsiders had no right to pry into them and that availability of information would help his competitors. Shareholders were deemed to be interested only in their dividends and in the market price of their shares; the profit figure given in the annual directors' report was merely an indicator of the maximum dividend payable, and shareholders had no concern with the manner in which it was arrived at. All that mattered was that the auditors should satisfy themselves that the profit, as reported, was fairly and honestly determined, and that it erred, if at all, on the side of understatement, and never of overstatement'.[13]

It would be incorrect to view the changes in accounting practice solely in terms of government regulation. The organisation of accountants into professional accountancy

institutes, with their own examinations of technical
competence, notably in Scotland in 1854 and in the 1870's
and 1880's in England, meant that the abortive attempt at
accounting and auditing regulation in 1844 could be re-
enacted in 1900 and 1908 with a greater chance of success.
From the last two decades of the nineteenth century,
legislators could call upon the expertise of professional
accountancy bodies, and individuals and companies were
entitled to expect competent professional advice from a
member of one of the professional bodies. However, it was
some fifty years before professional accountancy bodies
began to take any noticeable interest in accounting
reporting standards which went beyond the minimal legal
requirements. In their early days, most of their work was in
connection with liquidations, bankruptcies and taxation
advice, rather than the problems of company auditing and
accounting. The initiative for the examination of these
problems passed to the United States of America following
the Wall Street 'crash' of 1929. The Institute of Chartered
Accountants in England and Wales issued its *Recommendations on Accounting Principles* from 1942 onwards, and
these were supplemented by research reports, until the
whole debate was given added impetus by the Institute's
Statement of Intent on Accounting Standards in the 1970's.
This was issued in 1969 with the aim of reducing the large
number of different ways in which a particular item could
be reported. Since then, by a joint effort of the major British
accountancy bodies, many *Exposure Drafts* leading, often,
to *Statements of Standard Accounting Practice* have been
published.

The Stock Exchange and the City have been, and
continue to be, important in influencing accounting
standards. The Stock Exchange requires certain information to be disclosed before a company's shares can be
quoted, which, in general, reinforces the statutory disclosure requirements and those contained in the *Statements
of Standard Accounting Practice.* It performs an additional
function by requiring that the information issued to
prospective investors has to be as up to date as possible
before the quotation of the shares and that, after quotation,
interim half-yearly reports must be published in news-
papers. The Panel on Take-overs and Mergers was

established in 1968 to regulate merger and takeover activities, with a view to ensuring fairness of treatment among shareholders and the explicit statement of assumptions behind profit forecasts. The Panel issued the *City Code* which is frequently revised and which seeks to regulate, in a quasi-legal way, the activities of those concerned in mergers and takeovers. During the 1970's particularly, the debate on accounting practice has widened to include disclosure to trade unions, the social responsibilities of commercial organisations, worker participation and the increased involvement of government by way of direct nationalisation and the National Enterprise Board.

Nothing has, so far, been said about taxation and its relationship with accounting practice. The impression obtained from talking to owners of small businesses is that the main purpose of preparing annual accounts is as a basis for the taxation computation. As was suggested in an earlier section, the small trader believes that he keeps abreast of the affairs of his business, and does not need the annual accounts for this purpose. For the larger corporation, with a much greater duty of accountability, the relationship between accounting and taxation is more difficult to assess. The need for a taxable profit figure probably gives added impetus to the recognition of the importance of periodic income calculations, but no consistent theory of accounting is discernible in company law, taxation law, or accounting practice. Indeed, the piecemeal introduction of accounting practices and the underlying failure, on the part of the accountancy profession, to agree on what constitute the main purposes of accounting has left the profession open to criticism, to which it has only in the last few years begun to respond.

Notes and references

1   See M. Chatfield, *A History of Accounting Thought*, The Dryden Press 1974, pp. 24-29. The quotation is from p. 25.

2   For more detail see J. Freear, 'Robert Loder, Jacobean Management Accountant', *Abacus* VI 1970, pp. 25-38.

3   See particularly J. O. Winjum, *The Role of Accounting in the Economic Development of England: 1500-1750*, Center for International Education and Research in Accounting 1972, Chapter 3;

and B. S. Yamey, 'The functional development of double-entry book-keeping', *The Accountant*, 2 November 1940, pp. 333-342.

4   See G. A. Lee, *Modern Financial Accounting*, Nelson 1976, 2nd edn, for a more detailed explanation of double-entry book-keeping.

5   It seems probable that single-entry book-keeping was developed from double-entry book-keeping, not the other way round. See B. S. Yamey, 'Notes on the origin of double-entry book-keeping', *Accounting Review*, vol. 22, 1947, pp. 263-272, especially pp. 264-265.

6   It may well be that balances were checked by listing on loose sheets of paper which have since been lost.

7   See B. S. Yamey, 'Scientific book-keeping and the rise of capitalism', *Economic History Review*, 2nd series, 1949, pp. 99-113 and reprinted in W. T. Baxter and S. Davidson, *Studies in Accounting Theory*, Sweet and Maxwell 1962, pp. 14-43; B. S. Yamey, 'Accounting and the rise of capitalism: further notes on a theme by Sombart', *Journal of Accounting Research*, II, 1964, pp. 117-136; J. O. Winjum, *op. cit.*, Chapter 2; J. O. Winjum, 'Accounting and the rise of capitalism: an accountant's view', *Journal of Accounting Research*, IX, 1971, pp. 333-350; B. S. Yamey, 'Notes on double-entry book-keeping and economic progress', *Journal of European Economic History*, vol. 4, no. 3, Winter 1975.

8   For more detail on this important topic see Chatfield *op. cit.*, Chapters 12 and 13, and S. P. Garner, *Evolution of Cost Accounting to 1925*, University of Alabama Press 1954.

9   See Chatfield, *op. cit.*, p. 114

10 See R. Brief, 'Nineteenth century accounting error', *Journal of Accounting Research*, III, 1965, pp. 12-31.

11 See Brief, *op. cit.*

12 See T. A. Lee, *Company Financial Reporting*, Nelson 1976, pp. 30-33, for a summary of the major cases.

13 See G. A. Lee, 'The concept of profit in British accounting, 1760-1900', *Business History Review*, XLIX, 1975, pp. 6-36. The quotation is from p. 33.

2

A short survey of the accounting profession

MICHAEL RENSHALL

Partner, Peat Marwick Mitchell & Co.; formerly Technical Director, Institute of Chartered Accountants in England and Wales

'. . . accountancy . . . the new great professtion' — Lord Goodman

Foreword

An American observer has characterised British essays as long on argumentation and short on facts. Mindful of the stricture, the writer has in this piece concentrated on producing a factual description of the present state of the accounting profession in Great Britain — that is, England, Scotland and Wales — using evidence from a variety of published sources, with a minimum of surmise and opinion. The essay is divided into four main sections: (1) structure, numbers and growth; (2) central organisation and finance; (3) membership profile; and (4) a comparison of affinities and disparities. The statistics quoted relate mainly to 1975; the material was mainly prepared before 1976 figures became available.

Structure, numbers and growth

The primary and secondary registers, and total numbers. The present state of the British accounting profession can briefly be described as populous, pluralistic, and fragmented. At the end of 1975 there were at least ten separately identifiable registers of accountants in Great Britain and Ireland with a total of 129,000 names inscribed on them;

their associated student registers had 138,000 names inscribed.

Nine of the ten registers are maintained by separate autonomous accounting organisations; the tenth register is maintained by the Department of Trade under Section 161(1)(b) of the Companies Act 1948. The ten registers can be divided into two classes. The primary registers are those maintained by the six leading British and Irish accounting bodies.[1] At the end of 1975 they aggregated 113,000 members and 119,000 students (table 1).

In addition to the dominant set of six bodies, there is a

Table 1   Year of formation, membership and registered students of the six principal British and Irish accounting bodies at 1 January 1976

	Year formed	Members	Students
		(thousands)	
The Institute of Chartered Accountants in England and Wales	1880	62	15
The Association of Certified Accountants	1903	16	61
The Institute of Cost and Management Accountants	1919	15	35
The Institute of Chartered Accountants of Scotland	1951[a]	9	2
The Chartered Institute of Public Finance and Accountancy	1885	8	4
The Institute of Chartered Accountants in Ireland	1888	3	2 (Est)
Totals		113	119

Source: Annual Reports

[a] Society of Accountants (Edinburgh) formed 1853, chartered 1854. The Institute of Chartered Accountants of Scotland was granted its Royal Charter in 1951, amalgamating the three separate Chartered Institutes of Edinburgh, Glasgow and Aberdeen.

subsidiary set of accountants inscribed in a separate set of secondary registers. These consist of the Association of International Accountants, the Society of Company and Commercial Accountants, the British Association of Accountants and Auditors, and persons individually authorised by the Department of Trade under Section 161(1)(b) of the Companies Act 1948 to perform company audits. At the end of 1975 these four groups totalled 16,000 names. All save those entered on the Section 161(1)(b) register have their student cohorts, sometimes considerable: the Association of International Accountants is estimated to have some 14,000 registered students, most of them overseas (table 2).

The total of 113,000 names inscribed on the five principal British registers does not, of course, represent the total number of accountants active in Great Britain, because it not only includes retired members and persons resident outside Great Britain, but also includes a significant

Table 2   Secondary registers of the British accounting profession: year of formation, registrants and students at 1 January 1976

	Year formed	Registrants	Students
		(thousands)	
Society of Company and Commercial Accountants	1974	9	5 (Est)
Authorised by Department of Trade under Section 161(1) (b) of the Companies Act 1948	1948	4	—
Association of International Accountants	1931	2	14 (Est)
British Association of Accountants and Auditors	1923	1	—
Totals		16	19

Sources: *'The Accountant'*, 8 July 1976; *Companies in 1975*, Department of Trade Annual Report for year ended 31 December 1975

Table 3 Estimate of members of five principal accounting bodies active in Great Britain, 1 January 1976 (thousands)

	Total	ICAEW	ICAS	A Cert A	ICMA	CIPFA	ICAI
Total registrants	113	62	9	16	15	8	3
	—	—	—	—	—	—	—
Less							
ICAI	3	—	—	—	—	—	3
Resident overseas	15	8	2	3	2	—	—
Retired	11	5	1	2	2	1	—
	29	13	3	5	4	1	3
	—	—	—	—	—	—	—
	84	49	6	11	11	7	—
	—	—	—	—	—	—	—
Less dual memberships	5	—	—	2	3	—	—
	—	—	—	—	—	—	—
Members active in England, Scotland and Wales	79	49	6	9	8	7	—
	—	—	—	—	—	—	—

Source: Annual reports[3] and estimates based on NOP Readership Survey[4,5,6]

number of persons inscribed on two or more registers.[2] If adjustments are made for these factors (and ignoring for this purpose ICAI, which has its headquarters in the Republic of Ireland) it is estimated that there are about 79,000 members of the five main British bodies (i.e. those located in England, Scotland, and Wales) active and resident in Great Britain (table 3).

International comparisons. For reasons which remain inadequately explained, the English-speaking nations have developed their accounting organisations far more vigorously than other nations. As a generalisation it may be said that accounting as a separate recognised profession is more prominent in the Western bloc than the Eastern, in the developed countries than the developing countries, and in the English-speaking than in the non-English-speaking world. Table 4 compares the unadjusted total of 110,000 accountants inscribed in the five principal British registers with major bodies in other leading nations.

The contrast is most striking if the British accounting population is compared with those of its immediate peer group of European economies, France and Germany (England, Scotland and Wales 110,000, France 9,000, Germany 4,000, see table 4). There are two principal reasons for the discrepancy. First, the accounting profession in the English-speaking world is 'fused', that is, the profession groups together those working in public practice with those employed in finance, commerce, industry, education and government, whereas a number of non-English-speaking countries restrict membership of the profession essentially to those engaged in public practice. Again, the English-speaking accountants in public practice include taxation, management and other services in their briefs, whereas in other European countries some, if not all, of these functions tend to be differentiated from those of the accountant in public practice, who often inclines to confine himself to the more traditional or classic functions of accountant and auditor.

In sum, it can be said that the English-speaking nations use the term 'accountancy' to mean a multi-dimensional service, whereas other nations tend to treat it as having a more limited and conventional meaning. After all is said, however, there remains a substantial unexplained numerical discrepancy between the number of accountants estimated to be engaged in public practice in Great Britain (31,000) and, for instance, the total membership of the Institut der Wirtschaftsprufer in Deutschland (4,000 — see tables 4 and 9).

Rate of growth. The British accounting profession has shown a prodigious growth in the first three-quarters of the 20th century. One leading body alone, the ICAEW, has grown from fewer than 3,000 members in 1900 to 62,000 at

Table 4   Membership of major accounting bodies — international comparison end 1975 (thousands)

United States of America
American Institute of Certified Public Accountants	122	
National Association of Accountants	81	
Association of Government Accountants	9	212

United Kingdom (major five in Great Britain, table 1)		110

Australia
Institute of Chartered Accountants in Australia	8	
Australian Society of Accountants	42	50

Canada
Canadian Institute of Chartered Accountants	24	
Certified General Accountants Association of Canada	6	
Society of Industrial Accountants of Canada	9	39

France Ordre des Experts Comptables et des Comptables Agrees		9

Netherlands Nederlands Instituut van Registeraccountants		4

Germany Institut der Wirtschaftsprufer in Deutschland		4

Sources: Annual reports and 'EEC Company Law and its implications for UK Accountancy Practice and Standards' CCAB evidence to House of Lords Sub-Committee, 1975

the end of 1975 (63,000 at end 1976). At the end of 1975 the five major British bodies numbered 110,000 members (table 1). If their rate of increase in the six years 1970-1975 (4.5% per annum) continued unchanged, within a decade the English Institute alone would have 100,000 members and the six major bodies together almost 200,000 members.[7]

Students. The strong growth of the profession is reflected in a substantial student body, which has more than doubled in a decade and totalled 117,000 at the end of 1975 (table 5). The distribution of students among the leading bodies is strongly biased towards the A Cert A and ICMA.

The A Cert A has roughly as many registered students (61,000) as the English Institute has members. ICMA too has a substantial student body (35,000). Details are not available, but it is believed that overseas students constitute a majority of the total in both the latter cases.[9] The English and Scottish Institutes require students to be contracted to practitioners in the UK, so there is no significant overseas element in their totals. Moreover, their totals are probably understated by comparison with A Cert A and ICMA because they do not include students who have served out their required training periods but have not yet qualified. These may have numbered another 7,000-8,000 English Institute students in 1975, indicating a total number of English Institute aspirants of the order of 22,000-23,000.[10]

Table 5   Registered students 1965—1975 (thousands, at 31 December)

	1965	1970	1975
ICAEW	10 (Est)	12 (Est)	15
ICAS	2	2	2
A Cert A	15	23	61
ICMA	20	26	35
CIPFA	2	5	4
	49	68	117

Sources: Solomons Report[8] and Annual Reports[3]

Central organisation and finance

The five major British accounting organisations under review are, as noted, autonomous and conduct their affairs independently of the government and of each other. Private bodies with public responsibilities, they are classic examples of those independent self-regulating institutions on which the British especially pride themselves. Constitutionally, they are alike in being incorporated by Royal Charter.[11] They each have their own governing council, and each maintains its independent headquarters establishment to administer examinations, admissions, registrations, discipline, and services for members. Behind these apparent similarities the manner and terms of appointment to the governing councils and the style, financing and policies of the organisations differ substantially. Though objective analysis and comparison are not easy, the simplest approach is to compare the information contained in the annual reports and accounts.

The general impression given by the annual accounts is one of financial stability, thrift and prudence. The five major British bodies had gross revenues of almost £7 million in 1965 and they returned an aggregate surplus of £600,000. There are three principal sources of income: members' entrance fees and annual subscriptions, student and examination fees, and income from sales of publications, courses and other activities. However, there are marked differences between the bodies as to their principal sources of income. For instance, whereas members' entrance fees and annual subscriptions were the main sources of income for the English and Scottish Institutes (45% and 40% respectively), student and examination fees contributed some two-thirds of the revenue of A Cert A and ICMA; CIPFA was the most successful operator of marketed activities, achieving 65% of its gross income from sales of publications, courses and other activities. 40% of the income of ICAEW came from sales of publications, courses and related activities (table 6).

The most striking feature of the income and expenditure accounts is the powerful stream of income the Association of Certified Accountants derives from its vast international

Table 6 Income and expenditure, five principal British accounting bodies, 1975 (£ thousands)

	ICAEW	ICAS	A Cert A	ICMA	CIPFA
Income					
Subscriptions and entrance fees	1374	271	298	250	122
Student and examination fees	406	183	1197	581	99
Publications, courses and member services	1176	181	334	13(d)	458
Property and investment income	117	37	47	40	28
Other	7	—	18	—	—
Total income	3080	672	1894	884	707
Total expenditure	2795(a)	628(b)	1604(c)	879	722
Surplus/deficit for the year	285	44	290	5	−(15)

Notes (a) After adding back £406,000 relating to student and examination fees; any surplus on student account (£42,000 in 1975) is held available in trusts on that account for future years.
(b) After adding back revenue and costs of the Accountants Publishing Co. Limited (£112,000) and grant to meet deficit (£4,000).
(c) Including income and expenditure of Certified Accountants Educational Trust.
(d) Net.

Sources: 1975 Annual Accounts[3]

student body of over 60,000 (65,000 at end 1976[3]). Its income from this source in 1975 was £1.2 million, four times its subscription and entrance fees. The Association's 1975 surplus of £281,000 almost offset the entire subscription income from members (£298,000; in 1976 the surplus was £852,000, more than the entire surplus for all five British bodies in 1975).

A curious aspect of the financing of the accounting bodies is the modest level of the annual subscriptions of members. The highest rate of annual subscriptions in 1976 was paid by practising members of the Scottish Institute (£42 per annum); the highest rate paid by practising members of the English Institute was £29 per annum (plus £14 for a practising certificate); ICMA members paid a maximum of £26 per annum, CIPFA members a maximum of £20 per annum. It is instructive to compare these amounts with the British 1976 annual licence fees of £18 for colour television and of £40 for private cars.

Because of differences of presentation, it is more difficult to compare the pattern of expenditure of the accounting bodies than patterns of revenue. Not all disclose numbers of employees, or employment costs, nor can the amounts spent on major activities be clearly identified and compared. Ideally, one would wish to be able to ascertain and compare such key figures as the amounts spent on general administration, research and technical activities, education and the enforcement of ethical standards. Partial comparisons only are possible. The best that can be done is to select such figures as are available for comparison. Of the two numerically largest bodies, the English Institute in 1970 had 230 staff and the Association 115 (table 7). The higher ratio of staff to members of the latter is presumably accounted for by the vast student body of the Association. Employment costs as a proportion of gross revenue were 41% for CIPFA, 32% for ICAEW, 30% for ICAS but only 16% for A Cert A. Expenditure by ICAEW on technical activities (e.g. accounting and auditing standards, guidance to members on matters of professional practice, and representations to government) was £210,000, equal to 7% of gross revenue. In addition, £66,000 was granted by the English Institute's associated trusts for research and related technical purposes. It is not possible from the published information to make

Table 7   Numbers of staff and employment costs of five
principal British accounting organisations 1975 (£ thousands)

	ICAEW	ICAS	A Cert A	ICMA	CIPFA
Staff numbers	230	n.a.	115	n.a.	n.a.
Employment costs	£996	£203	£311	n.a.	£288

Source: Annual Reports[3]

direct comparisons with the amounts expended by the other
bodies on research and technical activities, though given the
size dominance of the English Institute it is unlikely that
any are in a position to exceed that body's technical
resources in absolute terms. The Scottish Institute's
accounts show £42,000 attributable to research and technical activities, which at 6% roughly matches the English
Institute's expenditure of 7% of gross revenue.

The Association differs significantly in its operating
policy from the four other major British bodies in three
respects. First, as noted, it services a far more numerous
student register than any of the other bodies, absolutely and
in proportion to its membership (approximately four
students to every member, against two per member for
ICMA, and about one student for every four members for the
English and Scottish Institutes). The latter two organisations particularly insist that every student is under the
direct tutelage of a member engaged in public practice, and
they also limit the number of students per firm. Second, the
Association has pursued an active policy of recruiting
students resident overseas. The only other body which has a
significant number of students resident overseas is ICMA.
The English and Scottish Institutes insist that their students
must acquire their training wholly or mainly in the UK
(though in 1977 the English Institute proposed relaxations
to allow training in EEC countries). Third, the Association
has developed subsidiary qualifications separate from and
inferior to those of its members — the Certified Diploma in
Accounting and Finance, a study programme for non-
accountants, and the Institute of Accounting Staff, a junior
qualification not conferring membership of the
Association. At the end of 1975 there were 500 holders of the

Diploma; in 1977 it was reported the IAS had 800 members and 7000 students. (CIPFA has established a class of non-corporate member with the title 'accounting technician'; this too is a form of junior qualification, but fully integrated with CIPFA's organisation. At the end of 1975, 700 accountant technicians were on the register. ICAEW and ICMA too have been considering schemes for a less advanced grade of qualification.)

The English Institute is alone in disclosing the amount spent on maintenance of professional and ethical standards (£34,000 gross in 1975, £55,000 gross in 1976). In 1976 the problem of enforcing professional standards created concern and the English and Scottish Institutes and the Association established an independent joint Committee under the Chairmanship of Lord Cross to review investigatory and disciplinary procedures. Published figures shed little light on the problem. The annual reports for 1975 show that misconduct was established in 58 cases involving members of the English Institute, five involving members of the Scottish Institute and two involving members of the Association. There were no reports of misconduct actions by ICMA or CIPFA. The information is summarised in table 8.

Table 8   Members disciplined 1975

	Number of cases		
	ICAEW	ICAS	A Cert A
Reported cases in which misconduct established	58	5	2
Judgements			
Expelled/excluded	9	1	2
Membership suspended	1	—	—
Practising certificate withdrawn/withheld	5	1	—
Censured/fined	43	3	—

Source: Annual Reports[3]

Membership profile

As noted, there are some 79,000 qualified accountants active in England, Scotland and Wales. The basic occupational division is usually taken to be between those engaged in public practice and those employed in other activities (primarily finance, commerce, industry and government). Estimates suggest that (after adjusting for multiple memberships) some 29,000 accountants are engaged in public practice (as principals or employees) and 50,000 in industry, commerce, central and local government and other occupations (table 9).

ICAEW is more public practice oriented than any of the other bodies (49% of its active members are engaged in public practice). Next comes the Scottish Institute (40% engaged in public practice[6]) and the Association (about 30%[13] in public practice).[14]

If CIPFA is ignored, British accountants show a marked preference for the private against the public sector. In 1975 only 3% of the members of the four non-CIPFA bodies worked in central or local government. The English Institute's members in particular are resolutely wedded to the private sector — only 1% of its members are in government service[4,5] (In fact there are fewer than 1,000 qualified accountants in the British Civil Service, and barely half of these are engaged in 'pure' accounting activities.[15])

Broadly, British accountants are distributed across the whole spectrum of organisations ranked by size. Roughly one-third work in organisations with fewer than 100 employees, one-third in organisations with between 100 and 1,000 employees, and one-third in organisations with more than one thousand employees.[4,5]

Whereas 50% of chartered and certified accountants work in organisations with fewer than 250 employees, 70% of ICMA members work in organisations with more than 250 employees. According to ICAEW data, those engaged in firms with fewer than 100 employees are predominantly in public practice.[4,5]

The age profile of the profession is young. This is particularly true of the English Institute, almost half of whose members are under 35, and three-quarters aged under 45.[3,5]

Table 9 Occupations of Accountants in Great Britain (thousands)

	TOTALS	ICAEW	ICAS	A Cert A	ICMA	CIPFA
Public practice	31	24	3	4	–	–
Finance, commerce, industry	40	22	3	5	9	1[a]
Central/local government	8	–	–	1	1	6
Other (including education, consultancy)	6	3	–	2	1	–
Totals	84	49	6	11	11	7

Numbers do not add owing to rounding.

[a] Author's estimate – Solomons[8] found 15% of CIPFA members employed in public boards and other public service organisations.

Sources: Estimates based on NOP Readership Survey,[4] ICAEW *Survey of Members Active,*[5] and ICAS *Continuing Education – The Way Ahead*[6]. See also Monopolies Commission report.[12]

Whereas the median age of chartered accountants is in the range 30-39, the median age of members of A Cert A and ICMA appears to be five or six years higher, in the range 40-49 years (in 1972 median ages were: ICAEW 36, A Cert A 42, ICMA 40, CIPFA 39).[4,8]

It is also a male-dominated profession. 97% of ICAEW's 1975 membership consisted of men, though there are signs of change: in the same year 15% of the student contracts registered by ICAEW were for women.[5]

In general, it is not a graduate profession though the two bodies of chartered accountants are moving strongly in that direction; the Scottish Institute has established graduate-entry requirements and the English Institute 'encourages' graduates. In 1975, 17% of ICAEW members had a university degree though a major shift in this direction is shown by the fact that in the same year 54% of training contracts registered were by students holding university or CNAA recognised degrees.[5] In contrast, in 1966 graduates comprised only 10% of contracts registered. It is noteworthy that the normal age of admission to the principal British accounting bodies is lower than in most major European countries. Thus the normal age of admission of chartered accountants in Britain is 23—25 years, whereas in France the normal age of admission is 28—35 years, and in Germany 30—35 years.[16] The age profile of A Cert A and ICMA members suggests a later age of admission than for chartered accountants.[4] It may be speculated whether the recent deliberate elevation of entry standards in Britain and the general trend towards a longer educational period in the Western world may force a shift towards the European pattern of higher average ages of admission.

The English Institute has published more information about its members than the other bodies and from this it is possible to construct a profile of the typical English chartered accountant in 1975. On average, he is male, in his thirties, and was admitted to membership since 1960. He qualified between the ages of 23 and 25, did not have a university degree and most likely served a five year training contract with a firm with fewer than nine partners — Solomons found that over 50% of ICAEW members in 1972 were trained in firms with three or fewer partners.[8] As noted, the typical non-chartered accountant (A Cert A,

ICMA or CIPFA) is on average older than chartered accountants (over 40 rather than under) and qualified at a later age than the chartered accountant — probably around 30 (this estimate is based on age distributions[4]). CIPFA apart, the non-chartered accountant is also less likely to be a university graduate. (In 1972, 31% of ICAEW student registrations were graduates; in 1975 they numbered 54%. By comparison, in 1972, 3% of A Cert A student registrants had university degrees, 10% ICMA and 34% CIPFA.)[5, 8]

The essence of the British profession is generally considered to be enshrined in its firms in public practice. Chartered accountants dominate and typify the profession in the public mind and they share one major characteristic: their training in practising offices. The typical practising firm has no more than five partners (70% of principals in the English Institute practise in firms of fewer than 10 partners). But a significant number (one in five) of English Institute principals practise in firms of more than 20 partners.[5] The half dozen largest practising firms in Britain will typically employ over 2,000 partners and staff; they all have substantial international connections and if partners and staff are aggregated on the basis of world-wide associated firms they can count numbers of the order of 15,000.[17] The writer knows of no other profession which has organised its units on such a large and international scale.

The most visible function of practising firms is to act as auditors of listed companies. While the half dozen largest British firms dominate the audits of the 3,000 British listed companies, they by no means monopolise them, and many smaller firms are still to be found as auditors of listed companies. It is noteworthy that this situation differs from the position in the United States where there is a clear separation between the major firms who audit SEC (Securities and Exchange Commission) regulated companies and smaller firms who do not. A major reason for this is the high financial risk associated with audits of listed companies: in the US, because of securities legislation, class actions, lawyers' contingency fees, and the reluctance of the courts to award costs against unsuccessful plaintiffs, the environment is more favourable to litigation and offers prospects of lucrative reward in a way unknown in the UK. Smaller US firms are not willing or able to sustain such hazards and in consequence they tend to avoid an area which is notoriously subject to risk which can be catastrophic in financial terms.

The numerical dominance of chartered accountants in public practice is repeated in industry and commerce (25,000 out of 40,000 qualified accountants active in industry in Britain are chartered accountants, see table 9). This dominance is particularly marked in the senior ranks of major companies. Four out of five of the chief financial officers of the 300 largest companies in *The Times 1000* are chartered accountants.[18]

It is a pluralistic profession and this pluralism is reflected in the diversity of its skills and functions. Solomons in 1972 found only a limited number of points of substantial identity between members of the major bodies as to their dominant tasks. He identified three tasks as being accorded common priority by chartered, certified, cost and management and public financial accountants alike. These were: communication with non-accountants, forecasting, and budgetary control. More dominant with chartered accountants than others were tax planning and verification of assets and liabilities, i.e. auditing (Solomons Report,[8] Table B 31, page 192, see also ICAEW survey[5]).

In its 1975 survey of members' activities the English Institute discovered a curious fact which underlines the diversity of accountants' functions. This was that for every major task rated important in their daily work by a significant number of chartered accountants there was always a counterbalancing significant number who rated the same task irrelevant. Thus, although 42% of respondents rated the preparation of accounts for publication as 'most important', 28% rated it 'irrelevant'; 40% rated preparation of accounts for management 'most important', but 20% rated it unimportant. There was no task rated so high that it did not have a significant minority which rated it irrelevant.[5]

Affinities and disparities

Periodically throughout its comparatively short history the British accounting profession has explored the possibility of unifying itself into a single centrally organised institution. The latest attempt was made in 1968—1970, when a scheme for integrating the six major British and Irish bodies into three national chartered institutes (England and Wales, Scotland and Ireland) was accepted by the five smaller bodies but decisively rejected by the members of the dominant English Institute.

The dream of unification persists, but the different sets of accountants are in their attitude towards each other akin to the nation states of Europe. They sense an affinity and yearn for a closer relationship, but nevertheless pursue their individual organisational aims in a strong if covert spirit of competition and self-interest. Examination shows that below the surface similarities there are significant differences of membership characteristics, institutional policies towards recruitment, education and training, and occupational spheres of interest. Some of the major points of similarity and dissimilarity are displayed in table 10.

The English and Scottish Institutes are public practice-based and public practice-oriented. All their members, without exception, are trained in practising offices, and a high proportion are engaged in public practice (49% in the case of the English Institute — 24,000 members active in Great Britain — and 40% in the case of the Scottish Institute). They train no full time students outside the UK (though, as noted, ICAEW proposes to introduce provision for training in EEC countries). Although university graduates form a minority of their total membership, a majority of their new student registrations now have university degrees or their CNAA equivalent. This is not demonstrably true of the Association and ICMA.

Although a significant number of members of the Association are engaged in public practice (about one-third — say 4,000) and in numbers they rank second to the English Institute, it is not primarily a practice-oriented organisation. Their members' dominant occupational tasks identify them more closely with ICMA members than with the chartered accountants (see especially Solomons Report,[8] Table B 31).

CIPFA stands apart from the other four organisations in that its members predominantly inhabit the public sector whereas the members of the other bodies predominantly inhabit the private sector.

CIPFA especially predominates in local authority

Table 10 Salient characteristics of British accounting bodies compared

	ICAEW	ICAS	A Cert A	ICMA	CIPFA
Students and training					
Majority are graduates	✓	✓	—	—	✓
Training wholly or mainly in UK obligatory	✓	✓	—	—	—
Training in public practice obligatory	✓	✓	—	—	—
Normal age of qualifying over 25	—	—	✓	✓	✓
Members					
Average age over 40	—	✓	✓	✓	—
15% or more overseas	—	✓	✓	✓	—
65% or more non-practice based	—	—	✓	✓	✓
35% or more practice based	✓	✓	—	—	—
95% or more in private sector	✓	✓	—	—	—
50% or more in industry/commerce	—	✓	—	✓	—
50% or more in organisations with fewer than 250 employees	✓	✓	✓	—	—
Central organisation					
Main source of revenue:					
Members subscriptions	✓	✓	—	—	—
Student and examination fees	—	—	✓	✓	—
Sales of services	—	—	—	—	✓
Offers junior qualifications	—	—	✓	—	✓
Reports ethical enforcements	✓	✓	✓	—	—
Active teaching as well as examining body	—	✓	—	—	—
Formal CPE[a] policy for members	✓	✓	—	—	—

[a]Continuing professional education[6]
Sources: see text.

finance. The main point of overlap with members of the other bodies is in the nationalised industries and other public service organisations, such as the National Health Service. Applying Solomons' 1972 data to 1975 membership totals suggests that there are about 1,000 CIPFA members engaged in public administration outside local government, almost as many certified accountants, and not significantly fewer chartered accountants.[5,8]

Four out of five ICMA members are engaged in industry and commerce in Great Britain (9,000). They outnumber members of the Association in the same area (5,000) but both groups together are outnumbered by chartered accountants in this field (22,000 English and 3,000 Scottish Institute members — table 9).

Chartered accountants differ from the members of the other three bodies in numbering among their dominant professional tasks taxation and auditing. They also predominate as chief financial officers in major British companies.[8,18]

Nevertheless, despite these differences, there are plain affinities among the whole order of accountants. During this century various attempts have been made to restrict by statute the use of the designation 'accountant' and to unify the profession: as noted, all have failed. If sets were to be grouped, the most suitable and obvious marriage would be between the two great British bodies of chartered accountants, the English-Welsh and the Scottish. But even the bold integration proposals of the late 1960's stopped short of creating such union, and its likelihood has not increased with the rise in nationalist feeling since that date. In current circumstances, amidst disenchantment with size and centralisation, the prospects of an amalgamation of the British accounting profession appear remote; and the differentiation of the major organisations in the fundamental areas of recruitment, training and education seems to be increasing when, if unity was envisaged, it should be decreasing.

It remains only to ask whether the profession can continue its numerical increase at the pace set throughout the 1970's. There seems no reason in principle to doubt it unless the progressive elevation of admission standards restricts access (1976 examination results suggest this may be happening in the case of the English Institute). The demand, if not the supply, seems assured, and the proportion of accountants to total population in Britain remains much lower than in Australia. The accounting profession first emerged in organised form in the nineteenth century as part of what can now be seen as the starting point for the development of an information-based economy. Today the production and processing of information and information systems is the dominant characteristic of developed societies. The appetite for information for use in control systems and policy analysis is insatiable and growing. Unlike animal appetites, it seems incapable of surfeit. Unlike material goods, its production is modest in its consumption of irreplaceable fossil fuels, and it can be stored (in giant data banks) or disposed of without creating consequential problems for succeeding generations. The auguries for the accounting profession, as for all information-based industries, appear on the whole auspicious.

Notes and references

1   They are: The Institute of Chartered Accountants in England and Wales (ICAEW), The Institute of Chartered Accountants of Scotland (ICAS), The Institute of Chartered Accountants in Ireland (ICAI), The Association of Certified Accountants (A Cert A), The Institute of Cost and Management Accountants (ICMA) and The Chartered Institute of Public Finance and Accountancy (CIPFA). Together they comprise the Consultative Committee of Accountancy Bodies, which acts as a forum for the expression of joint views on matters of common interest. This piece is principally concerned with the five bodies based in Great Britain, i.e. excluding Ireland and ICAI.

2   Dual or multiple memberships amongst the five principal British bodies are frequent. Six to seven per cent of chartered accountants are estimated to be members of one or more of the other four bodies. About 20% of ICMA and A Cert A members are estimated to have dual or multiple memberships.[4][5] The estimate in table 5 has been made by ignoring CIPFA and arbitrarily eliminating ICMA members who are members of any of the three other bodies (ICAEW, ICAS or A Cert A and ICMA).[4] Solomons[8] found lower rates of dual or multiple membership — 5% of ICAEW members, 17% of A Cert A members, 16% of ICMA members, 9% of CIPFA members were members of one or more of the other bodies. ICAEW's own data tends to support NOP's results, showing 6% of members with dual membership.[5] Whichever figures are used, a similar answer of some 5,000—6,000 multiple memberships is reached.

3   Institute of Chartered Accountants in England and Wales, *Annual Report and Accounts 1975 and 1976*.

Institute of Chartered Accountants of Scotland, *Annual Report and Accounts 1975 and 1976*.

Association of Certified Accountants, *Annual Report and Accounts, 1975 and 1976*.

Institute of Cost and Management Accountants, *Annual Report and Accounts, 1975*.

Chartered Institute of Public Finance and Accountancy, *Annual Report and Accounts, 1975*.

4   NOP Market Research Limited, 'Qualified accountants readership survey 1976', *Accountants Weekly*, 27 Sept. 1974. (Analyses by age, occupation and size of firm are mainly based on the 1974 NOP Survey.)

5   *Survey of Members Active in the UK*, ICAEW 1977.

6   *Continuing Education — The Way Ahead*, ICAS 1977.

7   For comparison: membership of some other leading British professional bodies at end 1975 was as follows: British Medical Association 50,000; Law Society (England and Wales) 38,000; Royal Institution of Chartered Surveyors 35,000: British Dental Association 13,000; Bar 4,000.

8   David Solomons with T. M. Berridge, *Prospectus for a profession — Report of the long-range enquiry into education and training for the accountancy profession*, Advisory Board of Accountancy Education 1974. Although the data relates to 1972, Appendix B together with Berridge's separately published *Summary Tables*, remains seminal for any survey of the British accounting profession.

9   60% of new student registrations of A Cert A in 1976 were reported to relate to overseas residents (*Accountancy Age*, 15 April 1977, page 3).

10 Solomons estimated the total number of ICAEW students at 20,000 in 1970.

11 Essentially, all the members of all the bodies are 'chartered' accountants, though only the members of the English and Scottish Institutes are entitled to use that description.

12 Monopolies and Mergers Commission, *Accountancy Services — A report on the supply of accountancy services in relation to restrictions on advertising*. Cmnd 6573, HMSO 1976. A curiosity, more notable for its errors and omissions than for the light it sheds on the British profession. It underestimated ICAEW members engaged in public practice by 10,000 and has not been relied on by the author save as a secondary corroborative source.

13 20% according to Solomons 1972 findings.

14 For comparison, 58% of the American Institute of Certified Public Accountants' members were engaged in public practice in 1976 (*source*: Annual Report).

15 K. J. Sharp, 'Financial management in the civil service — the role of accountants', *Public Finance and Accountancy*, January 1977, reprinted in *Management Services in Government*, May 1977.

16 *Training for the Profession — A Comparative Study*, UEC 1977.

17 See for instance, the statement of John C. Biegler, senior partner of Price Waterhouse (USA) before the Metcalfe Committee of the US Senate, 10 May 1977, and the interview with Douglas Baker of Touche Ross (UK), *Accountancy Age*, 25 March 1977.

18 *Profile of the Chief Financial Officer in Great Britain and his American Counterpart.* Findings of a study of the chief financial officers of the United Kingdom and the United States largest industrial companies, Heidrick and Struggles 1976.

3

The development of standard accounting practice

PETER BIRD

Professor of Accounting, University of Kent

A word with several meanings

A standard was originally the military emblem or banner beneath which an army took its stand, the rallying point to which you came back from the fray to 'stand hard'. The word has developed in at least four directions from there. Its uses today for (1) personal or official flags and for (2) upright things on poles (e.g. standard lamps and standard roses) are clearly not relevant to the problems of accounting practice; but the other two are both relevant and liable to be confused with each other.

A standard is (3) a measure to which other measures are expected to conform. This can be a simple measure such as the standard yard from which all other measures of a yard derive their authority and against which these others can be checked. It can also be a more complicated convention concerned with the characteristics to be measured as well as the units in which measurement takes place; and it can include standard methods of converting unlike measures into units of a common denominator. This sense of the word may be derived from the reference point idea of the military banner or from the fact that a standard measure was originally just as much the "King's standard" as his personal flag; clearly the notion of institutionalised authority is dominant in both of these possible derivations.

46

This meaning should not be confused with (4) the level below which it is unsatisfactory to fall. The origin of this meaning is not clear, though it may be connected with the Christian doctrine that in relation to God's standard of perfection we are 'non-standard' by being 'sub-standard' (See Romans 3.23). But the word is also now used to indicate the maximum tolerated amount of some undesirable feature, such as pollution in the river, lead in petrol, radioactivity to which people may be exposed.

The main difference between meaning (3) and (4) is that in a meaning (4) situation there is no penalty for doing 'better' than the standard, but where meaning (3) applies a result deviating from the standard in any direction is unsatisfactory — though not necessarily equally seriously at fault. The locomotives which competed in the Rainhill trials of the Liverpool and Manchester Railway in 1829 were required to be capable of drawing three times their own weight on the level at ten miles per hour; this was a type (4) standard and the 'Rocket' was not disqualified from winning the competition because it reached 12½ miles per hour with this load. But if the engineer who laid the track at Rainhill had been so anxious not to fall below the standard gauge between the rail centres of 4ft 8½in. that he had laid them 4ft. 11in. apart, he would have been guilty of failing to comply with a type (3) standard — and the competing locomotives, which had been built to the 4ft. 8½in. standard, would have fallen into the excessive gap between the rails.

Quality control standards

Standards used in quality control are sometimes type (3) and sometimes type (4).[1] 'Recipe' requirements are usually closed at one end only, either a minimum or a maximum. Petrol has a minimum octane rating, minimum anti-knock properties, maximum lead content; 'overkill' in meeting these requirements does not offend the standard, though it may carry a cost penalty. Such type (4) standards would constitute constraints in a mathematical programming formulation of a problem situation. The standard divides all possibilities so that each falls into one of two 'half-spaces' one of which satisfies the standard and the other of which does not.

But there are other quality control requirements that cannot be satisfied by being on the right side of the fence. The specification for a component may require it to be machined to a diameter of 2in. ± 0.03in; such a component will be rejected if it exceeds the standard tolerance of 0.03in. either above or below 2in.

Statistical sampling tests in auditing are a particular example of quality control which can use either type (3) or type (4) standards.[2] Acceptance sampling seeks to establish with a given level of confidence that the rate of error in a set of data does not exceed a specified (standard) limit; the auditor is not interested in the question of how far below that limit the actual error rate may be. But in estimation sampling the auditor seeks evidence to assure him that an amount falls within a range bounded both sides which can then be compared with the amount shown in the accounts; this type (3) standard is much more demanding and tends to make estimation sampling prohibitively expensive as an audit technique.

The reasons for setting up type (3) standards are different from those which form the justification for type (4) standards. Type (4) minima or maxima are established because things which fail to satisfy them are judged to be un-satisfactory at doing their job. A locomotive with no pulling power, a petrol which poisons the atmosphere with lead, a set of accounting data which is full of errors are all useless or worse; standards are established to try to eliminate these sub-standard products.

But there is nothing inherently better about a 36-inch yard, or a 4ft 8½in. railway gauge, or 2in. diameter component than about alternative standards that could have been established. There is, however, in all these cases a clear need for prior agreement on what standard should be used. This need is concerned with compatibility either in the physical sense (as in the situation where components have to fit together or trains fit on to railway track) or in the intellectual sense of comparability between one measured yard and another.

It could be argued that these type (3) standards are more of a requirement than those of type (4). Where there is clearly a better and a worse, there is hope that the better will drive out the worse (though, of course, we might find the reverse, as in

Gresham's Law, which observes that bad, debased money tends to drive good money out of circulation). But there is no reason to hope that, in the absence of standard setting, we would ever settle on a 'right' gauge for railway track or length for a yard, simply because there is no 'right' answer.

Which type of standards in accounting?

At the end of 1969 the Institute of Chartered Accountants in England and Wales issued a *Statement of Intent on Accounting Standards in the 1970's*.[3] After several intermediate stages of development the Accounting Standards Committee which was set up to carry out this intent is now a joint committee of all six major professional accountancy bodies in the British Isles.[4]

The first question to ask about this development is whether it is working towards type (3) or type (4) standards. In seeking an answer to this question we will look at three pieces of evidence: (a) the Statement of Intent; (b) the stimulus for the Statement; (c) the activities and achievements of the Accounting Standards Committee. It is not surprising that we should find that this evidence does not give us an unequivocal answer to the question. Most real situations contain something of both meanings, though one may in practice dominate the situation. Even the illustrations we have used so far (which have been chosen to be as melodramatically clear contrasts as possible) have not avoided this; a railway gauge of 4ft 8½in. is not clearly superior to one of 4ft 11in. but it has in most circumstances very real advantages over one of 3ft or of 7ft.

The Statement of Intent has a preamble which shows it is concerned with standards of financial reporting by companies. The main text then states that

It is the Council's intention to advance accounting standards along the following lines:

1 Narrowing the areas of difference and variety in accounting practice. . . .

2 Disclosure of accounting bases. . . .

3 Disclosure of departures from established definitive accounting standards. . . .

4   Wider exposure for major new proposals on accounting standards. . . .

5   Continuing programme for encouraging improved accounting standards in legal and regulatory measures.[3]

The first of these intentions relates to type (3) standards whereby practice is made more uniform; its place at the head of the list may be significant. The second item in the list is a

specific proposal for a type (4) standard on the basis that such disclosure is better than non-disclosure. Items 3 and 4 are concerned with the processes of developing and operating accounting standards. The last item in the list seems to relate to type (4) standards since it seeks to encourage 'the improvement of accounting standards.'

The Statement of Intent was the Institute's reaction to a substantial volume of adverse criticism of company accounting reports and of the accountants and auditors associated with them which built up during the years 1966 to 1969. Complaints in the financial press ranged widely and included as grounds for complaint inadequate quantity and quality of information disclosed and inadequate quality of audit work. But the criticisms which carried most weight were those of Sir Frank Kearton, as Chairman of the Industrial Reorganisation Corporation, and Lord Shawcross, as Chairman of the City Panel on Takeovers and Mergers. Both commented on the difficulties and confusion caused in takeover situations by the existence of many different professionally acceptable accounting treatments for the same situation. Both suggested that it was up to the Institute of Chartered Accountants to do something about the situation.[5] The substance of the complaint was under-lined by some facts in the GEC takeover of AEI in this same period.[6] Before the takeover AEI had forecast its pre-tax profits for 1967 (then in its tenth month) at £10 million. After the takeover GEC announced that AEI had made a loss of £4.5 million in 1967. GEC stated that, of the difference of £14.5 million between forecast and actual, £5 million related to matters of fact and the other £9.5 million to 'adjustments which remain matters substantially of judgement'.

Thus the main weight of the stimulus to the professional development of accountancy standards in Britain was a complaint by users of accounts that comparability was being made difficult by the absence of type (3) standards. Users had suddenly become aware that accounting rules were far less precise and the numbers derived by using them far less accurate than they had previously believed; they reacted by registering strong dissatisfaction at the accounting scene as they now understood it.

The working of the Accounting Standards Committee

The Accounting Standards Committee (ASC) has consisted entirely of accountants representing the professional bodies which have been associated with it at the time. But there is also a 'Consultative Group' of representatives of interested non-accounting organisations which is consulted by the Committee.[7] For most topics the first publication of the ASC is an exposure draft (ED) of a proposed statement of standard accounting practice (SSAP). Presumably, internal discussion papers are prepared at an earlier stage of consideration of each topic, but these have only been published in the case of three subjects (inflation accounting, taxation under the imputation system in company accounts and *The Corporate Report.*).

An open invitation is issued to comment on the exposure draft within a specified period of between three and six months. The draft may then be modified in the light of comments and a firm statement of standard accounting practice is usually then issued. In two cases to date the modifications were so substantial that the ASC decided to issue a revised exposure draft before proceeding to a SSAP. And in one case (ED3 — *Accounting for Acquisitions and Mergers*) comment was so adverse that the Draft was not followed up, though technically it is still (1977) an open matter lying on the table awaiting further action.

In quantitative terms the achievements of the ASC to the end of 1976 are 18 exposure drafts issued of which:

1 has been left as uncompleted business   (ED3)
2 have been superseded by revised ED's   (ED5, 14)
4 have been issued in 1975 and 1976 and have not yet proceeded to SSAP stage   (ED15, 16, 17, 18)
11 have resulted in SSAP's, of which four have been revised or amended since their original issue[8]

All the SSAP's now in issue are set in the context of the historic cost basis of accounting. But ED18 proposes the abandonment of the historic cost basis in favour of current cost accounting. If the latter is adopted as standard practice, amendment or replacement will be needed of all but one of the existing SSAP's (SSAP[5] on *Accounting for Value Added Tax*).

The topics tackled by the ASC are a mixture of those with varied existing practice from which the ASC was trying to select one type (3) standard practice, and those where an improvement in the general level of practice was being sought by the imposition of a type (4) standard. But even in SSAP's of the latter type there has been a noticeable effort to define terms precisely and to prescribe one standard method only for each defined set of circumstances. For instance, SSAP 1 standardised the reflection of undistributed earnings of associated companies, which was not common practice before the issue of the statement; in the related exposure draft an associated company was defined as one in which 'not less than approximately 20% of the equity voting rights' is held, but the word 'approximately' does not appear in the SSAP.

It should be noted in passing that mainland European efforts toward standard accounting are of long standing and are almost exclusively of the type (3) variety. Economic statisticians have been the dominant influence on accounting rules and they have insisted on standard definition of terms and usage as they do in any other branch of statistics. A similar emphasis is noticeable in centrally planned economies, communist and non-communist.[9] In the United States of America on the other hand, a strong accounting profession has resisted type (3) uniformity standards[10] and has issued type (4) standard statements which often list several alternative acceptable accounting methods. This bias may also be partly explained by the fact that the American accounting profession was first pulled into the standard-setting role after the stock-market crash of 1929; users of accounts, led by the New York Stock Exchange, asserted that sub-standard accounting (such as treating depreciation expense as an optional charge to be recorded only when profits were big) had contributed to the occurrence or at least the magnitude of the crash.

Justification for standard accounting practice?

The Accounting Standards Committee and, to a slightly lesser extent, its American equivalent have been on weak ground when they seek to lay down improved accounting standards of type (4). This is because they are not building on any agreed statement about the purpose of accounting reports. There is therefore no criterion against which to judge whether any proposed type (4) standard is really an improvement or not. It was noticeable that in its first list of eighteen topics to be considered the ASC listed in twelfth position 'fundamental objects and principles of periodic financial statements'. A good deal of academic attention has been given to this basic topic[11] and seems to have had some influence on *The Corporate Report*, a discussion paper published in 1975 by a working party appointed by the

ASC.[12] But none of the SSAP's or ED's to date can be said to
be based on this paper which has received only guarded and
qualified acceptance from the ASC.[13]

When we turn to the type (3) uniformity standards, we
note first that we live in an age in which it is fashionable to
try to impose uniformity on various aspects of our lives, in
the mistaken belief that this is the best way of achieving
equality. It is therefore not unreasonable to start with the
assumption that the accountancy profession is merely
joining this fashion and to ask for some fairly strong
arguments before we can be convinced that accounting
practice needs to be made as uniform as it is possible to make
it.

Why uniformity?

Before we can make any judgements about movements
toward uniformity in accounting reports, we will have to
take the first step along the road to deciding what these
reports are intended to do. This first step has not been
accepted explicitly by the accounting profession, but seems
likely to be entirely indisputable once it is stated.
Paragraph 1.1 of *The Corporate Report* states that such
reports 'should seek to satisfy, as far as possible, the information needs of users'. It follows that accounting reports are
intended to be channels of communication from people
with information to those who have previously lacked that
information. For present purposes we do not need to
consider who these people are or what information they
need; it is enough to acknowledge that we are concerned
with a communication process and so need to study the
nature and problems of communication processes.

For convenience we will describe the transmitter of
information as the 'accountant' and the receiver of information as the 'reader'; but the process we are analysing is of
much broader application than merely accounting
statements. In what circumstances is it worth having (and
paying) an accountant to provide information? It is
certainly not worth it unless the reader finds the information helpful in taking some decision that he faces. But even
then it is only worth it if one or more factors prevent the
reader from discovering the information for himself.

Examples of such factors are lack of right of direct access to the information, lack of time to review all the information available and lack of expertise to undertake such a review. All of these factors apply to most investors and other 'outsiders' in relation to the companies in which they are interested; they combine to form an effective brick wall between them and information about the company. The job of the accountant, who is on the inside, is to pass information over the brick wall to the readers on the outside. This would be a simple, though voluminous, task if he could just give a verbatim running commentary on what is going on in the company to those beyond the brick wall. But there are several interconnected reasons why this will not do.

It is just not technically feasible to give a complete statement of what is happening in a complex organisation in real time; it would take so long to assemble and transmit that it would get further and further behind — one day's events might take a week or more to transmit. But even if this problem could be overcome the reader would not be satisfied, because he suffers from lack of time to assimilate information and lack of expertise to select from its great volume what is important for him. And all readers have, in varying degree, the problem of limited mental capacity to assimilate information. So the accountant must compile from a vast store of information available or potentially obtainable within the company a relatively small package to throw over the wall; if the package is too big it will give the reader not information but concussion.

There are two ways in which the accountant gets his accounting report package down to a suitable size. First, he selects some aspects of the affairs of the company for inclusion in his accounts and excludes others altogether. He needs to talk over with readers of accounts how he should decide what to include and what to exclude. At the time he is preparing the accounts he is cut off from readers by the brick wall; but it is possible at other times to meet representatives of readers to talk about what are effectively type (4) standards of financial reporting.

The accountant can get more into his communications package, without overloading the readers' capacity to assimilate its contents, if he uses technical terms as a sort of shorthand code. If one word or phrase can be used instead of a long explanation, that leaves more capacity for other information to be transmitted. Accounting terms such as 'profit', 'capital', 'assets', 'depreciation' are all more or less precise codes for ideas that can only be expressed otherwise at considerable length. 'SSAP8' saves a lot of capacity compared with 'the statement of standard accounting practice concerning the treatment of taxation under the imputation system in the accounts of companies'.

The process we have described can be doodled like this:

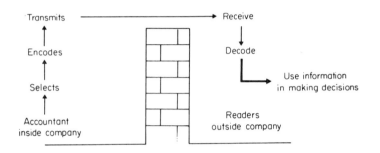

It can be seen that this leaves the readers with the task of decoding the package they have received. To do this effectively they have to be provided with a 'code manual', and accountants must agree to use that same manual in their encoding process. We must all agree beforehand what we mean by 'depreciation' and 'SSAP8'. And that is what uniform accounting standards are all about. They are an agreed code to enable limited communications capacity to be used more effectively. Note that there is no guarantee that the decoded information will be useful to the reader — the selection process may have gone wrong. But note also that, however good the selection process, the reader will not receive any information at all if he cannot decode with confidence the messages received from the accountant.

A standard which is merely a convenience to increase usage of capacity can, of course, be overridden in exceptional circumstances provided that full explanation and justification are provided. This is clearly envisaged by professional statements about the status of accounting standards.[14]

But uniform standards are useful also for reasons of comparability; this is the point which was made in the late 1960's in relation to takeover situations and which did most to provoke the accountancy profession into establishing the ASC. A company reports only about itself, but most readers read the accounts of a number of companies and derive most value from comparing the results shown by each of them. Such comparisons are worse than useless if the bases on which the accounts are prepared are strictly not comparable. Deviation from accounting standards should therefore be undertaken only with considerable reluctance.

People concerned with investment and finance on an international basis need comparable accounting information beyond the sphere of influence of any one professional body. In response to this need, the International Accounting Standards Committee (IASC) was established in 1973 by the professional bodies of the British Isles and eight other countries; a number of other countries have become associated with the work of the Committee since its foundation. The IASC is undertaking a programme similar to that of the British ASC and has to the end of 1976 produced three international accounting standards and a further five exposure drafts.[15] There is obviously the possibility that conflicting uniform practices may be laid down by British and International Standards; this problem has not yet arisen, but would have to be met either by double-reporting or by graceful withdrawal by one party — presumably the national deferring to the international.

It seems that the accountancy profession is fully justified in trying to establish uniform practice standards, though it would be on stronger ground if it made explicit its reasons for doing so, i.e. to enable users to receive intelligible messages on comparable bases. But this is only half the battle; it will ensure that clearly understood information is received, but a further process of setting type (4) standards on a firm foundation is needed before there is assurance that the most useful information is being transmitted and received.

This will necessitate occasional review and revision of SSAP's. Even when they do come to represent the 'best' practice at one time, circumstances and our ideas of what is best are likely to change over time, making further amendment necessary. Fears have been expressed that the ASC would be reluctant to vary standards once established and that practice standards would therefore tend to stagnate. But the record to date indicates that the ASC does not regard its own pronouncements as being like the laws of the Medes and Persians, and is willing to supplement and revise them quite frequently if necessary.

The stimulus to the development of accounting standards arose in respect of accounts for the shareholders of quoted companies. Standards designed with this context in mind are not necessarily appropriate for the accounts of non-company organisations, for accounts designed for other users (e.g. employees and their representatives), or even for the accounts for shareholders of small family companies. If accounting standards are to command the level of respect which they deserve, the ASC must devote attention to these other organisations and users as soon as it has recovered from the massive task of weaning companies from historic cost to current cost accounting.

Notes and references

1 See, for instance, M. K. Starr, *Systems Management of Operations*, Prentice Hall 1971, Chapter 13.
2 See, for instance, H. Arkin, *Handbook of Sampling for Auditing and Accounting*, McGraw-Hill, 1963; T. W. McRae, *Statistical Sampling for Audit and Control*, Wiley 1974.
3 Institute of Chartered Accountants in England and Wales, *Statement of Intent on Accounting Standards in the 1970's*, 1969, reproduced in *Accountancy*, January 1970, pp. 2-3.
4 That is, the three Institutes of Chartered Accountants (in England and Wales, of Scotland and in Ireland), The Association of Certified Accountants, The Institute of Cost and Management Accountants, and the Chartered Institute of Public Finance and Accountancy. Until 1975 the Committee was called the Accounting Standards Steering Committee.
5 See, E. Stamp and C. Marley, *Accounting Principles and the City Code*, Butterworth 1970, Chapter 9.
6 See, Sir Joseph Latham, *Takeover*, Iliffe 1969, Chapter 5 and Appendix 3. Note that this was the first contested takeover bid in which the Industrial Reorganisation Corporation intervened and that Lord Shawcross was a director of AEI before the takeover.
7 The 22 organisations represented on the Consultative Group are listed in *Accountancy*, August 1976, p.6.
8 A listing of the current position of ASC subjects (showing SSAP's issued, ED's still current and future programmes) can be found in the most recent exposure draft.

9   See, G. G. Mueller, 'International experience with uniform accounting' in *Law and Contemporary Problems*, 1965, pp. 850-873; A. J. H. Enthoven, 'Standardised accountancy and economic development', in *Management Accounting* (USA), February 1976, pp. 19-23; Peter Bird, 'Standard accounting practice' in H. Edey and B. S. Yamey (eds) *Debits, Credits, Finance and Profits*, Sweet and Maxwell 1974.

10 See T. A. Wise, 'The auditors have arrived' in *Fortune*, November-December 1960, reprinted in J. W. Buckley, *Contemporary Accounting and Its Environment*, Dickenson 1969, pp. 39-67.

11 See, for instance, American Accounting Association, *A Statement of Basic Accounting Theory*, 1966; Bryan Carsberg, Anthony Hope and R. W. Scapens, 'The objectives of published accounting reports' in *Accounting and Business Research*, No. 15, pp. 162-173; Peter Bird, 'Objectives and methods of financial reporting' in *Accounting and Business Research*, No. 19, pp. 162-167; *The Corporate Report: an academic view*, Institute of Chartered Accountants (E & W) Research Committee Occasional Paper No. 8, 1976.

12 The American Institute of Certified Public Accountants is in a somewhat stronger position following the publication in 1973 of the 'Trueblood Report' on *Objectives of Financial Statements*.

13 See ASC statement in *Accountancy*, August 1976, p.4.

14 'Explanatory foreword to Statements of Standard Accounting Practice', reproduced in *Accountancy*, February 1971, p.61; *The Effect of Statements of Standard Accounting Practice on Auditors' Reports*, Statement on Auditing No. 17, reproduced in *Accountancy*, March 1971, p.154.

15 A listing of the current position of IASC subjects can be found on the back cover of the most recent IASC exposure draft.

4

Accounting in Europe

R H PARKER

Professor of Accountancy, University of Exeter

The title of this chapter is Accounting in Europe rather than European Accounting for a very good reason: there is no such thing as European accounting. The countries of Europe have in fact very little in the way of a common accounting heritage. All use, of course, the techniques of double entry first worked out by the Italians around the year 1300, but so also does the rest of the world. Professor G. G. Mueller, a leading American authority on international accounting, argues that there are four patterns of accounting development: accounting within a macroeconomic framework; the microeconomic approach to accounting; accounting as an independent discipline; and uniform accounting.[1] These are pure types and most countries show traces of at least two of them. What is important to note here is that examples of all four can be found in Europe. Professor Mueller regards Sweden as the best example of accounting within a macroeconomic framework; the Netherlands as the best example of the microeconomic approach; the UK as a good example of accounting as an independent discipline; and France and West Germany as good examples of uniform accounting. Mueller's classification ignores the accounting systems characteristic of communist countries. These include a very large part of Eastern Europe.

The quality of company financial reporting in Europe varies considerably. Table 1 shows how the quality was

Table 1 Assessment of quality of reports and accounts, by country (figures refer to the number of managers and analysts reporting)

Country	Very high	High	Fair	Poor	Total
Belgium—Luxembourg	—	2	10	7	19
France	—	3	15	11	29
Germany	2	8	19	2	31
Italy	—	1	2	20	23
Netherlands	9	20	2	—	31
Switzerland	1	1	7	15	24
United Kingdom	12	17	1	—	30
USA	19	12	2	—	33
Japan	3	5	9	1	18

Source: D. C. Corner and D. C. Stafford, Open-End Investment Funds in the EEC and Switzerland, Macmillan 1977, p. 113.

assessed by the managers and analysts who completed a questionnaire sent out by Corner and Stafford of Exeter University. It will be noticed that the financial reporting of the United States is more highly regarded than that of any European country and that, within Europe, the UK and the Netherlands are the most highly regarded, followed by West Germany. British and Irish accounting — and perhaps Dutch also — is more closely linked to that of North America and Australasia than to accounting in the rest of Europe.

There are, however, two important European bodies of accountants: the EEC Accountants Study Group (Groupe d'Etudes des Experts Comptables de la CEE), consisting of representatives of the professional accountancy bodies of the nine member states (Belgium, Denmark, France, German Federal Republic, Ireland, Italy, Luxembourg, the Netherlands, UK) and the UEC (Union Européenne des Experts Comptables, Economiques et Financiers), a union of 21 professional accountancy bodies from 17 European countries (the nine member states of the EEC plus Finland, Greece, Norway, Portugal, Spain, Sweden, Switzerland and Yugoslavia). The membership of the International Accounting Standards Committee (IASC) is not, however, limited to Europe.

Table 2 European stock exchange statistics

	Equity stocks: market valuation		Equity stocks: market valuation as % of London		Market valuation: Equity stocks as % of fixed interest stocks		Equity stocks: turnover as % of market valuation	
	1975 £m	1976 £m	1975 %	1976 %	1975 %	1976 %	1975 %	1976 %
Amsterdam	9,404	11,589	22	28	108	101	26	29
Brussels	3,720	5,829	9	14	n.a.	34	18	7
Copenhagen	2,105	977	5	2	13	5	1	3
London	42,490	40,997	100	100	120	97	21	17
Madrid	15,241	13,892	36	34	285	213	4	6
Milan	4,790	4,823	11	12	17	13	25	16
Paris	17,754	15,874	42	39	63	63	16	15
Stockholm	4,999	6,062	12	15	33	29	5	5
West Germany (all exchanges)	24,001	27,667	56	67	38	35	20	20

Source: The Stock Exchange Fact Book, 31 March 1976, 1977
N.B. Market valuations are for domestic securities only, except that the London figures include all
UK and Irish stocks.

The diversity of European accounting has not gone unnoticed and attempts are being made to limit it, especially within the EEC. The harmonisation of accounting standards must of necessity work through the major sources of such standards. The most important of these are: stock exchange regulations; company legislation; tax legislation; recommendations and standards issued by professional accountancy bodies; the rules of governmental regulatory agencies; and national accounting plans. The *order* of importance differs quite considerably from country to country.

Although stock exchange regulations are not the most important source of accounting standards in any country, the existence of such exchanges is of great importance. In Britain the Stock Exchange has a few requirements that go beyond those of company legislation (e.g. the disclosure of a geographical analysis of trading operations) and insists that all listed companies comply with the standards laid down by the Accounting Standards Committee.

All other things being equal, one would expect better financial reporting in countries with large and lively stock exchanges.

Size for our purposes is best measured by the market valuation of equity stocks. Liveliness can be gauged by looking at the relative importance of equity stocks and fixed interest stocks and by the turnover of equity stocks as a percentage of their market valuation. Some relevant statistics are given in table 2. Two points especially worth noting are: the market valuation of equities quoted in London is greater than that of all other EEC exchanges combined, excluding West Germany; in all EEC exchanges except London and Amsterdam fixed interest stocks are much more important than equities.

Company legislation is the dominant source of accounting standards in West Germany and is also very important in the UK. Table 3 provides information regarding the number of public and private companies in the UK, West Germany and France. Aktiengesellschaften (AGs) and sociétés anonymes (SAs) have been taken as the approximate equivalents of public companies, and Gesellschaften mit beschränkter Haftung (GmbHs) and sociétés a responsibilité limitée (SARLS) as the approximate equivalents of private companies.

Table 3   European company statistics

	UK (31.12.1975)	W. Germany (31.12.1975)	France (1.1.1971)
Public companies (AGs, SAs)	15,590	2,189	83,356
Private companies (GmbHs, SARLS)	576,653	133,382	130,826
	592,243	135,571	214,182

Sources: UK, *Companies in 1975*, Department of Trade, London
W. Germany, *Statistisches Jahrbuch 1976*, Statistisches Bundesamt,
Wiesbaden. France, *Annuaire Statistique de la France 1976*, INSEE,
Paris.

In Britain the Companies Acts 1948 to 1976 require
published financial statements to show a 'true and fair view'
but give no guidance as to the meaning of the phrase except
that certain items must be specifically disclosed. The law
allows for the possibility that there may be occasions when
non-disclosure of some of these items may still lead to a true
and fair view. In contrast, the German Companies Act
(Aktiengesetz) of 1965 requires that the financial statements
conform to 'proper accounting principles' (undefined) and
give as sure a view as possible within the framework of the
valuation provisions of the Act. These provisions are quite
detailed and are a compound of historical cost and conservatism. The British Acts on the other hand do not prescribe
valuation methods: historical costs, replacement costs, net
realisable values and historical costs adjusted by a general
index are all permissible.

Both German and British company legislation prescribe,
with exceptions that are different in the two countries, the
publication of consolidated accounts (the company laws of
many European countries, including France and Italy, do
not at present so prescribe). The German legislation also
prescribes standard forms of balance sheet and profit and
loss account. The British Acts exempt certain companies
from some of the disclosure requirements, e.g. companies
with a turnover of less than £250,000 need not disclose its

amount. The accounting requirements of the German 1965 Act originally applied only to Aktiengesellschaften (the approximate equivalent of British public companies) but they were extended by the 'Publicity Act' of 1969 to all business organisations, including partnerships and sole traders, above a certain size. German 'private companies' (GmbHs) are governed by a separate statute.

In the rest of Europe, company law is important in Ireland (where the situation is much the same as in the UK), the Scandinavian countries and the Netherlands. In the Netherlands accounting was hardly regulated by company law at all until the Act on the Annual Accounts of Enterprises of 10 September 1970. The emphasis of this Act (now incorporated in the Dutch Civil Code) is on disclosure rather than prescribed forms of statement and rules of valuation.

Throughout most of Europe, with the notable exceptions of the UK, Ireland and the Netherlands, the requirements of *tax legislation* have a profound effect on company financial reporting. In France and Germany, for example, most tax benefits can only be obtained if certain entries are made in the books of account and the published financial statements. In France the form of the financial statements and the rules of valuation required by *company* law depend on the *tax* decree of 28 January 1965. In Britain tax law is an indirect influence. LIFO as a method of stock valuation, for instance, would be much more popular (despite the opposition of the accountancy profession) if it were allowable for tax purposes.

A major aim of the EEC is the establishment of one internal market with a free flow of reliable and consistent financial information. The EEC Commission is therefore attempting to harmonise both company and tax legislation, although progress has so far been rather slow.

The proposed fourth directive on company law deals with the coordination of national legislation regarding the annual accounts of limited liability companies. It was first issued by the European Commission on 16 November 1971, i.e. before the enlargement of the EEC from six to nine members. An amended version was issued on 21 February 1974 and is expected to be approved by the Council of Ministers in 1977. Each member state will have to have appropriate new legislation in force within thirty months of the date of approval. The proposed fourth directive does not cover groups of companies; these are dealt with in the proposed seventh directive issued on 28 April 1976.

The fourth directive will increase the importance of company law in accounting in all member states. Its general philosophy is largely a compromise between the German and British approaches. Annual accounts must give a true and fair view of a company's assets, liabilities, financial position and results and be drawn up clearly and in conformity with the provisions of the directive. It is not clear whether, as in Britain, a true and fair view is the overriding requirement or, as in Germany, conformity to the detailed rules comes first.

Following German company law, the proposed fourth directive has a very prescriptive approach to valuation methods. It is expressly stated that valuation must be on a conservative basis; that formation expenses, research and deveopment costs and goodwill must be written off over a maximum period of five years; that fixed assets must be valued at purchase price or production cost; that production cost must be calculated by adding to the purchase price of the raw and auxiliary materials the manufacturing costs directly attributable to the product in question and a reasonable proportion of the manufacturing costs which are only indirectly attributable; and that current assets must be valued at purchase price or production cost less value adjustments and using weighted average cost or FIFO or LIFO or some similar method.

As a result of mainly Dutch and British pressure, clauses have been added making possible some form of current cost accounting or current purchasing power accounting.

Again following German company law, the fourth directive prescribes standard forms of balance sheet and profit and loss account. These are set out in considerable detail. Some of the detail may be avoided but the basic frameworks are compulsory. The balance sheet may be in statement or account form. This choice is also allowed for the profit and loss account, the classification in which may be either 'natural' or 'functional'. There are thus $2 \times 2 = 4$ possible layouts for the profit and loss account.

The fourth directive applies to all companies but

exemptions are granted according to size. There are three categories of companies which can be called large, medium and small. Large companies (excluding banks and insurance companies, which are not covered by the directive) are subject to all the requirements. Medium companies can, if a member state so wishes, publish their profit and loss accounts in an abridged form. Small companies can be exempted from publishing a profit and loss account at all and need publish an abridged balance sheet only. There is nothing in the proposed directive to prevent a member state from requiring all three categories of company to comply with all the requirements of the directive.

Company size is measured by three criteria: balance sheet totals, net turnover and number of employees.[2]

The proposed fourth directive is not concerned with taxation as such but there has been an attempt, more important for countries such as France and West Germany than for Britain and the Netherlands, to ensure that the effects of taxation are *disclosed*. If, for example, fixed or current asset items are the subject of exceptional value adjustments solely for the purpose of tax law, the amount of the adjustments and the reasons for making them, together with the relevant future taxation, has to be indicated in the notes to the accounts. The notes must in any case indicate the amount of the changes in the profit or loss for the year due to the application of tax laws.

In several European countries *the recommendations and standards issued by professional bodies* are very important. In Britain, for example, the equity method of accounting for associated companies, the disclosure of accounting policies, the disclosure and method of calculation of earnings per share and the publication of funds statements are all dependent not upon legislation but on statements of standard accounting practice promulgated by the Accounting Standards Committee. The accountancy profession is also very influential in the Netherlands and in West Germany. In the Netherlands, company law provides that valuation rules must comply with 'standards that are regarded as being acceptable in economic and social life'. What these are is decided by the Dutch profession in association with representative associations of employers and

Table 4 Chart of accounts

	FINANCIAL ACCOUNTING								COST ACCOUNTING	SPECIAL ACCOUNTS
	Balance sheet accounts					Management accounts		Trading and profit and loss accounts	Cost accounts	Special accounts
Class 1	Class 2	Class 3	Class 4	Class 5	Class 6	Class 7	Class 8	Class 9	Class 0
Permanent capital accounts	Fixed asset accounts	Stock accounts	Personal accounts	Financial accounts	Expense accounts by type of expense	Income accounts by type of income	Trading and profit and loss accounts	Cost accounts	Special accounts
10 Capital	20 Organisational costs	30 Goods purchased	40 Suppliers	50 Borrowing repayable within one year	60 Purchases	70 Sales	80 Trading account	90 Reciprocal accounts	00 Contingent liabilities
11 Reserves	21 Fixed assets	31 Raw materials	41 Trade debtors	51 Loans due within one year	61 Wages, salaries and payroll charges	71 Trading subsidies received	81	91 Cost & reclassifications 92	
12 Retained profits brought forward	22	32 Supplies	42 Employees	52 Bills and warrants payable	62 Taxes	72 Sales of scrap and returnable containers	82		
13	23 Fixed assets under construction	33 Scrap and rejects	43 Government	53 Bills and warrants receivable	63 Outside supplies and services	73 Allowances against sales	83	93 Manufacturing costs	
14 Equipment grants received	24 Fixed assets by acts of war	34 Semi-finished goods	44 Partners or shareholders	54 Cash in transit	64 Travelling and transport costs	74 Discounts, rebates and allowances received	84	94 Permanent inventory accounts	
15 Provisions for losses and costs	25 Loans due after one year	35 Finished goods	45 Subsidiaries (or parent company)	55 Government and other marketable	65	75	85	95	

	repayable after one year	work in progress	debtors and creditors	postal cheque accounts	...tive costs	income	company exchanges and services	cost variances
17 Branch and intra-company accounts	27 Deposits and guarantees	37 Containers	47 Accruals, deferred income etc.	57 Cash in hand	67 Financial costs	77 Financial income	87 Profits and losses	97 Cost variances
18	28	38	48 Prepayments etc.	58 Administration advances and letters of credit	68 Depreciation, amortization, transfers to provisions	78 Work done by the enterprise for itself. Work and costs not chargeable to current trading	88 Profit/loss before appropriation	98 Manufacturing profit and loss account
19	29	39	49 Suspense accounts	59 Internal transfers	69	79	89 Balance sheet	99 Internal transfers

Total of the debit balances of accounts in classes 1 to 5 (assets)   + ...

Total of the credit balances of accounts in classes 1 to 5 (capital and liabilities)   − ....

Net profit (+) or net loss (−)   .... = Net profit/loss

Total of class 7
− Total of class 6
± Stock difference

Trading profit/loss   .... = Balance of account 80

± Profits/losses other than from trading

.... = Net profit/loss   = Balance of account 87

trades unions. In West Germany the role of the profession is more that of a commentator on legislation which, as we have seen, tends to be more detailed and comprehensive than in the other member states.

The EEC Accountants Study Group has been very active in relation to the proposed fourth directive and is specifically referred to in the explanatory memorandum to the amended proposal. The European Commission appears very willing to listen to it on matters which have no political implications. All that is required is agreement among the professional representatives from nine member states! The Study Group does not itself issue accounting standards. The UEC is concentrating its attention upon auditing standards.

Some countries have a *government regulatory agency* with the power to lay down or influence accounting standards. The most notable example is outside Europe: the US Securities and Exchange Commission. The most influential such body in Europe is the French Commission des Opérations de Bourse (COB) which controls the issue of prospectuses and has been largely responsible for the great increase in France in recent years in the number of consolidated financial statements published. A similar commission was recently established in Italy: The Commissione nazionale per le società e la borsa (CONSOB). It is too early to forecast how influential this body will be. A Companies Commission has from time to time been recommended in the UK but it now seems unlikely that one will be established.

In at least two countries in Europe — France and Belgium — financial accounting and reporting is greatly influenced by the rules of a *national accounting plan*. Such plans are not simply charts of accounts; they also contain model financial statements and detailed valuation rules. In France accounting plans based upon the national one are being developed for each industry. The official diagram of the national plan is reproduced in English translation on pages 68-9 as table 4. There has been no attempt by the EEC Commission to suggest a harmonised national accounting plan, although, of course, the prescription by company law of model financial statements and of valuation rules is in accord with the general philosophy of such plans.

Summary

The twin themes of a study of accounting in Europe are diversity and harmonisation. There is nationalism in accounting and financial reporting as in many other spheres and unity and uniformity are still a long way off.

Notes and references

1 G. G. Mueller, *International Accounting*, Macmillan, New York 1967.
2 It is possible to measure company size by balance sheet total because balance sheets have to be drawn up in a standard form. Turnover is net of VAT.

Suggested further reading

Detailed studies of accounting and financial reporting in leading European countries are being published by the Institute of Chartered Accountants in England and Wales in its *European Financial Reporting Series*. Volumes published to date are:

I   West Germany (1975) by J. H. Beeny
II   France (1976) by J. H. Beeny
III Italy (1976) by M. I. Stilwell

The Netherlands volume is due for publication in 1977. The proposed 4th and 7th Directives on Company Law are available as supplements to the *Bulletin of the European Communities*.

5

Accounting and changing prices

TONY HOPE

Senior Lecturer in Accounting, University of Manchester

Introduction

Let us suppose that you were asked to prepare a statement, in money terms, of all your assets and liabilities as at today's date, and also a statement showing the changes in your assets and liabilities from the position which existed, say, one year ago. Let us further suppose that you were not told the purpose for which these statements were required. How would you approach the matter? It is quite likely that your approach would depend on whether you possessed any knowledge of accounting.

If you possessed little or no knowledge of accounting you would probably first list all your physical (and perhaps non-physical) assets and second try to attach some money equivalent to each of them. The first part of the task would be easier than the second part. It always is. The attachment of money figures to the assets would probably be done on the crude basis of their worth or value to you as at today's date, (i.e. at their 'current value'). Correspondingly, the statement showing the changes in your assets over the last year would probably reflect in some way the changes in their 'current values', either because you had used them during that period and therefore they were worth less than they were one year ago, or simply because the process of time had made them more or less valuable. My assumptions about the way you might prepare your statements are supported by observations. I asked six of my friends, who profess to know nothing about what accounting is and about how accountants act, to tell me how they would place money equivalents on their assets. Every one made an independent stab at a 'current value'! I think this observation is important.

The reason I think my observation is important is that if you acted in the same way as my friends, it is most unlikely that your two statements of current financial position and changes in financial position would be based on the prices which you originally paid for your assets (even if you could remember what these were), except in so far as any of your assets had been bought shortly before today's date. And yet it is precisely this idea of 'valuing' assets at their original, historical cost which accountants still employ as the basis for preparing their financial statements.

The gist of my argument is simple. It is this. When people are faced with questions as to the preparation and, by implication, the meaning of financial statements, they think in terms of 'value' and 'worth' rather than in terms of past costs. I infer from this that the reason they think in terms of 'values' rather than 'costs' is because it is intuitively more meaningful and informative to do so. One would perhaps reasonably expect statements of financial position (balance sheets) and statements of changes in financial position (profit and loss accounts) to show monetary amounts which, in some sense, reflect 'current' values. There is however much evidence to show that people *believe* they do reflect current values. However, generally speaking, accounting statements do not reflect current values. They reflect depreciated and undepreciated past costs. Indeed an historic cost balance sheet is precisely what it purports to be; a sheet of balances extracted from the books at the end of the period, representing all items which have not been transferred to the profit and loss account. Let us spend a few moments trying to understand why this is the case.

Why accountants use historic costs

We could begin by saying that it is only very recently (in the 1970's) that accountants have used the criteria of meaningfulness and usefulness for particular purposes to determine how they should value assets and liabilities in balance sheets. This is primarily because the subject of accounting has never been based on any satisfactory theory (unlike, say, economics or physics) but rather it has evolved in a piece-meal way over time. Existing accounting practice has been augmented by additional legislation, with little or no thought being given to the overall purpose of the exercise. The result of this form of evolution has been that certain beliefs and dogmas (as distinct from theories) have become accepted by accountants and have been codified into what we might call accounting practice. Indeed, especially in the USA, accounting reports prepared for company share-holders are often said to be prepared on the basis of 'generally accepted accounting principles'. Few have questioned whether such generally accepted principles provide information which is useful to its recipients.

Perhaps the most pervasive belief of the accountant relates to the acceptance of the convention of historic cost as the most generally appropriate method of showing the financial results of the entity for which he or she is responsible. The entity could be a cricket club, a large public quoted company such as ICI Ltd., a charitable organisation or even the accountant himself. The distinction between the various possible types of entity has, until recently, been unimportant to the accountant; historic cost has been the chosen 'valuation' method.

The historic cost convention rests on one basic principle, which is commonly termed 'the realisation rule'. There are other principles associated with historic cost accounting, for instance the matching principle, the accruals principle and the conservatism principle, but it is the notion of the realisation rule which sets it apart from other measurement methods. This rule has the effect of preventing the accountant from recognising in the accounts any changes in the value of the entity's assets, irrespective of the size of such changes, until they have been realised by transaction (normally by sale). This refusal to recognise unrealised value changes means that only a part of the total increase in value accruing to the entity during an accounting period — the profit — is reported. The reported profit figure of any single year is therefore the result of a mixture of transactions which have occurred in *different* years, as a result of *different* decisions, probably made by *different* managements.

The part which is not recorded (i.e. the unrealised gains arising from the holding of assets whose prices have increased we might term the unrealised 'holding gain'. The recognition and treatment of holding gains forms the basic difference between historic cost and current value accounting.

We may question why this belief in historic cost accounting has persisted for so long without serious criticism from accountants. After all, historic cost is simply a man-made 'convention'. It has no natural claim for inclusion in accounting reports. If the common sense approach to asset valuation is to think in terms of current values, whereas the accountant deals in past costs, some reasons must exist as to why historic cost is preferred. We might perhaps detect at least three reasons for its continued use.

First, the accountants might tell us that they continue to use historic cost because that is the method of recording which is used in the entity's books of account, and the entity's balance sheet and profit and loss account are prepared directly from the books of account. In fact we might hear the reply that the recording technique of double-entry book-keeping is inseparably linked with historic cost; indeed, that double-entry relies on historic cost for its success. But we might counter this argument by saying that there is no logical reason why financial statements should not be prepared from books of account which contain information based on conventions other than historic cost. (Nor indeed is there any logical reason why entities should use profit and loss accounts and balance sheets to report their progress. For example, cash flow statements could quite easily be used instead of or as well as the traditional documents.)

Second, we might be told that in periods of stable prices, which have persisted in the United Kingdom for much of the twentieth century (though not during the last ten years), there is little difference between historic and current asset values. This argument could prevail even if there is a considerable time span between the purchase date of an asset and its balance sheet reporting date. However, the rates of price change experienced in the United Kingdom during the 1970's would appear to cast some doubts on the validity of this reply.

Third, the accountants may tell us that historic cost accounting has 'stood the test of time' and that any other proposed valuation convention must be shown to be demonstrably superior to historic cost.

The third argument is a good argument. How can we judge one accounting valuation method to be in some sense 'better' than another method? So far we have talked almost solely in terms of intuition and common sense, and even then largely in terms of observations from people who have little or no knowledge of accounting. To be more specific in answering the 'test of time' argument we must return to the point made earlier: that we can choose between different accounting conventions only in the light of some defined purpose, a definition which accounting has lacked.

The last ten years have seen many attempts to define an accounting purpose, particularly in the USA, in Australia, and in the United Kingdom. A common consensus view might now state that the function of accounting is to 'record, measure and communicate useful information to enable users to make informed decisions'. The most important word in this definition is the final one; the 'decision-taking' view of accounting information is the 'new' approach. If there is a difference between the original and the current cost of an asset, as might be the case with a fixed asset such as plant and machinery, then a choice must be made on the basis of the likely usefulness of the valuation for particular decisions of particular users.[1] We will see that this particular approach has been endorsed by a committee set up by the UK Government to investigate appropriate reporting methods.

It is perhaps no coincidence that these recent attempts to define the purposes of accounting have been paralleled, in the United Kingdom at least, by increased dissatisfaction with existing accounting practice, and therefore, by implication, with historic cost accounting. Indeed, one might say that the attempts at a definition of accounting were brought about by the dissatisfaction with practice. Nor perhaps is it a coincidence that the degree of criticism of accounting practice has also been paralleled by the largest increases in price inflation experienced in the Western world for many decades.

The motivation for change in the UK

Most of the theories of accounting which have been developed by academics have failed to obtain general support from the accounting profession. However, the rapid escalation in the rates of general inflation and in specific asset price changes which began in the late 1960's has focussed the attention of the accounting profession on the problems and potential inadequacies of historic cost. The profession has therefore had to look much more closely at the nature of its main products, the balance sheet and profit and loss account.

This re-appraisal of the nature and contents of the main accounting reports was initiated in the United Kingdom by a series of so-called 'accounting scandals' in the late 1960's which triggered off a public reaction against the apparent ease with which companies could manipulate their accounting profits. The response of the accounting profession was to set up, in December 1969, a Standards Committee, which decided to look initially at twenty potentially contentious areas of accounting practice. The procedure followed by the Committee was to issue an exposure draft on each topic for general comment, followed some months later by the issue of a standard of accounting practice on the same topic.

The most contentious exposure draft, ED8, issued in 1973, represented the profession's response to pressure to deal with the problems generated by the use of the historic cost convention during inflationary periods. It is very important to realise that Exposure Draft 8 was issued long before the profession had formulated its ideas as to what particular purposes accounting documents, whether or not adjusted to take account of changing prices, should seek to serve. (The purposes of accounts were eventually discussed in *The Corporate Report,*[2] prepared by a working party of the Standards Committee.)

ED8 advocated one possible method of incorporating the effect of changing prices into accounting reports. The method it laid down as being the appropriate model for accounting reports was almost exactly the same as that advocated by the American accounting profession in 1969. The method is known as *general* price-level accounting, or as it became known in the United Kingdom, CPP (current purchasing power) accounting.

The fundamental nature of the method, which we will explore in more detail later in this chapter, entails the updating of all the historic cost data in the accounts by means of a general price index, such as the Retail Price Index. The purpose is to show all figures in the profit and loss account and balance sheet in terms of 'current' pounds of the reporting date.

This method has not proved to be universally popular. Much criticism was directed at ED8, in particular by both the academic and the business communities, primarily on the grounds that updating all historic costs for *general* price changes may be quite inapplicable to entities which hold *specific* assets, the prices of which may each have changed at a different rate and, indeed, in a different direction from the general price level.

This barrage of criticism of the profession's proposed method of incorporating 'inflation' into published accounts prompted the UK Government to set up its own committee to investigate accounting for changing prices. The profession restricted itself to following ED8 with a provisional standard (PSSAP7), and that has since become defunct. Accordingly, an Inflation Accounting Committee was set up under Francis Sandilands to probe further the whole topic of how best to incorporate the effects of changing prices into accounting reports. This is the Committee to which earlier reference has been made. It is very important to note two things concerning the Sandilands Committee: first it was a government committee, and second it was not composed solely of accountants. Indeed, only three of the twelve members were accountants.

The Sandilands Committee reported its findings in September 1975.[3] It altogether rejected the ideas of ED8 (i.e. of general price level accounting) and recommended a complete system of current value accounting, called current cost accounting. Its recommendations were based on considerations as to what different user groups required from accounting reports,[4] and represented the most radical departure from the basis of historic cost accounting ever suggested by a non-academic body. At the time of writing

(March 1977) the suggestions put forward by the Sandilands Committee and its successor, the Morpeth Committee,[5] have not been implemented, but it seems likely that some form of current cost accounting will be compulsory in the United Kingdom within the near future.

Let us now proceed to explore in greater detail some of these alternatives to historic cost.

Possible alternatives to historical cost

Many theories of accounting have been advocated in the academic literature.[6] Most of these theories allow in some way for the incorporation of price changes into accounting statements. Some merely involve the updating (and therefore the retention) of historic costs, others advocate their abandonment for current values. The former group may be said to be primarily interested in incorporating in financial statements changes which arise because of the existence of inflation (i.e. from changes in the general level of prices), whereas the latter group of theories seek to incorporate changes which are caused by the movements in prices of the individual assets of the entity (i.e. specific price change accounting). Naturally, within these very broad definitions there is a number of alternatives, for example the use of either current buying prices or current selling prices in specific price change accounting. Most have in common the underlying notion of providing useful information to users.

As previously mentioned, the form of accounting advocated by PSSAP 7 is an example of general price level accounting, whereas the form of current cost accounting recommended in the Sandilands report is an example of current value accounting. These are 'extreme' examples of the two approaches. It is quite possible to have a 'hybrid' accounting theory which utilises both 'general' and 'specific' price changes whether of the buying or selling variety. For example, theories[7] have been developed which attempt to apply a general index to share-holders' funds while at the same time valuing the assets of the enterprise in terms of specific prices.

Our intention here is, in fact, to look at the two extremes, essentially because they represent approaches to accounting theory which have been considered by professional bodies as capable of implementation. We will try to point out, by the use of a numerical illustration, the different concepts underlying the theories of 'pure' general price level accounting (i.e. all figures in the accounts expressed in current *pounds*, rather than in current *values*) and 'pure' current value accounting, using current replacement costs. The Sandilands Committee anticipates that replacement cost will in most cases represent the appropriate measure of current value for reporting purposes.

We will use the following information to illustrate the points at issue.

Suppose a limited company starts operations on 1 January 19X1 with capital of £3300 made up of three types of asset, each purchased new at that date, as follows:

Plant and machinery	1000
Stock	2000
Cash	300
Total assets	£ 3300

Let us further suppose we have additional information concerning the assets as follows:

(a) The plant will last for five years and will lose value equally over the period of its life.

(b) The stock comprises two identical items, each having a cost of £1000.

(c) During the year from 1 January 19X1 to 31 December 19X1 work is performed upon only one of the stock items, the wages for which, amounting to £500, are paid on the last day of the year. On this same day the finished stock item is sold for cash of £2200, and is replaced by an identical unworked item costing £1500.

(d) The rate of general inflation, as measured by the Retail Price Index, is 20% for the year (i.e. the index was 100 on 1 January and 120 on 31 December.).

(3) The replacement cost at 31 December 19X1 of a new item of plant identical to that owned by the firm is £2000.

We now have all the data we need to explain the workings of the two alternative approaches. We shall do this by concentrating our attention on the firm's profit for the year under the different measurement concepts. We may define profit, in an accounting sense, as the amount by which the closing value of net assets exceeds the opening value of net assets, after allowing for any adjustments to opening net assets. Net assets are defined as being equal to the capital (or ownership equity) of the entity and the adjustments are known as capital maintenance adjustments; an understanding of them is fundamental to an understanding of competing accounting theories. Our definition of profit is identical to that founded in economic theory and used by the Sandilands Committee: the maximum amount the firm can distribute during a period and expect to be as well off at the end of the period as it was at the beginning. According to this approach, the amount of profit will depend on how we measure 'well-offness' — a measurement which we reflect in our capital maintenance adjustments. It is here that we can see most clearly the different ideas underlying general and specific price change accounting. The general price level notion of capital maintenance focuses on the owners of the entity. It is often termed a proprietary concept. This notion ensures that an entity cannot show a profit until the *purchasing power* of the initial capital as measured by some general price index, has been preserved. The specific price change method regards the firm as a separate entity from its owners, and is therefore usually termed an entity concept. It requires that the *productive capacity* of the entity's assets be preserved before profit can be struck. This means that all holding gains (increases in replacement costs) must be treated as additions to capital to ensure the maintenance of productive capacity. The specific price change method takes no account of the maintenance of shareholders' funds in terms of purchasing power.

Using our notions of capital maintenance and asset valuation we can now show the results for the year 19X1 based on the data given. At the end of the year the firm has the following assets:

(a) one item of plant which is one year old, and which is expected to last for a further four years.

(b) two items of stock, one of which was bought at the beginning of the period, the other at the end of the period.

(c) cash of £500, representing the balance in hand after the year's transactions.

We might therefore say that at the end of the year the firm has physical, or non-monetary, assets comprising plant and stock, and monetary assets comprising cash. These are unchangeable facts. Whatever measurement method we choose to value these assets, they will not change their form, and therefore whatever monetary equivalents are attached to them will still reflect the same underlying facts.

"..... And so, as you can see, the use of current cost accounting puts the results of this company in a much more realistic light."

Let us now see, after much (necessary) preamble, what profit figures are produced from the different accounting methods. Table 1 shows the profit figures under 'pure' historic cost accounting, 'pure' general price level accounting and 'pure' replacement cost accounting, derived from a direct comparison of the opening and closing capital subject to capital maintenance adjustments. Table 2 shows the same profit figures using the traditional method of

Table 1   Balance sheet comparisons of three alternative measurement
methods

	(1) HC	(2) CPP	(3) RC
Opening capital	3300	3300	3300
Add: Capital maintenance adjustment	—	660[a]	2000[b]
Revised opening capital (x)	3300	3960	5300
Closing capital (y) represented by:			
Plant	800	960[c]	1600[d]
Stock	2500	2700[e]	3000[f]
Cash	500	500	500
	3800	4160	5100
Profit for the year (y) − (x)	£ 500	£ 200	£(200)

[a] $660 = 3300 \times \dfrac{120}{100}$ (the change in the general price index applied to the opening capital)

[b] 2000 = Increase in replacement cost of plant   1000
Increase in replacement cost of stock

Used up 500
In hand 500 1000

    2000

[c] $960 = 800 \times \dfrac{120}{100}$

[d] $1600 = \dfrac{4}{5} \times 2000$ (i.e. four years remaining life of an asset having a replacement cost of £2000)

[e] $2700 = 1000 \times \dfrac{120}{100} + 1500$

[f] 3000 = Two items of stock, each having a replacement cost of £1500.

deducting the cost of input factors from the sales revenue realised.

A comparison of the results shown by tables 1 and 2 illustrates that it is possible to produce different profit and asset figures by applying different measurement methods to exactly the same transactions (i.e. column 1 shows a profit

Table 2 Profit and loss accounts of three alternative measurement methods

	(1) HC		(2) CPP		(3) RC	
Sales		2200		2200		2200
less:						
Cost of materials	1000		1200[g]		1500[h]	
Depreciation	200		240[i]		400[j]	
Wages	500		500		500	
Loss on holding cash	—	1700	60[k]	2000	—	2400
Profit/(loss)		£500		£200		£(200)

[g] $1200 = 1000 \times \dfrac{120}{100}$

[h] 1500 = replacement cost of stock item used

[i] $240 = 200 \times \dfrac{120}{100}$

[j] 400 = fall in value for one year (1/5) of replacement cost of £2000.

[k] 60 = decline in real value of cash during inflationary period

$\left(\dfrac{20}{100} \times £300 \right)$. The firm held £300 until the final day of

the year, during which time its value depreciated by 20%.

of £500, column 2 a profit of £200, and column 3 a loss of £200). These different figures are to be expected. What is perhaps less expected is the size of the difference between the methods, and in particular the discrepancy between the historic cost *profit* figure of £500 and the replacement cost *loss* figure of £200. 'Profit' and 'loss' are emotive words, and therefore the report that a business is making a loss (as measured in current terms) may lead to different decisions from those which would result from the report that a business is making a profit (from the same transactions), even though this profit is measured in historic terms. Emotion, in an accounting sense, may hopefully be cured by education, and there seems to be little doubt that a huge programme is needed to educate (or re-educate) accountants in the meaning and importance of different profit concepts.

An evaluation of the different concepts

But let us address ourselves more directly to an evaluation of the results shown in tables 1 and 2. We can see that the profit figures and, by implication, the returns on capital employed are very different (e.g. the business is earning a return of 13% on its closing assets as measured by using historic costs, approximately 5% using general price level accounting, but is shown by the use of replacement costs to be *losing* 4% on its (much higher) asset base). But what do the profit (and loss) figures shown in tables 1 and 2 signify? Which of the figures is the best one? Are the differences between the three figures important? The details of answers to such questions as these depend on how we stand in relation to the entity (e.g. whether we are managers or share-holders, creditors or employees), because our position in relation to the entity will determine the sorts of decisions, if any, we will make on the basis of the accounts, and these decisions may in turn be influenced by the available information. The managers of the company, for example, may be primarily interested in knowing whether they have made a profit after deducting the costs of those input factors they must replace if the firm (and also the management?) is to continue in business at the same volume of operations; the employees may be interested in knowing the same figure, as their prospects of future employment will be directly related to the firm's ability to maintain its operations (though in the short term they may also perceive the historic cost figures to be more congenial as a basis for pursuing wage claims); shareholders may be interested in knowing the efficiency with which management has handled the assets of the company as reflected in both the current net profit figure and also the current asset values at the end of the period, and creditors may wish to know most of all the current cost margin, as this affords some indirect indication of the likely future liquidity position of the business. It is not so easy to imagine situations in which users of accounts would prefer either the historic cost profit figure or the general price level profit figure, except perhaps to the extent that people prefer, as in our numerical example, to see profits rather than losses, however they are measured. And if that is the case we might say that those people are indulging in self-deception to the jeopardy of their longer term prospects.

In short we must conclude that on the basis of *a priori* arguments, which is the only possible basis for judging between alternative accounting methods unless we adopt an empirical approach to accounting theory, current value accounting represents the most useful method available of reporting profit and asset figures.

We have argued, at the start of the chapter, that, on the basis of casual observation of the reactions of individuals who possess no knowledge of accounting, current values represent the most *obvious* method of asset valuation, and we have closed with the view that current values also represent the *common sense* approach of users who possess some knowledge of accounting. And yet accounting is only now beginning, hesitantly, to shake itself free from the doctrine of historic cost. It is a perplexing situation. However, the work of the Sandilands and the Morpeth Committees encourage confidence that it can only be a matter of time before accounting rids itself of excessive emphasis on history and turns more realistically to the present and perhaps, in the fulness of time, the future.

Notes and references

1   For a summary of the possible approaches to the determination of an optimal reporting method see Chapter 7.
2   *The Corporate Report* produced by the Accounting Standards Committee in 1975 is a discussion document on the purposes and objectives of published accounts.
3   *Inflation Accounting*, the report of the Inflation Accounting Committee under Francis Sandilands.
4   See Chapter 5 of *'Inflation Accounting' op.cit.*
5   The Morpeth Committee (the Inflation Accounting Steering Group) was set up in 1976, to prepare a proposal for an exposure draft on current cost accounting to be based on the proposals of the Sandilands Committee. Its proposals were embodied in ED18, which was issued in November 1976.
6   For example amongst the better known are: R. J. Chambers, *Accounting, Evaluation and Economic Behaviour*, Prentice-Hall; E. O. Edwards and P. W. Bell, *The Theory and Measurement of Business Income* University of California Press 1961.
7   e.g. the work of R. J. Chambers, *op.cit.*

6

The modern audit function: a study of radical change

T A LEE

Professor of Accountancy and Finance, University of Edinburgh

Introduction

Throughout the past decade the company audit function has been the subject of increasing criticism. The main points of contention have been in two areas: first, the matters for which the auditor is responsible and, second, the persons to whom he has a duty of care. Much has been written and debated on these issues, but always in a fragmented way — each individual situation or case being scrutinised in detail as it arises. There has been little or no attention paid to the overall problems facing the auditor today. It is therefore the purpose of this essay to examine them generally in order to provide an overview of the company audit as it is presently constituted.

The importance of the audit function

Before proceeding to discuss the problems of responsibility now facing the company auditor, it is useful to take a pragmatic look at the importance of his function in relation to the needs of those persons assumed to rely on it. For example, the following statement would appear to express the current conventional wisdom of auditing:

> . . . no one would deny that the function of the auditor, in lending credibility to financial statements, has been

growing in importance, rapidly and steadily, over the last fifty years. . . . Such financial reports are relied on heavily by investors, creditors, security analysts, Government, and others. The role of the auditor, in lending credibility to these financial statements, is vital in establishing and maintaining confidence in the capital markets. Without such confidence the whole basis of our capitalist system would be destroyed. Thus, the continuing importance of the auditor's role is not in dispute.[1]

It is a statement of the *raison d'être* of company auditing and, from a review of the relevant literature,· appears to be generally accepted. Whether it should be is the subject for debate in the following section, for it makes the assumption that the use of financial information in decision-making activities depends to a large extent on the existence of a relevant audit function. This is an assumption which is often made, either explicitly or implicitly, without recourse to any supporting evidence. As such, it must remain as no more than a justifying statement for the audit function, and it would therefore appear to be appropriate to establish the truth of the matter before discussing the detailed problems of auditing responsibilities.

Use of financial reports

The auditor is concerned with examining, judging and giving an expert opinion on the quality of certain financial statements and reports published by companies for use by persons external to them. The first point of inquiry would thus seem to be whether or not these statements are used by those persons for which they are intended. This should at least give an initial clue as to the extent to which there is reliance on the work of the auditor. The available evidence is, however, scarce and limited.

The efficient markets evidence. Several studies have indicated the efficiency of American capital markets — that is, that share prices fully reflect all available information, and that no investor can therefore expect to use such information to obtain abnormal investment returns.[2] The speed of share price reaction to the publication of information is cited as evidence of market efficiency in this respect. In particular, the 'efficient markets' school has produced several interesting conclusions relevant to the importance of auditing:

(a) Interim financial reporting appears to have a far greater impact on investor behaviour than annual reporting. This is not surprising given the timeliness of the former data. Investors should be able to anticipate annual financial results by making use of interim data. However, quarterly or half-yearly financial statements are not normally subject to audit, which means that investors either are unable to distinguish between differing degrees of reliability in financial information or do not mind the lack of an audit opinion so long as the information is relevant to their needs.

(b) There is little evidence to suggest that the capital markets react naively to complex financial information. This appears to indicate a relatively sophisticated use of financial information by investors who should therefore appreciate the importance and meaning of the audit opinion, particularly if it is qualified.

(c) Certain findings show that investors tend to make use of a broad information set rather than merely published accounting data. A great deal of this information is unaudited, and often outside the control of the companies to which it relates. Again, this would suggest that investors are not as reliant on the work of the auditor as might at first be supposed.

Thus, in general terms at least, the American 'efficient markets' evidence indicates a relatively expert use by investors of all available financial information, with accounting data (often of an unaudited nature) occupying only a part of the total set. This tends to conflict with the traditional assumption of the investor relying heavily on audited financial reports.

Information needs of investors. A small number of studies have examined the information needs of investors in terms of the main factors for which accounting data are needed. Baker and Haslem,[3] in an analysis of 851 individual

investors, found that of the three factors rated by their
respondents as 'of great importance', two were related to the
future economic outlook of the company and its industry.
Of the next seven most important items, four related
specifically to the future. If information were to be provided
to satisfy these needs, it would presumably have to be of a
predictive nature and therefore not subject to the type of
audit scrutiny and opinion given to historic data. In
support of this, Baker and Haslem further found that 62% of
their respondents rated stockbrokers and other advisory
services as the most important information sources, with a
further 11% rating the financial press as the primary source.
Only 8% similarly rated financial statements which, in their
annual format, would be audited. None of these findings
lends much credence to the assumed importance of the audit
function in the use of financial information, although
audited data may be used indirectly in many of the unaudited sources. However, reliance on the work of the
auditor in these circumstances is, at best, second-hand.

  Baker and Haslem's work has been replicated by
Chenhall and Juchau.[4] Four out of the seven factors rated as
'of great importance' by their respondents would require
forecast data. In addition, although dealing with a
somewhat more sophisticated investment group than that
of Baker and Haslem, only 30% of the respondents rated
financial statements as the most important source of
information — 35% putting stockbrokers and advisory
services in that category.

  Thus, as with the 'efficient markets' evidence, the 'information needs' studies reveal serious implications for
auditing — investor needs tend to be directed at information
sources which are either unaudited or unauditable in the
conventional sense.

Evidence of reliance on audits. Surprisingly, little or no
research has been undertaken in the area of establishing
which sources of financial information are actually used by
investors and other persons interested in the financial
affairs of companies. Two UK studies and one Australian
study constitute the main evidence to date, and each
contains insights into a significant under-use of available
information by investors; particularly information of an
accounting nature accompanied by an audit opinion.

Clift[5] has carried out several studies in this area in Australia. In the first, in which he examined individual shareholder behaviour *vis-a-vis* the annual report, he found that only 36% of his respondents rated either the income statement or the balance sheet as the most interesting information source. In fact, the most popular statement was the directors' report, with one quarter of the responding group rating it in this way. Clift conducted this study in 1968 and again in 1974, and obtained almost identical results in both cases.

In a further study, this time of stockbroker behaviour, he found that only 47% of the interview group read and analysed thoroughly a large number of financial reports from companies. In addition, he established from an examination of the brokers' circulars to clients that approximately 45% of the data included in the circulars were derived directly or indirectly from financial reports. These results certainly do not indicate a heavy reliance on financial statements which have been subject to audit.

A similar conclusion has been arrived at in two recent studies of private shareholder behaviour in the UK.[6] Both involved shareholders in public companies and, in total, contained responses from 675 individuals. The following is a general summary of certain of the main findings of these studies which are relevant to this paper:

(a) The typical private shareholder appears to make his own investment decisions without help or advice from experts and without reference to any formal source of financial information about companies.

(b) Those individual shareholders making thorough use of annual reports from companies tend to be thorough users of other available sources of financial information. They also tend to be those with some significant experience of accounting and related matters.

(c) The two most extensively used sources of financial information were the chairman's report and financial press reports. Both were read thoroughly by a majority of shareholders in each study (just over 50% in all cases), but both are unaudited and may contain a great deal of subjective comment. On the other hand, it should be remembered that audited accounting data may be used by their producers at least as a background to their content.

(d)   The only audited financial statement to be extensively read by a significant number of share-holders in both studies was the income statement (by 47% in the first study and 39% in the second). Audited statements such as the balance sheet and the supporting notes to the accounts generally were poorly used, as were statements based on audited data such as the directors' report, the funds statements, and statements containing time series data.

(e)   The auditor's report was alarmingly ignored — only 17% and 16%, respectively, of the respondents in the two studies stating that they read it thoroughly; 44% and 48%, respectively, ignored it altogether.

(f)   The main reason for the avoidance of use of available financial information appeared to be its complexity and the technical language in which it was usually written.

None of these findings provides much evidence of the work of the auditor being relied on extensively by private shareholders and, as such, tends to confirm the evidence already gained from other studies of a considerable under-use of available information by investors.

Some reflections on the importance of auditing. Contrary to the usual view contained in the accountancy literature, the evidence which can be gathered together reveals that, at least amongst the investment community, the audit function is not as vital as some writers maintain. Of course, the very fact that it exists may give investors some confidence of the information's credibility without recourse to reading the audit report. But there is little evidence that they will use audited information in preference to unaudited information. In other words, if audited information is to be used extensively, it must not only be verifiable, but will also have to be relevant and understandable to its potential users. At the present time, investor preferences appear to be for data which are relevant and understandable. The fact that they are unaudited does not appear to inhibit their use.

These conclusions raise interesting questions regarding the future of the company audit, particularly with regard to the subject-matter of auditing and the persons to whom the auditor is responsible. If his work is directed at information which is little used by the investment community (as appears to be the case with many of the accounting statements in the annual report) then it becomes necessary to re-evaluate his role in relation to alternative audit areas, as well as in relation to the persons to whom his audit report should be directed. In other words, answers should be sought to the questions of whether he is auditing the most appropriate subject-matter on behalf of the most relevant interested persons. Not surprisingly, the main issues facing the audit today are contained in these related areas.

The subject-matter of auditing

Until relatively recently, the role of the auditor in corporate activity could be summed up reasonably as follows:

> Company auditing is concerned with the creation of belief and confidence in the financial accounting information which describes the use made of economic resources within a company over a stated period of time. By giving an expert and independent opinion upon the company's annual financial accounts, the auditor attests to the latter's credibility on behalf of the shareholders who rely upon this formal substantiation taking place, prior to making use of the information in their investment management activities.[7]

In other words, the company audit is generally regarded as a process concerned with the maintenance of an acceptable level of credibility in the published annual financial reports of management to shareholders. The auditor is attempting to give a reasoned opinion on the reliability of reported accounting data, thereby giving confidence to its users. This in no way should be taken as implying either that he gives a guarantee of the information or that he is certifying its accuracy. Such data contain too many subjective judgments to be regarded as accurate and, in any case, the auditor is in no position to undertake all the checking which would be necessary in order to issue an 'accuracy' certificate. At its most fundamental the company audit is an exercise in power and responsibility. Management is given the responsibility (usually at law) to produce reliable financial information annually for shareholders. However, because of its position, it also has the power to manipulate such information, to describe the financial results of the company as favourably as possible. The auditor is therefore appointed as a counter-balance to management in this respect, being given the responsibility to judge the quality of the reported data, and the power to state clearly and positively to the shareholders his expert opinion on their reliability.

It is this mixture of power and responsibility which has given rise to a growing debate about the acceptability of the role of the auditor in terms such as those expressed above. Largely influenced by a recent large increase in litigation against auditors in America and elsewhere, the main arguments have focussed on (a) the extent to which the auditor should seek evidence to support his opinion on the financial statements; (b) his specific responsibility for the detection of fraud and error; (c) the information on which he could give an opinion; (d) his position of independence; and (e) the persons to whom he can be held to have a duty of care.

In many ways, each of these areas concerns a possible extension or change in the role of the auditor as it is presently conceived, and reflects the need to regard his function as subject to the changing attitudes and needs of society. In particular, they all question the relevance of existing audit standards now used in the giving of expert opinions by professional accountants.

Responsibility for seeking evidence. One of the basic assumptions inherent in the audit function appears to be as follows:

> There is sufficient competent and reliable evidence available to allow the auditor to give an opinion on the credibility of the accounting information in the company's financial statements, and the auditor can

collect and evaluate it within a reasonable time and at a reasonable cost.[8]

Until relatively recently, the satisfying of this particular assumption did not appear to present the company auditor with too many difficulties. There seemed to be a generally accepted audit practice which was satisfactory to all concerned. However, this position was changed in the late 1960s by a number of court cases and incidents which, in effect, meant that existing audit standards were challenged, particularly by judges who tended to set higher standards than were generally accepted by the accountancy profession at the time. This situation has placed onerous burdens on auditors when deciding whether they have obtained sufficient evidence to support their opinion, and whether they have complied with acceptable audit standards.

The uncertainty in this area appears to have commenced with the American case of *Fischer v Kletz* (1967) 226 F. Supp. 180 SDNY (Yale Express) where the auditor was held to be negligent when he delayed reporting on accounting errors he had discovered in financial statements, having previously given an unqualified opinion on them. He delayed reporting on them until the following annual audit report even though they had been incorporated in un-audited interim statements in the meantime. He had therefore followed existing audit standards but these were found by the court to have been inadequate in the circumstances.

In *Escott v BarChris Construction Corp.* (1968) 283 F. Supp. 643 SDNY a similar situation arose. The auditor was found guilty of aiding and abetting in the issue of a false prospectus because he failed to re-audit financial statements on which he had previously reported. As a result, he failed to discover matters which should have been brought to light by evidence which only became available after his original report had been given. The need constantly to review previous audits in the light of new evidence was emphasised in a non-audit case, *SEC v Texas Gulf Sulphur Corp.* (1968) 401 F 2d. 833 2d. Cir. in which it was held that information found to have been omitted from previous financial statements should have been included in them, thereby implying that the relevant audit opinions, which failed to comment on the omission, were misleading. In other words, the Yale

Express, BarChris and Texas Gulf cases emphasised that the seeking of evidence to support an audit opinion did not cease at the time the opinion was given, and could therefore extend indefinitely into the future.

Several other recent cases have further complicated the auditor's position with regard to the seeking of evidence. The first stems from the Continental Vending case — *United States v Simon* (1968) CCA Fed. L. Re. 92, 511 United States District Court SDNY — in which the auditor was found guilty of criminal conspiracy when failing to verify and report adequately on the disclosure of certain loan transactions. Again, the auditor had followed generally accepted audit practice, and had not gone beyond the books and records of the company he was auditing in order to verify the uncertainty of recovery and security of a loan. In a rather similar way, the auditor of the Atlantic Acceptance Corp. Ltd had failed to go beyond the company to which he was appointed, and had relied on the opinions of other auditors of subsidiary companies. This was brought out in a Canadian Royal Commission Report on the affair, and since then most major professional accountancy bodies have attempted to specify guidelines for auditors to follow in such circumstances. In the Australian case of *Pacific Acceptance Corporation Ltd v Forsyth and Others* (1970), Supreme Court of New South Wales, the auditor was found to be negligent, inter alia, when relying on certificates from the company's stockbrokers relating to the existence and safe custody of securities. In addition, he had failed to investigate the reasons for qualifications in the reports of subsidiary company auditors.

In each of the above cases, there are clear indications to suggest that the modern auditor is now expected to go well beyond the confines of the particular company he is auditing in order to obtain evidence of the reliability of its financial statements on which he is giving an opinion. In particular, he appears to be expected, at least by courts of law, to investigate in some depth the credibility of relevant opinions given by other auditors and previous experts.

Responsibility for detecting fraud. The objectives of the earliest audits were concerned mainly with the detection of fraud and error — first, in relation to the safeguarding of business assets within the stewardship function; and second, as business accounting developed, in terms of preventing the publication of fraudulent or erroneous information in annual reports. In 1887, for example, the function was described as follows:

> The object of an audit is a two-fold one, the detection of fraud where it has been committed, and its prevention by imposing such safeguards, and devising such means as will make it extremely difficult of accomplishment, even if the inclination is in that direction.[9]

This particular approach to auditing persisted for several decades, until it became generally accepted that such a task placed impossible burdens on auditors. Fraud and error detection was relegated to a minor role, i.e. the auditor was expected to investigate the possibility of the existence of fraud and error only if his suspicions were aroused when using sound audit procedures in the normal course of his audit. The problem, however, has always been one of deciding at what point his suspicions are sufficiently aroused to warrant further attention and action before giving his opinion. Unfortunately, due again to recent law suits, it has become apparent that what the auditor regards as reasonable suspicion is not always the same as that perceived by investors and courts of law.

Evidence that there may be misunderstandings in this area is not hard to find. For example, in a UK study of individual perceptions of the role of the auditor in the late 1960s, it was found, in relation to the people questioned, that 86% of investors, 85% of company managers, and 85% of auditors believed fraud detection to be a main audit objective, with 12%, 34% and 23% of these groups, respectively, placing it as one of their major objectives.[10] Similarly, in a later study involving Australian private shareholders, it was found that 93% of the respondents expected the auditor to assure them that no fraud had been perpetrated by company officials.[11]

It is not surprising, therefore, that a number of cases have arisen recently which have caused auditors to reconsider their role *vis-a-vis* fraud and error. For example, in the Bar-Chris case mentioned above, the auditor did not detect fraud

in a prospectus because he failed to re-audit financial statements in the light of new evidence forthcoming since the
time of the original audit opinion. Similarly, lack of
sufficient checking in depth in the Continental Vending,
Atlantic Acceptance and Pacific Acceptance cases caused
auditors to be held negligent for failing to detect material
fraud. Finally, the failure of the Equity Funding Corporation of America in 1973, with its vast fraudulent activities,
was serious enough to warrant the appointment of a Special
Committee of the American Institute of Certified Public
Accountants to report on the adequacy of generally accepted
auditing standards, and in particular those relating to
fraud.[12] In the case of Equity Funding, the auditor failed for
several years to detect the overstatement of income and the
reporting of fictitious assets, involving by 1973 a required
write down of assets of $185.5 million. The Committee
concluded that generally accepted auditing standards were
sufficient to deal with a situation such as Equity Funding,
but it warned against failure to ensure that auditing
procedures were sufficient to detect a material fraud:

> In this respect, it seems quite clear that the auditor has an
> obligation to discover material frauds that are
> discoverable through application of customary auditing
> procedures applied in accordance with generally accepted
> auditing standards. The auditing profession should, on
> an on-going basis, continue to improve the efficiency of
> customary audit procedures to the end that probability of
> discovery of material frauds continues to increase within
> the limits of practicability.[13]

The problem, therefore, is one of attempting to improve the
probability of discovering fraud within normal audit
practice, and without recourse to the tedious and time-
consuming checking which characterised early company
audits. It would appear that auditors will require to
examine this aspect of their work much more seriously than
in recent years. The audit pendulum is now swinging back
in the direction of an audit role which has been allowed to
diminish in importance since the beginning of the
twentieth century.

Giving an opinion on other information. Arguably, the
most contentious area in auditing is likely to concern the

question of whether the auditor should give an opinion on reported information other than that of an accounting nature contained in the annual financial statements. Increasingly, in an age of pressure to disclose, companies are producing a substantial amount of information, much of which is not subject to audit. Obvious examples include interim financial statements, various parts of annual financial reports, press releases, and financial statements prepared specially for particular lenders, creditors, etc. In these situations, there is a feeling that unaudited information lacks the credibility of audited annual financial reports. Indeed, in America there appears to be pressure from the Securities and Exchange Commission and the New York Stock Exchange to have previously unaudited information audited. These pressures may grow rapidly if corporate reports expand their content in the way proposed by the UK Accounting Standards Committee in its publication *The Corporate Report*.[14]

The problem is that much of this information may be either more subjective or more qualitative than is the case with annual accounting statements and, for these reasons, it may not be possible to examine and report on an interim income statement or a chairman's report in the same way as is done for the annual income statement and balance sheet. Another related problem is the feeling that, particularly with the annual report, there may be a misapprehension by its users that the auditor's opinion on the annual financial statements covers other statements which contain accounting data. Thus, there is a fear that report users may believe unaudited data to have been audited, and may use them on that understanding. This may account for at least some of the relatively considerable use made of unaudited information by shareholders which has been commented on in an earlier section.

In order to clarify the situation, and to prevent any misunderstandings arising in the minds of report users, it has been suggested that auditors should attempt to give 'assurance' reports on reported information from companies which has not been subject to annual audit procedures.[15] This would involve a limited but relevant examination of the information and a suitable assurance of its reliability. This would not be the traditional audit report (that is, the 'true and fair view' opinion in the UK) but would be something far less precise. Much depends on the nature of the information being reviewed and the degree of uncertainty and subjective judgment associated with it. In the UK, the *City Code on Takeovers and Mergers* requires the auditor or reporting accountant to examine and report on the accounting bases and calculations used in the preparation of an income forecast for takeover or merger purposes. This is a form of assurance report, falling short of a full audit opinion, but intended to lend credibility to the forecast published by the company concerned. Much research has to be undertaken in this area to establish what form of examination and assurance report should be given in particular circumstances, but it appears that such an extension of the audit function is inevitable, given the assumed need to provide a level of credibility beyond that which already may exist in unaudited information. Although this will obviously add to the burden of auditors, it is not a function which is entirely new to them. For example, in the UK, they can be appointed as reporting accountants for the purpose of issuing a prospectus on a new issue of shares and, as already mentioned, they may also occupy a similar position in a takeover or merger situation. In both cases, their review is in addition to the normal annual audit and they are effectively giving assurance reports. In addition, within the terms of the annual audit, they are required to go beyond the traditional limits of evaluating historic cost information in order to ensure the company has properly applied its accounting in terms of the 'going concern' convention. This involves looking at economic and financial factors in a predictive sense in order to assess whether or not the company can be classed as a going concern. All in all, therefore, the company auditor should already have some experience of extending his function of verification beyond what has become generally accepted over the years.

Auditor independence

The accountancy literature has, for a long time, borne testimony to the continuing problem of auditor independence. The auditor's position of neutrality is one of the cornerstones of auditing thought and practice, and is generally assumed to be essential to maintaining the credibility of his opinion and, thus, of the financial information to which that opinion relates. However, it is easier to recognise the need for independence than it is to implement it in practice. Company legislation, professional regulations and unofficial rules of individual firms of auditors have undoubtedly helped to maintain the appearance of independence. However, much has been left to the individual auditor to be mentally independent when making his judgments and giving his opinions. But mental independence is not enough: there must also be tangible evidence. The auditor can be under considerable pressure if disagreement arises with a client company over accounting matters. He may be in a position of either agreeing with his client and thereby keeping the audit, or disagreeing and finding he loses the audit through dismissal or resignation. In other words, he tends to have responsibility without authority. As the courts appear to be increasing his responsibilities, attempts should be made to increase his authority by improving his position of independence. But here lies the crux of the problem — how to improve his appearance of independence so as to ensure a proper mental neutrality.

The American Institute of Certified Public Accountants has one of the strongest codes in this area, forbidding members who are auditors to give opinions in situations where they are not independent because of financial interests or employment connections with a client company.[16] Few professional bodies have gone this far in trying to establish auditor independence — in the UK much is left to the rather limited appointment provisions in the Companies Acts. However, the American provisions do not eliminate all dangers, in particular that relating to the provision of management services to companies by their auditors. The main issue involves the possibility of the auditor having to give an opinion on managerial matters which he may have initiated or helped to implement in a consultancy capacity. Unfortunately, these can create a further pressure on the auditor's position of independence — if management services are not given, or are insufficient, there is the danger that the audit might be given to another auditor who can provide them to the specifications required.

There have been several suggestions put forward to try to combat any lack of appearance of independence by the auditor — for example, the prohibition of management services by auditors; appointment, remuneration and dismissal of auditors by government or by government agency; rotation of audit appointments, say every five years; use of audit committees comprising non-executive company directors to review the audit and any problems arising from it before the audit report is submitted to shareholders; and the institution of an audit 'court' to give the ultimate audit opinion after submission of the audit evidence. Each of these solutions has certain advantages and disadvantages; none has obtained any general acceptance. It has therefore yet to be determined which are the most suitable and beneficial. Indeed, it has yet to be determined whether or not there is in fact a widespread problem regarding auditor independence from the point of view of financial report users, as there is little or no evidence on the matter.

Auditor responsibility

The final audit problem to be examined in this essay relates to the question of to whom the auditor is responsible. It has been accepted generally for many decades (both within the accountancy profession and in courts of law) that the auditor has a primary responsibility to a company's shareholders. In fact, he has been regarded during that time as the principal protector of the shareholders' interests *vis-a-vis* company management's financial reports. Today, there is little legal evidence to suggest that this is not still the case — the auditor's appointment, remuneration and dismissal all being matters for the approval of the shareholders, and there being no legal precedent indicating a wider responsibility.[17]

This is, in many ways, an awkward situation to resolve, as it is misleading to think solely of shareholders in relation to reported financial information and its audit. The 1970s are proving to be years of radical change regarding human relationships, particularly in the area of public accountability. A much wider disclosure and dissemination of financial information than ever before is now generally advocated, thereby acknowledging as of paramount importance the rights of the individual. This has resulted in a need for more communication, greater disclosure, and better accountability by business to persons interested in or involved with them.

Financial reporting has been affected by this widening emphasis, and a review of the recent accountancy literature provides evidence of this.[18] Report users can no longer be thought of solely in terms of the shareholder/investor group. Lenders, creditors, employees, trade unions, government, financial analysts, customers, and even the public at large are acknowledged as being interested in the activities of companies. The pressure is therefore to produce financial reports which are beneficial to these various interests. However, the question is whether the auditor of these reports should have a duty of care to each potential user group or whether it should remain primarily with shareholders.

The answer to this problem is not easy to find. There is no legal authority existing which can undeniably provide one, and the professional accountancy bodies have yet to formulate any suitable recommendations. The auditor is therefore left to decide for himself where his legal responsibilities lie when issuing his audit report. This is an unenviable task at a time when he is having to meet the challenge of numerous changes affecting his function — for example, the increasing size and complexity of corporate entities, and the volume of legal, professional and other regulatory provisions affecting the production of financial reports.

Widening the range of his responsibilities is one further complication in an already extremely complicated situation. However, it is a crucial complication because the credibility of reported financial information rests largely on the fact that it has been examined and reported on by a suitably qualified auditor. Does he therefore assume that every potential user may rely on his opinion, or that only certain specific ones will do so? If it is the former assumption then his responsibilities are limitless in the sense that he cannot foresee every user of the audited information and the degree to which the information will be relied on in practice. If, on the other hand, it is the latter assumption, then he is containing his duty of care to more manageable proportions; but he is still faced with predicting the outcome of possible reliance by users within a fairly wide range.

Obviously, the most sensible approach to this problem is to establish a limited yet acceptable duty of care. It is asking too much of any professional man to be open to possible negligence law suits for work which did not take into account the needs of a previously unknown report user. No auditor should be subjected to that amount of pressure. However, it must also be recognised by professional accountants that shareholders form only one of many report user groups which might rely on auditor's opinions. It therefore does not appear appropriate that the auditor should continue to think solely in terms of being responsible to shareholders. He must accept a wider responsibility to other known major user groups. This should not place intolerable burdens on him for, if he is satisfying his duty to shareholders in terms of the quality of his work, he should also be largely adhering to his responsibilities to other groups.

Conclusions

This has been a fairly wide-ranging commentary on the problems facing the company auditor today. It has been necessarily brief but, hopefully, has highlighted some of these problems. First, because audited financial reports may not be as widely read as might be assumed, the auditor's report does not appear to be relied on to the extent that is commonly supposed in the accountancy literature. Second, the modern auditor, faced with increasingly complex business situations in which to work, is having to cope with auditing standards (particularly with regard to the collection of suitable evidence) set by courts of law at higher levels than are generally accepted within the accountancy profession. Third, there appears to be a reversion to the somewhat obsolete fraud detection objective, largely as a consequence of the previous point, but which places additional onerous burdens on the auditor. Fourth, he is also under pressure at the present time to widen his function to encompass reported financial information previously published in an unaudited form. Fifth, the independence of the auditor is increasingly being criticised, and cognisance will have to be taken to improve his appearance of independence in order to improve the existing credibility of his audit opinions. And, finally, because of the increasing range of financial report usage, the auditor is now being asked to widen his duty of care beyond the traditional limits of the shareholder group.

In other words, at a time when his work does not appear to be relied on as heavily as it should, the auditor is under pressure to widen and deepen the scope of his function, taking on additional responsibilities and duties, and at the same time improving his position of independence. Radical changes must be implemented if these pressures are to be released. Modern auditing is in a period of serious turmoil and doubt. It will take many years to resolve the problems mentioned in this essay but they will have to be resolved if the audit function is to have any value in the future.

Notes and references

1   E. Stamp and C. Marley, *Accounting Principles and the City Code: the Case for Reform*, Butterworth, 1970, pp. 168-9.

2   For a recent summary and introduction to this research work, see W. H. Beaver, 'What should be the FASB's objectives?', *Journal of Accountancy*, August 1973, pp. 49-56.

3   H. K. Baker and J. A. Haslem, 'Information needs of individual investors', *Journal of Accountancy*, November 1973, pp. 64-9.

4   R. H. Chenhall and R. Juchau, 'Investor information needs — an Australian study', *Accounting and Business Research*, Spring 1977, pp. 111-19.

5   For a summary of his work, see R. C. Clift, 'Accounting information and the capital market', in *Australian Company Financial Reporting*, Australian Society of Accountants, 1975, pp. 83-98.

6   The results of the first study are contained in T. A. Lee and D. P. Tweedie, 'Accounting information: a study of private shareholder usage', *Accounting and Business Research*, Autumn 1975, pp. 280-91; 'Accounting information: a study of private shareholder understanding', *Accounting and Business Research*, Winter 1975, pp. 3-17; and 'The private shareholder: his sources of financial information and his understanding of reporting practice', *Accounting and Business Research*, Autumn 1976, pp. 304-14. The results of the second study are contained in T. A. Lee and D. P. Tweedie, *The Private Shareholder and the Corporate Report*, Institute of Chartered Accountants in England and Wales 1977.

7   T. A. Lee, 'The nature of auditing and its objectives', *Accountancy*, April 1970, p. 292.

8   T. A. Lee, *Company Auditing: Concepts and Practices*, Gee and Co. 1972, p. 61.

9   J. H. Bourne, 'Auditing', *The Accountant*, 4 June 1887, pp. 330-32.

10 T. A. Lee, *'An Inquiry into the Nature of Objectives Relevant to the External Audits of United Kingdom Companies'*, unpublished M.Sc. thesis, University of Strathclyde, 1969, p. 131. passim.

11 G. W. Beck, 'The role of the auditor in modern society', *Accounting and Business Research*, Spring 1973, p. 122.

12 'The adequacy of auditing standards and procedures currently applied in the examination of financial statements', *Report of the Special Committee on Equity Funding*, American Institute of Certified Public Accountants, 1975.

13 Ibid, p. 40.

14 Accounting Standards Steering Committee, *The Corporate Report*, Institute of Chartered Accountants in England and Wales 1975, particularly pp. 47-60.

15 See, for example, D. R. Carmichael, 'The assurance functions: auditing at the crossroads', *Journal of Accountancy*, September 1974, pp. 64-72.

16 'Reporting when a certified public accountant is not independent', *Statement on Auditing Procedure 42*, American Institute of Certified Public Accountants, 1970.

17 Although a non-accounting case, *Hedley, Byrne and Co. Ltd. v Heller and Partners Ltd.* (1963) 2 All ER 575; (1963) 3 WLR 101; (1964) AC 465, did suggest the possibility of liability to persons other than shareholders, there is as yet no firm legal precedent in th's matter — see 'Accountants' Liability to Third Parties — the *Hedley Byrne* Decision', *Accountancy*, September 1965, pp. 829-31.

18 For example, as in *The Corporate Report, op. cit.*

7

The information requirements of shareholders

JOHN ARNOLD

Professor of Accounting, University of Manchester

Introduction

The provision of information to shareholders has been a legal responsibility of large companies for many years. Recently, however, doubts have been expressed about whether the information provided is as useful as it might be, and a good deal of practical and academic research has been directed towards this question. The purpose of this chapter is to summarise the research which has been undertaken and to suggest directions for future investigation. The problem of selecting an optimal accounting method (i.e. of deciding which financial information ought to be reported) is complicated by the existence of a variety of users of accounting reports. Information which is useful to one user, or group of users, may not be useful to others. Although we concentrate on the requirements of shareholders, we include a brief discussion of the problems created by conflicts between users regarding the information which companies ought to provide.

Broadly, the approaches adopted in the literature to the problem of choosing between alternative accounting methods fall into two main categories: (a) efficient capital market approaches, which involve an examination of the efficiency of the capital market in incorporating accounting

(and other) information in share prices and are thus
concerned mainly with the allocation of investors'
resources; (b) user decision oriented approaches, which
involve the identification of the main groups of users of
accounting reports and an assessment of the ability of
alternative accounting methods to satisfy the information
requirements of each group. The assessment is often based
on an examination of users' decision models.

Efficient capital market approaches

Efficient capital market tests are concerned with the extent
to which accounting and other information is reflected in
current share prices.[1] Three forms of market efficiency are
generally hypothesised and tested — weak, semi-strong and
strong. The weak form of the efficient market hypothesis
asserts that current share prices fully reflect all past share
price behaviour; the semi-strong form asserts that current
share prices fully reflect all publicly available information;
the strong form asserts that current share prices fully reflect
all information, whether or not it is publicly available.
Various empirical studies, which are discussed at greater
length in the chapter on Accounting and Finance, have
examined different aspects of capital market efficiency with
respect to accounting numbers. For example, the studies
have been concerned with reaction of security prices to the
announcement of accounting numbers, or to changes in
accounting methods, and have so far been directed
primarily to the New York Stock Exchange. In general, the
tests undertaken to date provide support for the semi-strong
form of capital market efficiency at most.

As we have already noted, efficient capital market
approaches are concerned with the allocation of investors'
resources and, as such, are relevant to this chapter.
However, it is important to recognise that they are not
concerned with the allocation of the resources of non-
investors and are thus of little help in assessing the
usefulness of accounting reports to users other than
investors. In addition to their limited scope, efficient capital
market approaches suffer two main weaknesses as means of
choosing between alternative accounting methods. First,

they are concerned with efficiency at the aggregate level. So existence of the semi-strong form of efficiency, for example, would imply an allocation of resources throughout the capital market which fully reflected all publicly available information; new published information would be rapidly absorbed, and reflected in share prices. However, it is probable that only a limited number of those dealing in the market would receive and absorb the new information immediately, and only they would be in a position to make gains by buying or selling shares. No unambiguous method exists at present for comparing the utilities (satisfaction) different individuals enjoy or suffer as a result of financial gains or losses. Consequently it would not be possible to assess whether new publicly available information was beneficial to the whole investor group, or indeed to society in general. The problem of comparing inter-personal utilities (i.e. the problem of defining a 'social welfare function') is discussed later.

The second weakness arises because efficient capital market tests are concerned primarily with the efficiency of the market in processing available information. They are not concerned with alternative information (e.g. alternative numbers produced by using different accounting measures) which could be provided but which is unavailable at present. Thus capital market efficiency cannot, by itself, be used to asses the *desirability* of alternative reporting methods, although it may be of some use in assessing their *effects*.

User decision oriented approaches

A user decision oriented approach involves a consideration of the ability of alternative accounting methods to provide useful input to users' decision models. Initially, the information requirements of each user group are considered separately. When an optimal reporting method is agreed for each group, the further question arises as to whether the various methods can be combined into one general-purpose report or whether social welfare is better satisfied by the provision of a special report to each group. Broadly, the steps involved in applying a user decision oriented approach are:

1   Identify groups of users and determine the
    information requirements of each group;

2   Specify alternative accounting methods which might
    be used for reporting to users;

3   Specify a testing procedure for relating the available
    courses of action (alternative accounting methods) to
    the information requirements of each group;

4   Use the procedure developed in (3) to select an optimal
    reporting method for each group, after taking account
    of the cost of each alternative;

5   Assess the extent to which the various group-optimal
    reporting methods might be combined in a general
    purpose report.

The results of the above procedure are unlikely to remain
stable through time. For example, users' understanding of
accounting information may change as a result of which
their responses to alternative reporting methods may alter.
Thus it is important that the procedure should be regularly
repeated.

The Inflation Accounting Committee (the Sandilands
Committee), reporting in 1975, opted for a user decision
oriented approach, and identified the following user groups
for consideration:[2] shareholders; investment analysts; the
City (Stock Exchange, etc.); creditors and lenders; other
companies; employees; management; the government and
official bodies; the general public. Apart from the omission
of customers, the list appears sufficiently general to include
most potential users of accounting reports. Our main
concern in this chapter is with the first group listed, namely
shareholders. The size of the remainder of the list indicates
the extent to which a concentration on shareholders
represents only a partial analysis of the problem of choosing
an optimal accounting method. The first step in applying
the user decision oriented approach to shareholders is to
determine what information they require. Information
requirements may be determined empirically or
normatively, and we discuss both approaches in the
following two sections.

Information requirements of shareholders: the empirical approach

At least three variants of the empirical approach to the determination of shareholders' information requirements are available:[3] (1) ask a sample of shareholders what sort of information they require, using questionnaire and interview techniques; (2) conduct controlled experiments, by providing a sample of shareholders with alternative forms of accounting information and asking them to make hypothetical decisions on the basis of the information provided; (3) observe and analyse the actual decisions taken by shareholders in response to information which is publicly available.

None of the variants of the empirical approach is free from problems. For example, variant 1 involves selecting a representative sample of shareholders and designing an attitudinal questionnaire which does not bias respondents' replies; variant 2 relies on shareholders responding to hypothetical decision situations in the same way as they would react to real-world problems; variant 3 requires the researcher to distinguish between shareholder actions which are motivated by the provision of accounting information and those which result from other factors such as changes in general economic conditions. All three variants suffer a further serious disadvantage. Shareholders' responses may be conditioned by the sort of information they are receiving at present and have been accustomed to receive in the past. A reliable empirical experiment would probably involve providing a wide range of information for a long period of time before testing shareholder preferences for particular information, using one of the three variants described above.

Information requirements of shareholders: the normative approach

A normative approach to the determination of shareholder information needs requires the specification of a normative shareholder decision model. A major decision facing a shareholder (or potential shareholder) in a particular company is whether to buy, hold or sell shares in that company. In order to make the decision, the shareholder must estimate the value to himself of owning shares in the company and compare that value with the current market price of the shares. If the value of the shares to the investor exceeds their current market value he should buy shares and vice-versa. The most widely advocated normative share valuation model involves discounting expected receipts from a shareholding (dividends and capital distributions) to their present value using a rate of interest which is appropriate for the risk attached to the expected receipts. The model may be stated formally as:

$$V_0 = \frac{d_1}{(1+i)} + \frac{d_2}{(1+i)^2} + \frac{d_3}{(1+i)^3} + \ldots + \frac{d_n}{(1+i)^n}$$

$$V_0 = \sum_{j=1}^{n} \frac{d_j}{(1+i)^j} \qquad\qquad (1)$$

where V_0 is the current value of a shareholding to an investor, d_j is the receipt he expects from the shareholding at time j, n is the last time at which a receipt is expected from the shareholding and i is the appropriate discount rate.

In order to use the normative valuation model, a shareholder requires estimates of future receipts from the shareholding. He also requires information about the risk associated with the expected receipts in order that he may choose an appropriate discount rate. The measurement of the risk of a particular shareholding poses considerable problems. The most promising approach is offered by portfolio theory, which recognises the opportunities available to investors to reduce risk by diversification. The literature on portfolio analysis is extremely complex and we restrict ourselves to a simple example to illustrate the main principles involved.[4]

Suppose that an investor possesses £1000 cash and no other assets. He has the opportunity of investing his cash in one of three companies, or in a combination of two or three of the companies. An investment in each company produces a single return at the end of one year, but the size of the return depends on which of three sets of environmental circumstances (generally called 'states of the world')

Table 1

State of the world	A	B	C
Probability of state of the world	0.4	0.3	0.3
Company X	£1200	£ 700	£1700
Y	£1200	£1100	£1300
Z	£1200	£1700	£ 700

prevails. The possible returns expected, from an investment of £1000 in each company, are as shown in table 1.

The weighted average of the returns expected from an investment of £1000 is £1200 in each case. However, the risk associated with the average return is not the same for each company. The returns from an investment in Y vary less, depending on which state of the world prevails, than do the returns from investment in X or Z, and variability is normally regarded as a helpful measure of investment risk. Investment in Y produces the same average return and lower variability than investment in either X or Z. Does this mean that the investor should apply his £1000 entirely to investment in Y? The answer is no. So far we have considered separately the variability (risk) of the returns from each company. Suppose that the investor diversifies and invests £500 in company X and £500 in company Z. Whichever state of the world prevails he will receive £1200 after one year, i.e. the diversification strategy removes all variability (risk) from the expected investment returns. (The same result would be achieved by investing £833 in Y and £167 in Z.) Thus investment in X and Z (or in Y and Z) offers the lowest level of risk for a given return and is likely to be the option preferred by the investor.

The above illustration is an extremely simplified version of the opportunities facing an investor in practice. For example, there would normally be many investment possibilities available and many probable states of the world. Nevertheless, it illustrates the main principles of the portfolio approach. In particular it demonstrates that the risk associated with an investment cannot be determined independently — it depends on the relationship between the returns expected from the investment and the returns available from other opportunities. In our illustration, for example, investments X and Z and investments Y and Z are good hedges for each other; good returns on one investment arise under a state of the world which is associated with poor returns on the other and vice-versa. Such a relationship offers opportunities for risk reduction by diversification, and an investor will be interested in assessing the risk of an investment in the light of its diversification potential. This potential is captured by the statistical measure of

covariance.[5] A negative covariance between the returns of two investments indicates that when one investment does badly the other one generally does well.

Portfolio theory, based on the arguments outlined above, suggests that in order to assess the worthwhileness of an investment in a particular company a shareholder requires estimates of the cash flows expected from an investment in the company and estimates of the covariance of the cash flows with the cash flows expected from a market portfolio of investments. The shareholder may use these estimates, together with estimates of other market statistics, to calculate the minimum return he requires each year from the investment under consideration. The information will assist him in deciding whether his current portfolio is efficient, whether it is optimal with respect to his attitudes to risk, and whether it is likely to provide a satisfactory pattern of consumption over time.

As part of the process of estimating future distributable cash flows and their associated relative risk, a shareholder will require control information. The control information should consist of periodic reports explaining both differences between estimated and actual payments to shareholders and changes in expectations regarding future dividend payments. This sort of control information, involving the regular comparison of budgeted and actual performance, is a familiar part of internal planning procedures. It should be an equally important part of a shareholder's prediction and control process, enabling him to assess the efficiency of management.

The above analysis suggests that shareholders have two main, interdependent, information requirements — forecasts of future dividends and relative risk, and regular reports explaining both differences between forecast and actual dividends, and changes in forecasts if expectations have changed. Traditionally, reports to shareholders generally cover only past performance and the current position of the business, and no departure from this framework seems likely in the near future. Reports of past performance and current position cannot satisfy directly all of the shareholder information requirements outlined above, in particular those relating to predictions of future performance. However, they may do so indirectly by providing control information which will assist the shareholder's prediction process; they may provide information that will enable the shareholder to appraise the company's past performance and, from that appraisal, to form expectations about its future performance. Thus competing accounting methods may be assessed against two interdependent criteria: their usefulness in enabling shareholders to estimate future events of relevance to their decision models (their *predictive value*) and their usefulness in assisting shareholders to monitor a company's performance through time (their *control* properties).

Testing for predictive value and control properties

Earlier, we outlined the steps involved in applying a user decision oriented approach to the choice of accounting method. We now turn to a consideration of the requirement (in the third and fourth steps) of establishing and applying a procedure for testing the ability of alternative accounting methods to satisfy the information requirements of shareholders. We might attempt to test directly the usefulness of various accounting methods in predicting future cash flows and future relative risk. Alternatively, we might use another method of income measurement and asset valuation, believed to have high predictive value but, for some reason, thought to be unsuitable itself as a reporting method, as a bench-mark against which alternative feasible accounting methods may be assessed. Such a procedure might be described as an indirect test of predictive value.

In order to test the predictive value of alternative accounting methods, directly or indirectly, we need either real-world or simulated data. If real-world data are used it may be necessary to undertake predictive value tests for several samples of companies, operating in various industries and for various time periods, in order to generalise the results. The data needed for a single company may be both elusive and expensive. For example, information about expectations and details of data that would be needed to calculate a range of alternative accounting measures are generally not published by companies at present. Even if a company's managers are willing to cooperate in providing the necessary data, the preparation of accounts using various methods and covering a number of years may require a high input of time by the researcher. The problems outlined above are increased if the necessary calculations are to be applied to a variety of companies in various industries for various periods of time. If simulation is used, the data needed to undertake predictive value tests are created by the researcher. While this procedure is more feasible and less time-consuming than the use of real-world data, it is not without its limitations, which are discussed below.

Simulation enjoys other advantages over the use of real-world data. Even if companies are willing to cooperate in providing the data needed to undertake predictive value tests, the results, and in particular the relative performance of alternative accounting methods, may be affected by actual environmental conditions, for example the rate of inflation, relative price change rates, the level of unemployment, and changes in gross national product. For experimental purposes it is extremely difficult to control the impact of such factors on real-world data. Simulation, on the other hand, allows examination of a wide range of environmental conditions, whose impact may be controlled by the researcher. It also facilitates the manipulation of values given to particular parameters in the simulation model in order to assess the sensitivity of test results to changes in those values. Finally, simulation permits study of a time period far longer than would be feasible using real-world data.

The main limitation of simulation is that the test results may be influenced by the simulated environmental relationships chosen by the researcher. This limitation may be abated somewhat by choosing assumptions carefully, so that they are as realistic as possible, and by repeating the simulation a large number of times under varying conditions. In this way, the generalisability of the results is increased.

Despite its limitations, simulation is a powerful and useful research technique and, in view of the present difficulties involved in using real-world data, it provides a valuable means of testing the predictive value and control properties of alternative accounting methods. However, if simulation is used, disputes may arise about the appropriateness of environmental assumptions. Such disputes can probably be resolved only by real-world testing. Consequently, it seems likely that both real-world tests and simulation experiments have an important part to play in the search for an optimal accounting method.

Inter-group and intra-group conflicts

In our discussions of both the efficient capital market and the user decision oriented approaches to the choice of accounting method, we noted the problem caused by the existence of potential conflicts between groups and within groups about the information that should be provided in published accounts. Inter-group conflicts arise when the provision of certain information is beneficial to one group of users and harmful to another. For example, the employee group may require information on a plant-by-plant basis about the wage rates paid by the reporting company, in order that employees being paid less than the average rate for a particular job may negotiate wage increases. The shareholder group may oppose the provision of this information on the grounds that it could result in a reduction in the cash available for the payment of future dividends. Intra-group conflicts arise when information provision benefits certain members of a particular user group but is disadvantageous to other members of the same group. For example, certain members of the shareholder group may be better equipped than others to understand the accounting information currently published by companies and thus be in a better position to make gains by buying or selling shares. The introduction of a more easily understood accounting information system would erode the advantageous position enjoyed by the more sophisticated group of shareholders, thus reducing their profit-making opportunities while at the same time improving the opportunities available to other shareholders.

Inter-group and intra-group conflicts are inevitable in any attempt to choose a system for providing accounting information to users with a variety of decision models. The resolution of such conflicts requires some form of social value judgement, i.e. a judgement about whether the benefits to one group or sub-group arising from a change in accounting method outweigh the costs to others in social terms. Social value judgements may have to be made ultimately by government, or by another body, such as the accounting profession, with the implicit or explicit approval of government.[6]

Summary and conclusions

In this chapter we have considered the usefulness of both efficient capital market and user decision oriented approaches in choosing between alternative accounting methods, with particular reference to the satisfaction of the information requirements of shareholders. An important characteristic of both approaches is that they give rise to hypotheses that may be tested empirically, an essential quality if disputes about the relative merits of alternative reporting methods are to be resolved. Despite this, neither approach has yet provided a conclusive answer to the problem of choosing an optimal accounting method, and neither seems likely to do so in the near future. As we have noted, the efficient capital market approach is useful for assessing the effects of alternative accounting systems rather than their desirability; it is concerned with the aggregate impact of currently available information on the capital market rather than with the usefulness of alternative accounting methods to individual users. Furthermore, its scope is limited to one group of users of accounting reports, namely investors.

User decision oriented approaches involve an initial concentration on a particular group of users. A final recommendation depends on the informational preferences of all users, and may be affected by inter-group and intra-group conflicts. The resolution of such conflicts requires some form of social value judgement. In addition, attempts to determine the information requirements of any one group empirically are restricted by the problem that users may be pre-conditioned by the information they are receiving at present. Within the user decision oriented approach, the application of a normative model to the determination of shareholder information requirements suggests that shareholders require estimates of future dividends, together with the risk associated with them defined in terms of portfolio analysis, and regular control information. These requirements lead to the use of the interdependent criteria of predictive value and control in choosing between alternative methods of reporting to shareholders. However, virtually no reliable empirical support is available at present for these normative hypotheses and an urgent need exists for research in the area. We discussed the form that appropriate tests might take.

In view of the difficulties involved in applying the efficient capital market approach and both the empirical and normative variants of the user decision oriented approach, no one research method can be demonstrated to be superior to the others at present. All the approaches discussed in this chapter seem to offer opportunities for advancing the debate on the choice of accounting method. We stand at the beginning of what may turn out to be a very long research road.

Notes and references

1 For a summary and evaluation of the efficient capital market literature, see T. R. Dyckman, D. H. Downes and R. P. Magee, *Efficient Capital Markets and Accounting: A Critical Analysis*, Prentice-Hall 1975.

2 *Inflation Accounting: Report of the Inflation Accounting Committee*, Cmnd 6225, HMSO 1975, p. 43, para. 147.

3 All three variants of the empirical approach may also be applied to other user groups, with problems similar to those encountered in applying them to shareholders.

4 Two of the earliest and most influential articles on the development of the portfolio model are: H. Markowitz, 'Portfolio selection', *The Journal of Finance*, March 1952, and W. F. Sharpe, 'Capital asset prices: a theory of market equilibrium under conditions of risk', *The Journal of Finance*, September 1964. Both articles are reproduced in S. H. Archer and C. A. d'Ambrosio (eds), *The Theory of Business Finance: A Book of Readings*, Macmillan 1967. A short explanation of the main principles of portfolio analysis is contained in B. Carsberg, *Analysis for Investment Decisions*, Haymarket Publishing 1974, Chapter 14.

5 See Carsberg, *op.cit.*, Chapter 14 for an explanation of the calculation of covariances.

6 For a fuller discussion of this problem see W. H. Beaver and J. S. Demski, 'The nature of financial accounting objectives: a summary and synthesis', *Studies on Financial Accounting Objectives*, 1974, Supplement to *Journal of Accounting Research*, 1974.

Bibliography

Notes and references given in the chapter have been restricted as far as possible to avoid unnecessary disruption to the reader. However we list below a selection of the major works in the areas covered for the benefit of those who wish to pursue particular topics in more depth.

Accounting Standards Steering Committee, *The Corporate Report*, Institute of Chartered Accountants in England and Wales 1975.

American Accounting Association, *A Statement of Basic Accounting Theory*, American Accounting Association 1966.

Arnold, John and Hope, Anthony, 'Reporting business performance', *Accounting and Business Research*, Spring 1975

Ashton, Robert H., 'The predictive-ability criterion and user prediction models', *The Accounting Review*, October 1974.

Ball, Raymond J., 'Changes in accounting techniques and stock prices', *Empirical Research in Accounting: Selected Studies*, 1972, Supplement to *Journal of Accounting Research*, 1972.

——— and Brown, Philip, 'An empirical evaluation of accounting income numbers', *Journal of Accounting Research*, Autumn 1968.

Barton A., 'Expectations and achievements in income theory', *The Accounting Review*, October 1974.

Beaver, William H., 'The information content of annual earnings announcements', *Empirical Research in Accounting: Selected Studies*, 1968, Supplement to *Journal of Accounting Research*, 1968.

——— 'The behavior of security prices and its implications for accounting research (methods)', Supplement to *The Accounting Review*, 1972.

——— Kennelly, John W. and Voss, William M., 'Predictive ability as a criterion for the evaluation of accounting data', *The Accounting Review*, October 1968.

——— and Demski, Joel S., 'The nature of financial accounting objectives: a summary and synthesis', *Studies on Financial Accounting Objectives*, 1974, Supplement to *Journal of Accounting Research*, 1974.

Bierman, Harold, Jr., 'The implications of efficient markets and the capital asset pricing model to accounting', *The Accounting Review*, July 1974.

——— and Davidson, Sidney, 'The income concept — value increment or earnings predictor', *The Accounting Review*, April 1969.

Bonini, Charles P., *Simulation of Information and Decision Systems in the Firm*, Prentice-Hall 1963.

Brenner, Vincent C., 'Financial statement users' views of the desirability of reporting current cost information', *Journal of Accounting Research*, Autumn 1970.

Carsberg, Bryan, *Analysis for Investment Decisions*, Haymarket Publishing 1974.

———, Arnold, John and Hope, Anthony, 'Predictive value: a criterion for choice of accounting method', in Baxter, W. T. and Davidson, S. (eds), *Studies in Accounting Theory*, 3rd edition, Institute of Chartered Accountants 1977.

———, Hope, Anthony and Scapens, R. W., 'The objectives of published accounting reports', *Accounting and Business Research*, Summer 1974.

Clarkson, Geoffrey, *Portfolio Selection: A Simulation of Trust Investment*, Prentice-Hall 1962.

Demski, Joel S., 'Predictive ability of alternative performance measurement models', *Journal of Accounting Research*, Spring 1969.

———, 'Choice among financial reporting alternatives', *The Accounting Review*, April 1974.

Drake, David and Dopuch, Nicholas, 'On the case for dichotomizing income', *Journal of Accounting Research*, Autumn 1965.

Dyckman, Thomas R., 'On the investment decision', *The Accounting Review*, April 1964.

————, Downes, David H. and Magee, Robert P., *Efficient Capital Markets and Accounting: A Critical Analysis*, Prentice-Hall 1975.

Edwards, Edgar O. and Bell, Philip W., *The Theory and Measurement of Business Income*, University of California Press 1961.

Estes, Ralph W., 'An assessment of the usefulness of current cost and price-level information by financial statement users', *Journal of Accounting Research*, Autumn 1968.

Fama, Eugene F., 'Efficient capital markets: a review of theory and empirical work', *The Journal of Finance*, May 1970.

Forrester, Jay W., *Industrial Dynamics*, John Wiley & Sons 1961.

Foster, George, 'Quarterly accounting data: time-series properties and predictive-ability results', *The Accounting Review*, January 1977.

Frank, Werner, 'A study of the predictive significance of two income measures', *Journal of Accounting Research*, Spring 1969.

Gonedes, Nicholas J., 'Efficient capital markets and external accounting', *The Accounting Review*, January 1972.

————, 'Capital market equilibrium and annual accounting numbers: empirical evidence', *Journal of Accounting Research*, Spring 1974.

———— and Dopuch, Nicholas, 'Capital market equilibrium, information production and selecting accounting techniques: theoretical framework and review of empirical work', *Studies on Financial Accounting Objectives*, 1974, Supplement to *Journal of Accounting Research*, 1974.

Greenball, Melvin N., 'The accuracy of different methods of accounting for earnings — a simulation approach', *Journal of Accounting Research*, Spring 1968.

————, 'Evaluation of the usefulness to investors of different accounting estimators of earnings: a simulation approach', *Empirical Research in Accounting: Selected Studies*, 1968, Supplement to *Journal of Accounting Research*, 1968.

————, 'The predictive-ability criterion: its relevance in evaluating accounting data', *Abacus*, June 1971.

Hendriksen, Eldon S. and Budge, Bruce P. (eds), *Contemporary Accounting Theory*, Dickenson 1974.

Hope, Anthony, *Accounting for Price-Level Changes — A Practical Survey of Six Methods*, Institute of Chartered Accountants in England and Wales Research Committee Occasional Paper No. 4, 1974.

Inflation Accounting Committee, *Report of the Inflation Accounting Committee*, Cmnd 6225, HMSO 1975.

Jensen, Michael (ed.), *Studies in the Theory of Capital Markets*, Praeger 1972.

Kaplan, Robert S. and Roll, Richard, 'Investor evaluation of accounting information: some empirical evidence', *Journal of Business*, April 1972.

Libby, Robert, 'The use of simulated decision makers in information evaluation', *The Accounting Review*, July 1975.

Louderback, Joseph G., 'Projectability as a criterion for income determination methods', *The Accounting Review*, April 1971.

Markowitz, Harry, 'Portfolio selection', *The Journal of Finance*, March 1952.

May, Robert G. and Sundem, Gary L., 'Research for accounting policy: an overview', *The Accounting Review*, October 1976.

McDonald, Daniel L., 'A test application of the feasibility of market based measures in accounting', *Journal of Accounting Research*, Spring 1968.

Naylor, Thomas H, Balintly, Joseph L., Burdick, Donald S., and Chu, Kong, *Computer Simulation Techniques*, John Wiley & Sons 1966.

Pankoff, L., and Virgil, R., 'Some preliminary findings from a laboratory experiment on the usefulness of financial accounting information to security analysts', *Empirical Research in Accounting: Selected Studies*, 1970, Supplement to *Journal of Accounting Research* 1970.

Parker, James E., 'Impact of price-level accounting', *The Accounting Review*, January 1977.

Parker R. H. and Harcourt, G. C. (eds.), *Readings in the Concept and Measurement of Income*, Cambridge University Press 1969.

Revsine, Lawrence, *Replacement Cost Accounting*, Prentice-Hall 1973.

Schrieber, Albert N. (ed.), *Corporate Simulation Models*, University of Washington 1970.

Sharpe, William F., 'Capital asset prices: a theory of market equilibrium under conditions of risk', *The Journal of Finance*, September 1964.

Simmons, John K. and Gray, Jack, 'An investigation of the effects of differing accounting frameworks on the prediction of net income', *The Accounting Review*, October 1969.

Sterling, Robert R., 'Decision oriented financial accounting', *Accounting and Business Research*, Summer 1972.

Sunder, Shyam, 'Relationships between accounting changes and stock prices: problems of measurement and some empirical evidence', *Empirical Research in Accounting: Selected Studies*, 1973, Supplement to *Journal of Accounting Research*, 1973.

Wells, M. C., 'A revolution in accounting thought?', *The Accounting Review*, July 1976.

8

Information for trade unions

DAVID COOPER

Lecturer in Accounting, University of Manchester

Accountants are slowly turning their attention to the provision of information for trade unions and for employees in general. The recognition that unions might have rights to information is a reflection of changing social attitudes towards accountability. In this chapter we propose to consider some issues crucial to the debate about information disclosure and the provision of information for unions. We will firstly indicate the general nature of union decision-making and the role of unions in British society. We will then evaluate two approaches to information disclosure. Our preference for the decision oriented approach leads to a discussion of union decision models. Finally, in part due to the lack of development of such models, we consider an alternative (and rather radical) approach to the provision of information for unions.

Unions, information and decision-making

Information that is required for any organisation (and we may define trades unions as organisations) is related to the need of the organisation to make good decisions; decisions that enable the organisation to survive and prosper in its environment. The provision of information for trades unions may be taken to mean the provision of information to facilitate good union management.

We can thus see that information for trades unions is only a specific example of the accounting problem of the provision of information to aid good management. Accounting has been described as 'the process of identifying, measuring and communicating economic information to permit informed judgements and decisions by users of the information'.[1] Similarly, *The Corporate Report* states: 'the fundamental objective of corporate reports is to communicate economic measurements of, and information about, the resources and performance of the reporting entity useful to those having reasonable rights to such information'.[2] Accordingly, this is an area that has been the concern of accountants for many years: all the general exhortations about accounting information would therefore seem to be applicable. Information must be decision-relevant; information should influence actions and improve behaviour. When data are unintelligible, out-of-date or unassociated with the problem at hand, then they cannot be regarded as valuable information.

Unions are organisations whose purpose is to promote the welfare of their members; a function that can best be achieved by combination and concerted, unified action. A large proportion of the working population is unionised. The total trade union membership in the UK is now nearly 12 million, being over half the total labour force.[3] Union activity and decisions in which unions are involved affect all aspects of life.

Information for trades unions means, therefore, the provision of information that will allow effective management; management that includes the maintenance of the collective strength of the union and consideration of methods to enhance this strength. Thereby the welfare of the union members will be improved. Union officials do not normally think of themselves as managers, yet that is what they are. It is largely ideological confusion (i.e. the belief that managers *de facto* are capitalists) that limits the recognition that unions need to be managed and that managers in unions need (at the very least) the same sorts of information as managers in any other institution. Information about an organisation's objectives, the state of its environment and knowledge about the probable consequences of any action it might pursue is important to the management of any large organisation.[4]

There are two features about unions that we wish to emphasise. First, unions are not concerned with purely financial objectives. Many observers try to reduce the objectives of an organisation to a single 'maximand', typically the maximisation of cash resources; such a sleight of hand will not do for a union! Men and women are not economic objects to be bought and sold on the labour market; and if some would wish it so, unions do their best to minimise the inhumanity resulting from such an attitude. Unions are multi-objective organisations. In order to improve the welfare of their members union officials are concerned with wage levels, job security, working conditions, industrial and community health, industrial democracy, national income and quality of life.

The second feature about unions that requires emphasis is that their role in society varies from one country to another. In this chapter the emphasis is on UK unions and their role in a capitalist and so-called pluralist society. In the UK it is alleged that unions 'do battle' with other powerful interest groups (like the CBI, Employer Federations and large companies) and the outcome of such negotiations is determined through the market forces of supply and demand. Each major institution in a pluralist society is said to act in its own 'selfish' interests and these interests are accommodated through market forces.[5] The evidence about the distribution and workings of power in the UK make this position difficult to sustain.[6] The battle is decidedly one-sided: British society is controlled by a specific class whose interests are associated with capital and finance. If this latter view is correct, then unions should be concerned with changing the nature of society to one where their members' interests can genuinely be served.

These introductory observations emphasise the importance of the provision of information to enable the effective management of unions. The sort of information provided will, of course, depend on the decisions in which unions are expected to be involved. We now turn to an examination of two approaches to the provision of information to unions.

Alternative frameworks for information disclosure

The first approach may be regarded as the 'consumer sovereignty' approach to information disclosure. This framework is closely related to the notion of Britain as a pluralist society. Under this approach the unions, as a result of their perceived wants, press for increased information. Such demands, when taken with those of other 'interested' parties have resulted in a number of changes in UK law relating to information disclosure.

The Industrial Relations Act (1971), the Health and Safety at Work Act (1974),the Employment Protection Act (1975) and the Industry Act (1975) have all widened the scope of information disclosure to unions beyond the obligations stated in the Companies Acts. These pieces of legislation, which have come about as a result of union pressure, have been followed by more detailed statements by the Commission on Industrial Relations,[7] the Advisory Conciliation and Arbitration Service,[8] the Trades Union Congress,[9] the Confederation of British Industries,[10] and even the accounting profession.[11] Furthermore, the whole debate on information disclosure has been widened and enlivened by the Bullock Committee Report on Industrial Democracy.[12]

Yet the suspicion of accounting by unions and the lack of interest in employee information requirements by accountants may have resulted in deficient information that is unlikely to be useful or relevant to employees and their union representatives. This deficiency may be the result of a concern with servicing the desires or wants of employees. The 'consumer sovereignty' approach involves asking the consumers, in this case, employees or their representatives, what information they would find useful. The resulting 'shopping list' is compared with the information currently provided and with the information lists provided by other 'relevant' bodies. Political bargaining or lobbying results in some consensus about disclosure.

The result of such negotiations is marginal adjustment to the *status quo*. User demands for information will be based on perceptions of the sorts of information systems that are currently available. For example, a union official may want historic cost based information to help him formulate his claim. His demand is more likely to be based on the perception that historic cost information can be provided than on the belief that such information will be helpful to him in satisfying his need to formulate a claim advantageous to his members.

The second, and preferred, approach to the information choice problem may be called the decision oriented approach.[13] Information should be provided that is required as input to the decision model which enables a decision-maker to satisfy his goals and result in an improvement in his welfare. This approach implies that the accountant must act as an information educator, (i.e. he must work with the unions and indicate to them the potential uses of information).

The first requirement of the decision oriented approach is to ascertain the objectives of the decision-maker, in this case, the union. The objectives of any organisation involve both intention (as provided, for example, in official statements) and commitment (through, for example, the allocation of resources to satisfy the intention). Accordingly, we must look beyond official statements of objectives to the allocation of resources within unions. Indeed, use of the decision oriented approach requires some consideration of what these allocations 'should be'. Considerations of 'should be' necessitate an understanding of the role and function of unions in our society and in changing our society. These 'political' issues are not avoided by refusing to acknowledge them; such a refusal provides tacit approval of the existing role of unions. As we do not have the space to develop this argument further, we intend to boldly assume that existing official and semi-official union statements provide some clues about the current role of unions in our society. Official statements are likely to be influenced by the trade union leadership. This leadership, with notable exceptions, seems to adhere to the current organisation of society. Yet these statements are often heavily conditioned by official union ideology which includes an idea of what the role of a union should be. We hope some readers may be encouraged to consider more carefully what the role of unions ought to be and indeed what information would be needed to make such an assessment.

Many official and semi-official statements of objectives have been made by trade unions. The following definition of a trade union has been highly influential: 'a continuous association of wage earners for the purpose of improving their working lives'.[14] Although there are differences of emphasis, most commentators would agree that unions have broad organisational, political and social objectives as well as a concern to improve the economic security and status of their members.[15]

These objectives cannot be pursued independently of other groups in society; suppliers, customers, providers of finance and creators of the infra-structure for the nation are all relevant. Unions cannot in the long run pursue policies that completely alienate customers or investors or any other group associated with an organisation; if they do the organisation will cease to exist. Yet, this interdependence requires that models of union decision-making must take account of bargaining behaviour. The decision oriented approach necessitates the identification of decision models that relate union action to the satisfaction of the union's objectives.

Union decision models

Accounting — and industrial relations — have tended to look to economics for usable and appropriate decision models. Increasingly, however, the limitations of most simple economic models have become apparent in industrial relations — and to a lesser extent in accounting. A model is a representation of the world (or an aspect of it) and many economic models represent the world as being capable of accurate and complete representation. Classical economic analysis is frequently based on a decision model which states that choices (or actions) are made by individuals so as to maximise their subjective expected utility (SEU). Such an analysis involves the identification of all possible courses of action, assigning a value (or utility) to each possible outcome associated with an action and assessing the probability of its occurrence. The action with the highest expected utility is then chosen.

Information has two major roles in the SEU model, the implication being that accounting information has two functions to perform in improving decision-making. First, a decision-maker requires information to construct his model — to identify feasible actions, their associated consequences (or outcomes) and the likelihood of such outcomes occurring. For example, in making a decision about a pay demand, a union official may require information about the aspirations of the union membership and the ability (and willingness) of the organisation to pay a range of possible wage settlements.[16]

The second function of information in the SEU model is to provide feedback to the decision-maker in order that he may revise his model. Accounting is required to help the decision-maker learn from his experiences. Results of recent decisions may suggest that the original estimates of the members' militancy or the assessment of the organisation's ability and willingness to pay the claim, need to be revised.

The SEU model takes for granted the accurate and complete representation of the possible actions, the consequences of each action, the likelihood of each consequence occurring and the identification of a level of utility associated with each consequence of action. If we are to use models and produce prescriptions that are to be of use to a decision maker then we cannot ignore the evidence indicating man's inability to make accurate and complete representations of the world.[17] Further, experimental psychologists have demonstrated the inability of man to integrate actions, consequences and probabilities to achieve utility maximisation; man is not a very good intuitive statistician.[18]

Similarly, developments in game theory, although elegant, are not very relevant in a search for decision models useful to unions.[19] Game theory is concerned with decision situations in which the results are dependent on the interactions of two or more 'players'. Thus far, however, decision theorists have concentrated on analysing situations when the game is concerned to divide, by cooperative means, a fixed sum. The theory of games is largely undeveloped in the area of non-constant sum, non cooperative games.[20]

There is, however, a further role for information in gaming situations. Information may be used as part of the bargaining process in order to influence the other players' perceptions of the likely consequences. The threat of a strike, for example, may be used to influence an employer's perceptions of the consequences of refusing a pay demand. Similarly, the announcement by an organisation of reduced profits, a decline in sales or a cash crisis may alter the employees' perceptions of the consequences of pressing a pay demand.[21] Union decision-making is not likely to occur in cooperative situations where the bargaining is just about the share of a fixed 'booty' or cake.

The inapplicability of decision models based either on SEU or game theory may be clarified by a few examples. These examples of the range and complexity of union decision-making may also suggest the sorts of decision models that will be helpful to unions. Unions are likely to be involved in decision-making at the national, industry and plant level; all three levels may produce outcomes likely to affect the welfare of union members.

The TUC in its discussions with government, CBI and other bodies interested in national economic performance will be concerned with the size of the national cake (in terms relating perhaps to national economic growth figures) as well as the manner in which the cake will be distributed. For example, a decision by the unions, through the TUC, to support a particular set of distributive policies will depend on their attitude towards the economic strategy being pursued (e.g. no growth, high growth, reduced unemployment, etc.). Unions, like all the parties to such negotiations, need models of the economy that enable them to predict the consequences of alternative strategies they may pursue in the satisfaction of their objectives.

Full-time union representatives are frequently concerned with industrial agreements. Negotiations between union officials and a particular industry's employer federation or dominant firm will normally be concerned with basic wage rates, bonuses and overtime rates.[22] These negotiations may include detailed bargaining about changes in the industry's structure; this is particularly likely in industries which have one major employer — coal mining, electricity supply and steel production are obvious examples. As with negotiations at national level, unions will need models of industrial sectors that enable them to predict the consequences of their actions. It may also be worth emphasising that these negotiations are likely to be of a non-constant

sum variety where the amount produced will depend on the
bargain struck. If a low pay claim is achieved, then labour
productivity is likely to fall. This will result in lower
production. If a high pay claim is achieved, then the
amount invested in capital is likely to fall and also result in
lower future productivity. The effects of labour effort are
unlikely to neatly balance the effects of capital investment.
Indeed, many observers on both sides of industry would
regard the interests of labour and capital (represented by top
management) as fundamentally opposed. Negotiations are
decidedly non cooperative!

Unions are involved with plant level negotiations as well
as national and industry negotiations. The Donovan
Commission[23] drew widespread attention to the fact that a
great deal of industrial relations bargaining was conducted
at the plant level. Plant managers and shop stewards
bargain not only over basic pay but also over health and
safety issues and general working conditions.[24] Decision-
making by shop stewards requires a decision model that
encompasses demands for extra safety expenditure,
demands for real opportunities for job satisfaction, evaluations of potential closures and, in general, concern with
the overall management of the plant.[25] The conflict
inherent in these negotiations with plant managers again
emphasises the potentially non cooperative nature of
decision-making.

We would, however, be unwise to generalise from these
three examples — at national, industry and plant level —
about what the decision models of union officials should be.
The three examples may provide clues as to the type of
decision models that union negotiators might need to use.
The decision models ought to take account of the
complexity of the decisions and the nature of the decision-
makers.

Decision-makers are not omnisciently rational; models
based on such abilities will have limited usefulness to
decision-makers in unions (or anywhere else for that
matter!). Human decisions are intendedly rational yet
bounded by human capabilities.[26] An improvement in the
welfare of union members will be a satisfactory outcome for
a union decision-maker. Such an improvement will
probably be achieved through the use of simple decision

rules, 'rules of thumb' that enable a decision maker to cope with the complexity of his environment.

Models of decision-making based on the above ideas, known as 'bounded rationality', involve the following observations. A 'problem' requiring solution does not appear from nowhere and the nature of problem recognition needs careful consideration in any theory of decision-making.[27] Solutions to a problem are often inherent in the way the problem is identified. A union official's recognition, for example, that the union's members need more money, implies the 'solution' of obtaining more money. Rephrasing the problem as one of coping with a declining standard of living opens up possible solutions of price controls, tax adjustments and a general enquiry into the causes of the decline (and hence an enquiry into the issue of who benefits from decisions taken 'in the national interest').

The search for solutions and the identification of the consequences that might result from any solution are normally severely limited. Decision-making does not involve a ranking of all alternatives. Alternatives have to be found and generally the first alternative action that seems to be satisfactory will be undertaken. The search for a satisfactory alternative will be based on experience of past decision-making. Learning is difficult in an environment that is rapidly changing — the past, in such circumstances, is unlikely to be a good predictor of the future.

Decision models specific to union officials do not seem to be well developed. Nor is it clear whether the environment within which a union official makes decisions is either rapidly or only slowly changing. To resolve these sorts of problems will require research into union decision-making.

In the meantime, research is being undertaken which describes one specific union representative, the shop steward, and the sorts of information he would require in his decision-making. This line of research takes the role of the shop steward as given and then identifies the decisions associated with the shop steward roles of union administrator, pay bargainer and manager in the plant.[28] For the first role, that of union administrator, the shop steward seems to make decisions about inter-union disputes, recruitment and subscriptions. Information necessary to make such decisions relates to details of union membership such as manpower statistics.

In his role as pay bargainer, the shop steward makes decisions about how much he should claim and to what extent he should or can support the claim through union activity. Information related to the organisation's ability to pay the claim and information related to the sum that is minimally acceptable to his membership seem to be relevant in this context. Examples of such information include details of labour productivity, expected output, value added and the standard and cost of living of employees in the plant.

As a 'manager', the shop steward is concerned about the efficiency of the plant's operations both in an economic and social sense. He is concerned with decisions about how the organisation should be operated and the possibilities of plant closure or expansion. He is also concerned with the social performance of the organisation: he makes decisions about demands for health and safety expenditure as well as about the opportunities for job satisfaction in the organisation. These types of management decision require information about economic plans (including proposed investment and financing policies) as well as accident, noise, turnover and absenteeism records. We may summarise some of the implications that our tentative findings suggest for providers of information, as follows:

(1) Information should be future oriented. To assess an organisation's ability to pay, for example, the relevant concern in bargaining is the future ability of an organisation to pay a wage demand. To assess economic efficiency, future operating and investment plans of the organisation need to be considered. To assess social efficiency, the safety of machinery to be introduced must be evaluated. Such considerations and evaluations suggest that information should include an indication of the likelihood of various outcomes occurring in the future.

(2) Information should relate to specific decisions. Thus in the research mentioned above, plant level information was found to be of much relevance.

Industrial data are relevant to industrial bargaining and national data are probably most relevant to the bargaining involved in national decisions. Most published accounting information, however, relates to legal and not economic or social entities. In short, it is not decision oriented. Companies have been noticeably reluctant to disaggregate or 'break down' the information relating to the legal entity to information relating to the individual plants.

(3) Information should relate to the environment of the organisation. Information about the level of claim that is regarded as the minimum acceptable requires consideration of wage opportunities outside the specific organisation. Future economic and social plans can only be assessed in the light of the particular situation. It is highly probable that such information will not be purely financial: physical and social indicators are likely to be just as relevant to union decisions as is financial information.

These general statements about the sorts of information that might be relevant for union decision-making have been derived in a manner which falls far short of the ideals we set out in the opening sections of this chapter. There is a most pressing need for research into decision-making by trade unions. Statements about information for trades unions can only be very tentative at present.

Information or data for decision-making: 'opening the books'

Thus far we have not been careful in distinguishing between data and information. Yet the difference can be crucial. Data can be regarded as raw material out of which information can be created. Information, to be regarded as such, must have relevance to a decision. Indeed, if a message (which contains data) does not alter the decision-makers' beliefs about a situation, then the message is said not to have any informational content.[29]

In this chapter we have been concerned to indicate the way in which accountants might choose information which is relevant to unions. This choice of information has required a specification of the union decision models. We have seen the difficulty in specifying these models for unions. Perhaps a way forward is to provide unions with access to an organisation's records: to open the books. Access to the records may result in decision-makers being faced with more data than they can effectively handle. The resulting information overload can produce poor decisions. It is essential therefore that opening the books does not reduce the stimulus for accountants to understand the process of union decision-making.

A second reason for opening the books has been suggested by several prominent members of the British labour movement. In a situation of class struggle the unions cannot be expected to regard information provided by the opposing class, as unbiased, neutral or value-free.[30] It is therefore not surprising that 'Employee Reports', those glossy documents that some companies are now producing for their employees, are frequently viewed with disdain. They are usually a comic-strip version of the annual company reports, which themselves may be out-of-date, irrelevant and biased towards presenting a view for the owners (i.e. shareholders).[31] These observations help to explain why it has been found that shop stewards rate both information obtained from their union and from other shop stewards as more important in pay bargaining than company accounts or information provided by plant management.[32]

Not only is deliberate distortion of information suspected by unions but it also seems that most of the information currently collected by accountants bears little relation to the sorts of information unions may require. For example the shop stewards in the research survey cited above, said they wanted future oriented information — about expected lay-offs, production changes and takeovers.[33] Although we must be careful in interpreting such comments they do reinforce the demand to open the books. This demand 'does not mean as it has so much in the past, just the cooked up balance sheets ... It means that workers have full and detailed information concerning costing, marketing and all other essential financial details.'[34]

The demand is for access to a data bank that includes all the details of events potentially useful to unions. This may mean that the basis of the data bank is not related to a specific organisation; data about alternative employment opportunities may be beneficial. The mass of detail implied by the demand to open the books can be handled by computers. Moreover, it is not obvious that the centralisation of records in a computer will result in the centralisation of decision-making.

The sorts of data that are likely to be useful to unions may necessitate the creation of records on a basis different from the conventional accounting basis. At the present, accounting events are recognised or recorded when a transaction takes place. Yet many organisational activities do not result in transactions. The case of pollutants or dangerous diseases resulting from production is a classic example. Further, even when transactions occur, the 'price' at which the deal takes place may not take account of the value to the parties. The market price (most transactions occur in our society in a market context) may not fully reflect the activity. Under current accounting conventions, the activity of producing a product such as a motor car is recorded ultimately in the books of a firm as a sale at a market price. Yet the market price is a reflection of the private value of the motor vehicle; it does not include the public price of the product: potential fatalities, injuries, traffic congestion and general destruction of amenity.[35]

Unions might be expected to be concerned with many of these external effects and activities which are not neatly summarised in market transaction data. They will also be concerned with the effects on union members of organisational activities which do not involve transactions. Authoritarian management is likely to result in a reduction in employee welfare; lack of safety equipment may result in injury; failure to provide nursery facilities may result in a reduction in female labour. These events are currently not recognised or recorded by accounting reports. Unions will also be concerned with the effects of organisational activities on those who are not employed in the organisation. For example, wage settlements that involve reduced recruitment may result in effects on the wider community; especially potential workers and union members. Indeed the Transport and General Workers Union claim to ICI in 1971 is an example of both union concern about the community and of obtaining information about the effects of ICI activities on the community around it.[36]

Opening the books would enable union decision-makers to obtain access to potentially relevant data. This suggestion would require unions to employ specialists who can make sense of and use the available data. There is a need for accountants who are committed to the interest of unions. Employment of accountants by unions should reduce the problems of information overload. The accountant would be able to act as an information educator, indicating the potential use of data and alternative ways of combining and interpreting the data. This sort of partnership between accountants and union decision-makers is likely to result in rapid learning by decision-makers of the type of data which have relevance to them. In such a way, the lack of awareness as to what constitutes good union decisions can be partly overcome. Yet there can be no guarantee that unions will use the data to get the best possible benefit. We are not convinced that union officials are always concerned with the welfare of their members. They may be more concerned with their own welfare. Since union officials may not, for deliberate or non-deliberate reasons, use a data bank effectively, we still need to understand what union decision models ought to be.

It is our belief that accountants should investigate and clarify the nature of such models. That is why this chapter has been concerned as much with decision models as with information per se. Until we have knowledge of what constitutes good union decision-making and useful information for unions it may be premature to become involved in detailed measurement issues.

Notes and references

1 Committee to Prepare a Statement of Basic Accounting Theory, *A Statement of Basic Accounting Theory*, American Accounting Association 1966.
2 Accounting Standards Steering Committee, *The Corporate Report*, 1975 section 32.
3 R. Price and G. Bain, 'Union growth revisited: 1948-1974 in perspective', *British Journal of Industrial Relations*, 1976, vol. 14.
4 See, for example, H. Raiffa, *Decision Analysis*, Addison Wesley 1968

or P. Lawrence and J. Lorsch, *Organisation and Environment*, Irwin 1969.

5   See, for example, R. A. Dahl, *A Preface to Democratic Theory*, University of Chicago Press 1956 or M. Friedman, *Capitalism and Freedom*, University of Chicago Press 1963.

6   R. Miliband, *The State in Capitalist Society*, Weidenfeld and Nicolson, 1969 and J. Urry and J. Wakeford (eds), *Power in Britain*, Heineman Educational Books 1973.

7   Commission on Industrial Relations, *Disclosure of Information*, Report No. 31, HMSO 1972.

8   Advisory Conciliation and Arbitration Service, *Draft Code of Practice: Disclosure of Information to Trade Unions for Collective Bargaining*, HMSO 1976.

9   For example, Trade Union Congress, *Economic Review*, TUC 1976, pp. 43-45.

10   Confederation of British Industry, *The Provision of Information to Employees: Guidelines for Action*, CBI 1974.

11   Accounting Standards Steering Committee *op. cit.*, 1975 s.2.

12   Report of the Committee of Inquiry on *Industrial Democracy*, Cmnd 6706, HMSO 1977.

13   R. R. Sterling, 'Decision oriented financial accounting', *Accounting and Business Research*, Summer 1972.

14   S. and B. Webb, *History of Trade Unionism*, Longman 1920.

15   See, for example, the list produced by the Trades Union Congress, *Trade Unionism: Evidence of the TUC to the Royal Commission on Trade Unions and Employers' Associations*, TUC 1966, especially paras 97-98.

16   R. E. Walton and R. B. McKersie, *A Behavioral Theory of Labor Negotiations*, McGraw-Hill 1965.

17   A sample of such literature might include R. Cyert, H. A. Simon and D. B. Trow, 'Observation of a business decision', *Journal of Business*, vol. 29, 1956; R. Cyert and J. G. March, *A Behavioural Theory of the Firm*, Prentice-Hall 1963; H. A. Simon, *Administrative Behaviour*, 3rd edition, Collier Macmillan 1976.

18   C. Peterson and L. Beach, 'Man as an intuitive statistician', *Psychological Bulletin*, vol. 67, 1967.

19   For a recent review see B. Foley and K. Maunders, *Accounting Information Disclosure and Collective Bargaining*, Macmillan 1977.

20   A. Coddington. *Theories of the Bargaining Process*, George Allen and Unwin 1968.

21   K. T. Maunders and B. J. Foley, 'Accounting information, employees and collective bargaining' *Journal of Business Finance and Accounting*, vol. 1, 1974.

22   Government Social Survey, *Workplace Industrial Relations, 1972*, HMSO 1974.

23   Royal Commission on Trade Unions and Employers' Associations: 1965-1968 Report, Cmnd 3623, HMSO 1968.

24   Government Social Survey, *op. cit.*, 1974 and for evidence about the engineering industry, D. J. Cooper and S. R. Essex, 'Accounting information and employee decision-making', *Accounting Organisation and Society*, forthcoming.

25 D. J. Cooper and S. R. Essex *op. cit.*
26 For further development of these idea, refer to H. A. Simon, *Models of Man*, Wiley 1956.
27 W. F. Pounds, 'The process of problem finding', *Industrial Management Review*, Fall 1969.
28 D. J. Cooper and S. R. Essex, *op. cit.* Our research on the roles of shop stewards has been summarised in T. Climo 'The role of the accountant in industrial relations' *The Accountant*, December 16, 1976.
29 C. Shannon and W. Weaver, *The Mathematical Theory of Communication*, University of Illinois Press 1964.
30 M. Barrett Brown, *Opening the Books*, Institute for Workers Control, 1968.
31 P. Hird *Your Employers' Profits*, Pluto Press 1975, makes an attempt to de-mystify accounting and to show how to interpret and re-work company published accounts.
32 D. J. Cooper and S. R. Essex *op. cit.*
33 *ibid.*
34 H. Scanlon, *Workers Control and the Transnational Company*, Institute for Workers Control 1970.
35 These ideas have been discussed in T. Gambling, *Societal Accounting*, George Allen and Unwin 1973, especially in Chapter 5.
36 Transport and General Workers Union, *A Positive Employment Programme for ICI*, TGWU 1971.

9

Accounting to society

TREVOR GAMBLING

Professor of Accounting, University of Birmingham

'The public's concern for non-economic aspects of the quality of life appears strongly influenced by the health of the economy. Thus if the anticipated increase in real per capita income is not realised in the next decade then the public's concern for quality of life and ramifications of this concern (e.g. greater need for social accounting reports, demands for changes in working conditions, etc.) may not materialise.'[1]

I hope I am not too unkind in describing this as the conventional hard-liner's view — social concern is a froth on the surface of sated prosperity which disappears as soon as it becomes apparent that the second home can only be an alternative to the second power-boat! Of course, another scenario could be put forward — if we cannot have a second home we become more concerned with the environment surrounding our first one. Which is more true is not easy to demonstrate, but it seems reasonable to suppose that the issue would be much influenced by whether the society in question viewed social concern as a matter for public taxation or private charity and so as a 'charge against profit' or merely an 'appropriation of surplus'. This could provide the reason why interest in 'accounting to society' is not the same everywhere even amongst those countries which pursue the issue at all.

One cannot understand the American writings about
social accounting if one is unaware that the executives of
major companies in the USA are expected to devote a
considerable amount of time to community activities. One
could be naive or cynical about this aspect of American
business life and both attitudes are likely to be wrong. There
is an element of 'Small-town America' about it; local fund-
raising committees are the very places for the rising young
man to meet people and make his mark. At the same time, it
is true that until the 1930's in the USA, both state and
federal employees were few in number and of little
significance; not a few remain political sinecures to this
day. Thus, not only did the people turn to 'big business' in
the way that they had turned previously to landed magnates
in older countries, but business was able to supply
administrative apparatus on a scale beyond that possible to
landed gentry anywhere.

A number of American writers[2] have seen more positive
virtues in this arrangement. It is seen as providing
protection of civil liberty because it represents a denial of
further power to the central and local government. At the
same time it is claimed to be more efficient, because the
people involved are used to pushing through major
undertakings of all kinds and may be supposed to have
better education and training and pay than regular government employees. Against this, one must wonder whether
the fact that a man manages a big manufacturing plant in
Detroit makes him all that great an expert on, say, pre-
school play-groups for minority children. Also, one
supposes that the plant must have first call upon his
services, although the community work could take up the
slack which queueing theory tells us must exist in an
efficient organisation. This theme could be expanded, since
a good deal is on record about the involvement of American
business in social endeavours and in the whole range of
governmental and quasi-governmental agencies. However,
it is not necessary to analyse the comparative *efficiency* of
different ways of administering social agencies, but only to
mention the effects which they have upon a country's
approach to social concern and 'accounting to society'.

In a country where business enterprises regularly devote
so much time and energy to community projects, American-

style accounting to society naturally places emphasis on recording the expenditure of cash and effort in activities which are often tangential to the main purposes of the enterprise. In a European context such an emphasis would run a danger of having large sums of general administrative expenses disallowed against taxation! However, in the USA, it is part of the expected activity of business and seen by stockholders and others as proof that the enterprise has entered the major league. The most definite statement of this sort is to be found in Linowes' proposal for a Socio-Economic Operating Statement[3], which seeks to record all those things which a corporation did *which it was not required to do by law*.

Things order themselves differently again in Continental Europe. Thanks to such diverse talents as Napoleon and Bismarck there is a long tradition of authority in many of these countries, which is to say that the state lays down precise regulations for the conduct of business affairs. The incredible output of EEC regulations follows this tradition. Here too a certain cynicism is possible; enforcement of such a profusion of detail is sometimes erratic to say the least. The regulations often require elaborate returns to be completed; 'accounting to society' in these countries may take the form of substantial abstracts from these returns presented as supplementary information to the main accounts. Also there is still a strong element of paternalism in the relationship of worker and employer so that here 'social accounting' is more concerned with matters affecting employees than those affecting the community at large.[4] Again the efficiency of the arrangements do not really concern us, but only the effect of their existence on accounting to society.

By contrast, 'accounting to society' has no great history in the United Kingdom, where social enterprise has been left entirely to local and central government, or specific charitable trust-type organisations. Over the years, legislation has appeared about safety at work, pollution control, discrimination against minorities and the like, but on a less detailed scale than elsewhere. Some desire has been shown recently in this country for accounts which will show the dealings of enterprises with the community-at-large. The thing to notice is that it has come from the

community-at-large — and not from within the
organisation or from government agencies. There seems to
be a belief here that firms do not always conduct their affairs
in the best interests of anybody but senior management and
dominant shareholders or individual proprietors; workers,
customers, neighbours, the state and maybe even the
ordinary run of shareholders suspect that they occasionally
get short-changed by a smallish group which both controls
the publication of data about what is going on, and has the
power to make their own prophesies largely self-fulfilling!
To the extent that our industrial—social interface is less
institutionalised anyway, we seem to want to place just as
much emphasis on the control aspects of accounting as on
simple reporting functions.

This attitude has been succinctly summarised (by a
professor at an American university!) as demand for some
sort of 'social contract' whereby a community agrees that an
enterprise should be permitted to function in its midst
provided it shows on balance a satisfactory contribution to
social welfare.[5] There is no longer any general assumption
that what is good for General Motors must be good for
America or anywhere else. Social psychologists would see
this change as an advance in the general level of integrative
thinking, possibly in response to an increasingly complex
social environment. Throughout history we were deeply
concerned about the state of trade, the condition of the poor
and public health and by and large we made sincere efforts
to do something about them, but it is only lately that the
proposition that methods of trading, taxation and land-
tenures, can cause poverty and affect public health has
received general acceptance. It should be observed that the
use of more abstract, integrative models does not ensure
more useful results, although one can hope that they will
prove more fertile sources of possible strategies for dealing
with more complex problems. We now demand accounts
which show more rarified relationships between industry
and society than those provided by the price-mechanism.

So far, this demand for more information has not been
very specific about the form in which it should be given; one
might suppose that American and Continental institutions
are so different that their procedures will not prove suitable
for wholesale copying in this country. Accounting for share-

holders and trade unions has been discussed in the two preceding chapters of this book, and it may be that the probable shape of the regulatory instruments which will be forthcoming for these purposes can be forecast to some extent. Pressure for accounting to the more remote participants in the firm like customers, neighbours and the state is also substantial, but the form is harder to forecast at this time. A much undervalued document which attempts to do this is *The Corporate Report*[6] published by the English Institute, which sets out a number of supplementary statements which (one supposes) could be prepared without too much difficulty by most firms:

(a) A statement of value added
(b) An employment report
(c) A statement of money exchanges with the government
(d) A statement of transactions in foreign currency
(e) A statement of future prospects
(f) A statement of corporate objectives

One supposes that what inspired the choice of the suggested additional reports in *The Corporate Report* was their ready availability as much as their relevant nature. However, it will be suggested that these statements can be conceived in forms which would provide a most adequate account of the 'social contract' between the enterprise and its host society. Probably our traditional approach to social aspects of industry does not indicate any particular form of accounting. Thus we are able to make a fresh start of our own. It is possible for us to go back to first principles, and see what people *want* to know about and control within the relationship of business and society. This in turn requires us to consider what that relationship is. One can see how the 'model' of the relationship held in America and Europe has influenced the reports prepared in those countries. The models may be incomplete, but they provide rational criteria for choosing the form of accounting. The United Kingdom has not institutionalised this relationship to the same extent, so our model has to be of the relationship itself rather than of the institutions set up to regulate it! One way of seeking this model might be to have a look at the various attempts so far made *in practice* to provide some sort of social reckoning; these are certain aspects of human resource accounting, the social audit movement and maybe cost-benefit analysis.

Human resource accounting

Human resource accounting is a wide area and includes much that is false or at least mistaken, other matters which are more pertinent to operational research than to accounting proper and yet other aspects which require a better-developed science of social psychology than we are likely to have for some time.

These issues are peripheral to 'accounting to society', except to the extent that the human resource is a section of society with which the firm has a major relationship! However, another aspect of human resource accounting requires attempts to forecast the future demand and behaviour of the human resource by the firm. This could be called manpower planning 'with knobs on', a technique of operational research. To the extent that its purpose is to plan recruitment and the like, this is a correct description, but our researches have shown that manpower models are being built for purposes which extend far beyond this. Both legislation and a heightened social sensibility are pressing for the general de-casualisation of labour; people ought not to be hired-and-fired, maybe they ought not to be recruited to a dead-end job which does not constitute or lead on to a satisfactory career. An unexpected element is the use of such planning-models for dealing with racially mixed work-forces and women employees.[7] This is clearly accounting, or more correctly 'accountability'; managements are being asked to justify their exercise of authority on other grounds than profitability. The minority/female aspect of manpower-planning is extraordinarily fruitful for our purposes, because it underlines the fact that we are asking managers to account for their *policies*. Also it is not at all clear where the 'side of the angels' lies in many of these matters. Do we want 'equal opportunity' which just requires that anyone who applies for a job or for promotion should be treated equally, or is it 'affirmative action' of some sort which is needed, implying the use of quotas and targets of balances to be reached in future years? In the same way, a few firms are beginning to concern themselves with the personality characteristics of their work-force. In many ways it is the personality of the individual worker which determines the morale of the plant as a whole, and hence the best strategies for managing it. This is closely related to the workers' reactions to orders, criticism, feedback of data, budgeting and so on — and may thankfully be left for consideration under 'Accounting and Behavioural Science' in a later chapter. However, this is another morally sensitive development. *Ought* employers to mark employee records to the effect that a worker is 'black', 'female', let alone 'depressive'?

The social audit movement

Another field of practical application of 'accounting to society' has been through the 'social audit' movement, both in the United States and in the United Kingdom. A number of specialist organisations have emerged such as Arthur D Little and Abt Associates in the USA and Medawar's Social Audit Group in the United Kingdom. Although their approaches are markedly different, there seems to be considerable agreement over methodology. Because social data can be given a variety of interpretations, a firm should open its doors to a panel of 'experts' in social matters who would examine all the evidence and come to some conclusion about the social impact of the enterprise. The treatment tends to be episodic; the social auditor comments adversely, say, on the rejection of a Pakistani for a job as a book-keeper — presumably the firm could counter with its story of giving a job to a spastic West Indian. The point is that neither the auditors nor the firms seem able to *generalise* about social matters. Now this is significant, because the objective of the more familiar financial audit is to do just that with financial affairs; does a *system* exist for ordering and receiving goods, checking and paying invoices, so that a limited test-audit gives grounds for supposing that the *totals* of purchases and creditors are correct?

This difficulty is illustrated by an instance from one of the few specific 'social audits' conducted in this country. A group of workers believed that they were being required to handle potentially dangerous chemical substances, while the firm denied that dangerous forms of the chemical were in use at all.[8] If anything is to be made of this *in practice* it is necessary to be able to say exactly what chemical compounds were in use in which plants at what times. Moreover, if we want to establish responsibility we would need to establish the contemporary medical opinion about that compound at those times; if we want to establish entitlement to compensation, it would be necessary to establish exactly which workers were exposed to what concentrations of what substances and for how long. Social audit, like any other audit needs a comprehensive formal record which has been prepared under such circumstances as to support the possibility that it may be complete, in the sense that all items are correctly described, all items which have occurred have been recorded correctly and no items have been recorded which have not occurred.

It is possible that this approach is justified partially by the difficulty of applying a quantitative measure to the impacts of a firm's activities upon the social fabric. "Heat" can be measured in centigrade and 'noise' in decibels, but 'working conditions' can best be described as pleasant or unpleasant. Tolerances of heat and noise can be established but an attempt to weight them so as to arrive at a more general measure is bound to be contentious. Individual's preferences in these matters vary widely, and companionship and interest in the work at hand are in any case of at least equal importance and not at all readily quantified. Some of the largest investments made by developed countries have social rather than commercial objectives, and the probability is that these objectives can be 'achieved' (whatever that may mean!) in more than one way. This has led to the development of techniques such as program planning and budgeting systems (PPBS) and cost benefit analysis (CBA). The former emphasises the need, on the one hand, to see objectives in terms such as 'provision of leisure facilities' rather than 'maintenance of the Parks and Allotments Department'. On the other hand, it attempts to modify the generality of the former sentiments by insisting that some quantifiable variables should be identified by which both the progress of the project and its degree of success can be agreed to be measured.

Cost-benefit analysis

CBA is simply the conventional 'net present value' technique of capital project appraisal, which shows the projects which do not justify investment at all and helps in ranking those which do in some order of attractiveness. The peculiar feature is the necessity to place cash values on the costs and benefits which arise. This is not going to be easy, because the reason the objective is being pursued by a government agency of some sort is usually because private trading through the market system is not providing the services in question. In short, 'prices' do not really exist for these services, or the prices which do exist are defective reflections of the 'true' costs or benefits arising from them. Supporters of the technique used to say 'Any figures are better than no figures at all' — which is fine if it is said with a light laugh, but these figures are meaningless taken out of the context of the decision-model for which they are devised. This is the message of C. West Churchman's paper 'On the Facility, Felicity and Morality of Measuring Social Change',[9] which takes as an example the use (in the Roskill Report) of a rather low insured value as the 'cost' of destroying a Norman church to make way for the third London Airport. All sorts of other 'costs' could be calculated, such as replacement cost, the present value of the original investment, the present value of the future pleasure and inspiration and probably others; the real point is that a market in used churches does not exist. However, churches are occasionally bought and sold, but the 'price' has to be negotiated in each case — somewhere between the lowest price the vendor would take for it and the highest price the purchaser will pay. The various calculated prices of the church are no more than war-cries for use in the negotiations, which seek to arrive at political compromises about the issues. It is worth mentioning that this can also be true where market prices do exist. The assumption is that the market is a 'perfect' one which correctly discounts all the social and commercial issues affected by the transaction, so that the prices and costs take on a virtue of their own which does not have to defend itself by any more detailed model of cause-and-effect. Where the market is imperfect the validity of the prices is less self evident, and this is where the judgment of experts is needed.

Despite these problems it is now possible to suggest a scheme for accounting to society about non-financial aspects of a firm's activities. This does not differ significantly from the techniques needed to account for the financial activities themselves, which is not surprising because 'social accounting' is simply an extension of public concern about the firm beyond the traditional area of financial honesty, following a growing awareness that the market price-system does not adequately regulate some most important aspects of the firm's operations. The concerns are various: fair employment practices, pollution control, workers' safety, customer service, fair advertising are a few of them. The essence of accounting for anything (including financial honesty) can be summarised:

(a) There has to be a policy laid down for dealing with the item. The policy does not have to be particularly lovable; we can say we want to double-bill our customers or only hire Old Etonians and these are just as much 'policies' as more benevolent approaches to the same concern.

(b) There has to be a control system to ensure that the policy is being followed in exactly the same fashion with every case that comes along. The control system has to produce data relating to the transactions it carries out in this way; because they have been produced through a control, these data have a high degree of internal credibility.

(c) These data are then used to produce some sort of reckoning of what the current situation ought to be with regard to the item. Mostly this reckoning will be of a simple 'in', 'out' and 'balance' nature, like a cash-book ledger account or inventory. Thus the basic output of our employment policy control is a manpower inventory showing the present number of employees in their various grades. However, our policies are usually directed at the *quality* of these balances and inventories; our policies on race and sex should produce certain mixtures of race and sex on the various grades in the manpower inventory. The relationship of these qualities to the transactions can be more complex than a straight ledger-type operation; hours of exposure to chemicals over a certain period of time can be used to forecast levels of lead in the blood, for example.

(d) Finally, we usually seek external validation of these reckonings by taking a physical stock-taking to verify the balance.

Society is now asking business to demonstrate more than its commercial acumen and financial honesty. Firms are being pressed to establish policies about matters of social concern, to publish them and justify their decisions in the light of those policies. As we become more sophisticated politically, it is becoming clear that the 'unacceptable face of capitalism' does not lie in anything as constructive as grinding the faces of the poor or the exploitation of man by man. The unacceptable face is the blind and destructive panic of the well-to-do in the face of a threat to their interests. *In the absence of a definite policy* it *is* the sensible thing 'to get out from under' at the first sign of trouble; a proprietor or chief executive who insists on going down with his ship is more to be commended for his nobility than common-sense. Only a commitment to build a better mouse-trap in Ashby de la Zouch, plus a firm set of acceptable policies for achieving it, can provide society with the protection it is demanding against panic-striken 'decisions' to cut losses, move investment out of an area or even out of a country. It could be argued, and rightly, that long-term commitments do not always lead to the greatest economic efficiency. Probably firms who want to operate on a very limited time horizon have every right to do so, but their policies should be well-known to those who do business with them, including those who work for them. Individuals and society-at-large would need to be sure that they recover their costs rapidly and even build up fat against possible un-employment when treating with a firm of this type.

It should be noted that an enormous bibliography exists in this area, mainly of American origin. For the reasons mentioned in this chapter, the works are not discussed in great detail here. The interested reader can find the references from the various Committee Reports of the American Accounting Association published as supplements to *The Accounting Review*. Recent reports include *Environmental Effects of Organisation Behavior, Human Resource Accounting* (1973); *Measurement of Social Costs, Accounting for Human Resources, the Relationship of Behavioral Science and Accounting* (1974); *Social Costs* (1975); *Social Performance* (1976). A certain amount of 'continental' reference material is cited in H-M Schoenfeld's working paper.[4]

Notes and references

1   *Research Opportunities in Auditing*, Peat, Marwick, Mitchell & Co 1976, p.136.
2   For example, Peter F Drucker, *Management*, Heineman 1974, p. ix, and Philip C Cheng, 'Time for social accounting', *The Certified Accountant*, Vol LXVIII, October 1976, pp. 285-291.
3   David F Linowes, 'The accounting profession and social progress', *The Journal of Accounting*, July 1973, pp. 37-40.
4   Hans-Martin Schoenfeld, *Social Reporting — the Present State in West Germany, Austria and Switzerland*, Faculty Working Paper No 311, College of Commerce and Business Administration, University of Illinois, May 1976.
5   Kassaveri V Ramanathan, 'Toward a theory of corporate social accounting', *The Accounting Review*, Vol LI, July 1976, pp. 516-528.
6   Accounting Standards Steering Committee, *The Corporate Report* Institute of Chartered Accountants in England and Wales 1975.
7   Neil C. Churchill and John K. Shank 'Accounting for affirmative action programs: a stochastic flow approach', *The Accounting Review*, Vol L, October 1975, pp. 643-656.
8   Reported in *The Sunday Times* of 8 February 1976; a story on an investigation of Avon Tyres by Social Audit.
9   C. West Churchman, 'On the facility, felicity and morality of measuring social change', *The Accounting Review*, Vol XLVI, January 1971, pp. 30-35.

10

Accounting as a basis for taxation

J R MACE

Senior Lecturer in Accounting and Finance, University of Lancaster

Introduction

The objective of this chapter is to introduce readers to the use of accounting information for purposes of taxation. The development of taxation structures has been strongly influenced by the development of accounting practices and it is likely that the Inland Revenue will continue to be a major user of information from accounting reports. Accounting information serves two purposes in the administration of the tax system: first, it provides asset valuations and measurements of income which may be used in a routine way as a basis for determining liability for a number of taxes, and secondly, it provides information about the activities and progress of the accounting entities which enables the effectiveness of the tax to be monitored by the taxation authorities. Assessment of the effectiveness of the tax system for achieving its objectives would normally lead, albeit in an ill-structured way, to changes in the tax system which were designed to enhance its effectiveness. Changes which may be envisaged as a result of such monitoring could include alterations to the rates of tax which are charged or alterations in the legal definitions of the tax bases which are used. From time to time, new taxes are introduced and old taxes are abolished, or radically restructured as circumstances change, and the various objectives of tax systems are given new priorities.

In summary, we may say that accounting information has a programmed role in the routine computation of tax liabilities, and it has a non-programmed role in the design of systems of taxation. Through these intimate links with taxation, accounting information has a profound effect upon each one of us, for taxation is a part of the social and economic environment in which we both work and play.

Taxation is not passive but active within this environment and, in influencing personal and business decisions, it evokes new political and economic pressures for its own change in an unending process of mutual interaction.

Problems of tax system design

Before we look at some of the routine uses of accounting information for computing tax liabilities, we shall examine some of the factors which have led the designers of tax systems to make use of accounting information in defining a base for tax. Problems of tax system design are always current issues because changing requirements lead to changing solutions. The fundamental requirement of a tax system is that it should raise revenue to pay for the machinery of government, for defence, for the maintenance of law and order and for various other public purposes which may be formulated from time to time. The pioneering economist, Adam Smith, addressed himself to the problems of tax system design in his book, 'An Inquiry into the Nature and Causes of the Wealth of Nations'. His four maxims with regard to taxes in general are almost as valid today as when they were first published in 1776, despite the vast changes in society and in the role of government which have taken place since that time. Adam Smith believed (according to his first maxim) that the subjects of every state ought to contribute towards the support of the government, as nearly as possible, in proportion to their respective abilities; that is, in proportion to the revenue which they respectively enjoy under the protection of the state. He likened the expense of government which falls upon the individuals of a great nation to the expense of management which falls upon the joint tenants of a great estate, and he thought that the individuals in the nation, like the tenants of the estate, should be obliged to contribute in proportion to their respective interests. Ideas concerned with equity in taxation are closely associated with this first maxim of Adam Smith's and we shall return to the topic shortly.

His other maxims about taxes in general are concerned with the attributes of a tax system which would endure because of its general acceptability to those affected by it. These characteristics are still thought to be desirable, but more modern writings have given greater emphasis to the use of taxation systems for the achievement of short-term objectives of public policy than to the creation of a durable system. Smith's second maxim was that the tax which each individual is bound to pay ought to be certain and not arbitrary as to its time of payment, manner of payment and the quantity to be paid, and that these matters ought to be clear and plain to the contributor, and to every other person. His third maxim was that every tax ought to be levied at the time or in the manner in which it is most likely to be convenient for the contributor to pay it for that is when he is most likely to have the wherewithal to pay it. The final maxim was that a tax which was equal, certain and convenient should cost as little as possible to its contributors above what it brought to the public treasury of the state.

Communication through the medium of a tax system

In his elaboration of the final maxim, Smith makes an important point which continues to operate as a constraint upon the design of a tax system. He suggests that the obligation upon individuals to pay tax may diminish or destroy some of the funds which might enable them more easily to pay those taxes and he draws attention to the fact that the community may benefit more from the way in which individuals choose to employ their capital than from the way it is employed by the state. The levying of a tax may, for example, in Smith's words 'obstruct the industry of the people, and discourage them from applying to certain branches of business which might give maintenance and employment to great multitudes'. This illustrates the nature of the tightrope upon which tax designers must walk. Some tax payers are in the position of the goose which is laying golden eggs for the benefit of society, and yet any impatience by taxation authorities to raise more revenue may have adverse effects upon the morale of the goose — if it does not kill it! The taxation authority is able to use the tax system as a means of communication with the tax payer. The tax payer has no obligation to refrain from altering his behaviour when there is a tax change, and he is entitled to adapt his personal and business affairs so as to maximise his well-being after all taxation. Individuals normally act in ways to further their own self-interest and for any given structure of taxation, the taxpayer may perceive incentives for particular kinds of actions.

The taxation authority may take advantage of the taxpayer's perceptions and mould the tax system to encourage the taxpayer to behave in a socially desirable way. It is able to do this by providing relief from taxation in respect of some activities which are to be encouraged and withholding relief in respect of others (examples are given later in the chapter). By this means, the structure of the tax system would communicate to taxpayers the nature of those activities which are to be fostered.

Changes in an existing tax system provide messages to taxpayers of other kinds, in that they herald changes in the policies, intentions and attitudes of governments. Even small changes in tax systems can have potent effects upon the morale and confidence of tax payers, because of the effect they have upon tax-payers' expectations about the future. The psychological impact of new taxes can be particularly severe upon such groups in society as the proprietors of small businesses who may be inclined to perceive non-existent threats to their survival, and to exaggerate the real dangers of change.

Smith may have been unduly pessimistic in assuming that taxation could only discourage private action, but his comments opened the way for successive governments in recent years to seek to prove him wrong. They have tried to use the tax system in a number of ways to provide incentives to taxpayers to act in socially desirable ways — of which perhaps the most important has been the succession of attempts to encourage industrial investment. We should perhaps emphasise that some of the incentives perceived by taxpayers from their observations of a tax system may not have been communicated intentionally by the designers of the system. It is for this reason that the monitoring of taxpayer behaviour by the tax authorities is important, for without such monitoring, the tax authorities would be unable to detect any adverse or unexpected consequences which may arise or to correct any anomalies which may develop.

Equity as an objective of taxation

The most important intention of tax system designers over many years appears to be that which has been expressed in the first of Adam Smith's maxims. Indeed much of the development of tax systems has centred upon a search for fairness or 'equity' in taxation. We may distinguish two types of fairness in relation to taxation: a fairness between those tax-payers of equal taxable capacity which requires that those in similar circumstances should pay similar amounts of tax (horizontal equity), and a fairness between those taxpayers of unequal taxable capacities which requires that the amounts of their tax payments should be properly differentiated (vertical equity). It is easier for the problem to be stated than for a definitive solution to be found. Achievement of horizontal equity requires that all components of the taxable capacity of taxpayers should be measured and aggregated on a common scale. Achievement of vertical equity requires that appropriate rates of tax should be charged at each level on the scale of taxable capacity. The measurement of the taxable capacity of taxpayers is usually undertaken in a way which takes into account the needs of the taxpayer as well as his means. The results are, first, that a taxpayer with greater needs is considered to have a lower taxable capacity than that of another with equal means, and secondly, that a doubling of a taxpayer's means with no corresponding change in his needs would more than double his taxable capacity. Taxable capacity may thus be considered to be related to the excess of means over needs. Achievement of vertical equity is thought to justify the imposition of higher rates of tax upon higher taxable capacities — a phenomenon known as 'progressive taxation' — but the selection of appropriate rates is particularly controversial and in this chapter we shall concentrate our attention more upon the efforts to achieve horizontal equity in taxation.

The first problem is to identify the components of taxable capacity which are to be measured. The list of components is continually subject to revision as the nature of taxable capacity is constantly an issue for discussion. It seems to be agreed, however, that (subject to certain safeguards in each case for assessing his needs) it would be possible to assess a taxpayer's means from an examination of either his expenditure, his wealth, or his income. In practice, taxation is levied at the same time upon all three of these possible bases. Some theorists have argued, however, that it would be desirable to base all taxation upon a single one of these bases, and the choice has frequently fallen upon income as such a base. The taxation of income often proceeds, in practice, as if taxable income were in fact the sole measure of taxable capacity although it is recognised that a more comprehensive definition of income would be necessary if horizontal equity is to be achieved from the taxation of 'income' alone.

Early attempts to relate taxation to the taxable capacity of tax payers were frustrated by an unwillingness of taxpayers to disclose financial information to persons outside their businesses. The result was that the taxation of income proceeded *indirectly* through the imposition of taxes on items of luxurious expenditure and upon such things as would be likely to be an indication of the taxpayer's income like the number of servants he kept, or the number of windows in his house. We have now identified that the objectives for the equitable taxation of income are that income should be comprehensively defined to include all components of the taxable capacity of taxpayers and that the measurement of income, when so defined, should be in terms which allow comparison to be made between the taxable capacity of one taxpayer and the taxable capacity of another.

It is the unique contribution of accounting to matters of taxation that it should provide the information upon which such measurements and comparisons may be made. The process remains imperfect and inexact for many reasons but the use of accounting measurements of income is arguably an improvement upon indirect methods of evaluating the taxable capacity conferred by income.

Income tax

Let us examine the methods by which accounting information is presently used in routine ways for determining liability to taxes on income. British tax law does not provide the comprehensive definition of income for tax purposes which we have said would be desirable, but instead, it defines income by classifying the sources of income in a number of schedules and cases, as follows:

Schedule A: annual profits or gains arising from ownership of land in UK

Schedule B: income from the occupation of woodlands in the UK managed on a commercial basis and with a view to the realisation of profits (unless the occupier elects for taxation under Schedule D Case 1)

Schedule C: income from 'gilt-edged' securities. (i.e. from UK government loans, etc.)

Schedule D: annual profits or gains from any kind of property subdivided as follows:

Case 1   profits of trades and businesses

Case 2   profits of a profession or vocation

Case 3   interest from which tax has not been deducted by the payer (e.g. bank deposit interest)

Case 4   interest on certain foreign securities

Case 5   income from possessions (including shares) located outside the UK

Case 6   annual profits or gains not falling within any other case or schedule (including rents from furnished accommodation)

(Case 7   This case was originally used for the taxation of short-term capital gains. It was introduced in 1962 and abolished in April 1971 when such gains became taxable under the provisions of Capital Gains Tax)

(Case 8   This case was used for the taxation of income from land and buildings until Schedule A

was reinstated in April 1970, seven years after
some earlier provisions for the taxation of
land under Schedule A had been abolished)

Schedule E: Cases 1, 2 and 3 of this schedule deal with the
taxation of earned income (wages and salaries) from any
offices or employments of various taxpayers in various
parts of the world.

Schedule F: dividends and other distributions of a
company resident in the UK

A system of taxation based upon such classification of
income according to its source is known as a 'schedular
system' of income taxation.

It permits different treatment of incomes from different
sources either in the method of computing income or in the
rate of tax which is applied. In some instances, a distinctive
treatment is believed to contribute to a fairer measure of
taxable capacity, than would a simple aggregation of
amounts derived from different income sources. For
example, the distinction of income which is 'unearned' or
derived from investments from that which is 'earned' by
work has, for long, been an important feature of the British
tax system. The persistence of the distinction is based upon
the belief that a given money income from investments
confers a different taxable capacity upon the recipient from
that conferred by a similar money income from a job. It has
conventionally been thought that the former confers more
taxable capacity than the latter, though the extent of the
differential between them has varied from time to time —
and in some countries the possibility of making such
distinctions is ignored and incomes from all sources are
treated identically under a system known as a 'global
system' of income taxation.

Example of an Income Tax Computation

Consider as an example of the British system, the
computation of the income tax liability of Mr Tumbril.
Detailed changes occur in the tax rates and in the amounts
of allowances from year to year, but the basic structure of the
computation changes less frequently. The example given is

Income tax computation for Mr Tumbril 1975–76   £

Earned Income   6,695

Investment Income:
   Building Society Interest   (see note 1)
          Mr Tumbril   960
          Mrs Tumbril 340
                   1,300
Add notional basic rate tax

    $£1,300 \times \dfrac{35}{65}$ 700   2,000

   Dividends   (see next sub-section)
          Mr Tumbril 3,250
Add tax credit

    $£3,250 \times \dfrac{35}{65}$ 1,750   5,000   7,000

                                   13,695
Less Mortgage interest   1,500
Total Income   12,195

Less personal allowance   (see note 2)   955
       child allowance   240   1,195
Taxable Income   £11,000

Tax payable   (see note 3)

	£
4500 @ 35%	1,575
500 @ 40%	200
1000 @ 45%	450
1000 @ 50%	500
1000 @ 55%	550
2000 @ 60%	1,200
1000 @ 65%	650
£11000	5,125

Investment Income surcharge   (see note 4)

		£
1000 @ Nil	0	
1000 @ 10%	100	
3500 @ 15%	525	625
5500		5,750

Less Life Assurance relief   (see note 5)
       17½% × 1000   175

                                      5,575
Less Tax Credit on Dividends   1,750
       Building Society Interest Credit (see Note 1)   700   2,450
Net Tax Payable   £ 3,125

for 1975-76 (the tax year ends on 5 April), in which year a man's taxable income was defined as his total income *plus* the investment income of his wife *less* the personal allowances to which he was entitled. Special rules would have applied for the calculation of income tax on the earned income of Mr Tumbril's wife, so for simplicity in the example, we shall assume that she had none. Apart from his salary of £6695, Mr. Tumbril had cash income for 1975-76 which consisted of £960 Building Society interest and £3,250 dividends from ordinary shares in several companies. His wife's only income consisted of £340 Building Society interest. He paid £1,500 interest on a mortgage for the purchase of his house and £1,000 allowable life assurance premiums on qualifying policies. Mr and Mrs Tumbril have one child born in December 1970. The computation of Mr Tumbril's income tax liability is given on page 161 and additional words of explanation are given in the notes which follow.

Note 1: Building Societies have a special arrangement for the payment of tax which means that the interest they pay on money deposited with them is free of income tax at the basic rate (35% in 1975-76) in the hands of depositors. Mr and Mrs Tumbril have received a total of £1,300 of such interest but for purposes of calculating tax at higher rates and for calculating the surcharge on investment income, the notional amount of basic rate tax must be added into the computation of taxable income. This process is known as 'grossing-up' since income net of tax is being converted into an equivalent 'gross' amount. The notional basic rate tax (calculated as £700 in the example) is not paid or payable by Mr Tumbril and reappears as a deduction in the computation of net tax payable.

Note 2: The allowances which are deducted from total income at this point in the computation are intended to reflect the taxpayers needs. His total income may be said to represent his means, so the deduction of the allowances from means will produce a 'taxable income' which is an approximation to taxable capacity. A married man whose wife was living with him or wholly maintained by him throughout the year was entitled in 1975-76 to deduct a personal allowance of £955 from total income. There was also a child allowance for each child of the taxpayer living at any time within the year (and also for other children in specified circumstances) which consisted of a deduction from total income of £240 when the child is under eleven (£275 if between eleven and sixteen and £305 if over sixteen). The child allowance was to be reduced by the excess (if any) of the income of the child in his own right above £115 per annum. The personal allowance for a single man in 1975-76 would have been £675.

When they were first introduced, the personal allowances had the administrative advantage of causing small incomes (below the aggregate amount of allowances) to be totally exempt from income tax. The distribution of incomes is skewed with relatively large numbers of small incomes, so the existence of personal allowances considerably reduced the numbers of potential taxpayers. It thereby avoided the costs of assessing and trying to collect very small amounts of money from large numbers of people, most of whom would probably not have been in a position to pay the tax anyway. In recent years, however, some other features of the allowances system have become prominent in discussion. One of these controversial issues concerns the fact that allowances have not been increased in line with the change in the general level of prices, and that more and more people have become payers of income tax in consequence, despite the fact that they are the relatively poor members of society. If the levels of allowances were directly linked to an index of prices, this would alleviate the problem, but such a solution has not yet been adopted because *inter alia* it would reduce the flexibility which Chancellors of the Exchequer presently have in framing proposals for changes in the tax system; it would make it more difficult to raise required amounts of public revenue from taxes on personal incomes or to change the levels of allowances in real terms to reflect changing living standards; and in the views of some people, the indexing of a single aspect of income tax alone would create more inequity in the tax system as a whole than the inequity it removed.

A second controversial issue concerned with the allowances system has developed from the fact that the marginal value of an allowance to a particular taxpayer is dependent upon the rate at which he pays income tax on marginal increases in his taxable income. Thus, in our example, the value of the child allowance to Mr Tumbril is £156 (65% of £240) because he would pay £156 more tax if he had no child allowance. At the lower extreme, where total income is less than the allowances, an addition to the level of allowances would provide no marginal benefit to the 'taxpayer' because he is paying no income tax anyway. Since the marginal value of an allowance to a taxpayer depends upon his marginal rate of tax, and the marginal tax rates paid by many taxpayers now exceed the basic rate (because the progressive scale of tax rates expressed in money terms has become steeper in real terms as price levels have increased), it has become increasingly apparent that the child allowance cannot in all circumstances be related to need in the way that was once claimed. Several solutions to this problem have been proposed, including the suggestion that payments should be made to those taxpayers whose total incomes were below the total of their allowances. Such payments would have been proportionally related to the shortfall of the taxpayer's income below his needs, as measured by his allowances, and would have ensured that changes in allowances provided some benefit even to the poorest members of society. It appears that the problem is to be tackled (at least as regards the allowances for children, if not for other allowances presently available) by the phasing out of the present child allowances for tax purposes and their replacement by non-taxable child 'benefits' paid in cash directly to the mothers of the children. The subsidy in respect of each child would ultimately be unaffected by the level of the taxable income of the parent when the substitution of child benefit for child allowance has been completed. Such a result may well be desirable, but it is to be hoped that it can eventually be achieved without the inefficiency which appears to derive from extracting a few extra pounds of tax each week from a husband merely to pay back a roughly similar number of pounds to his wife.

Note 3: The scale of rates of tax exhibits the characteristic of progressive taxation to which reference was made earlier in the chapter. The scale is intended to achieve vertical equity in taxation but the disincentives to certain taxpayers from the higher rates (rising to 83% on earned income in 1975-76 when taxable income exceeds £20,000, and to 98% on investment income after taking the investment income surcharge into account) are argued by some to have social disadvantages which outweigh the social advantages of an appearance of vertical equity.

Note 4: The investment income surcharge (an extra tax on investment income) reflects the belief, previously discussed, that investment income represents (pound for pound) a higher taxable capacity than earned income. In our example, the grossed-up investment income of £7,000 (refer to the computation) is reduced by the £1,500 of interest payable by Mr Tumbril on the mortgage for the purchase of his house before the investment income surcharge is calculated. The first £1,000 of the surchargeable investment income is surcharged at a nil rate (it would have been the first £1,500 in 1975-76 if either the taxpayer or his wife had been aged sixty-five or more in the tax year), the balance up to £2,000 was surcharged at 10%, and any excess over £2,000 was surcharged at 15%. By granting exemption from surcharge to the lowest band of investment income, the system ensures that the surcharge is paid primarily by those with the largest concentrations of income-earning wealth. In this way, the present surcharge fulfils some of the objectives which would otherwise be achieved by the existence of an annual Wealth Tax, and it implies a recognition that the extra taxable capacity associated with unearned income is consequential upon the concentration of income-earning wealth in the hands of one taxpayer, rather than upon the mere existence of such wealth in the hands of taxpayers generally.

Note 5: There was in 1975-76 a deduction of half basic rate tax on qualifying life assurance premiums which applied to the whole of such premiums where they exceeded £20 per annum. This aids taxpayers who make regular savings through the medium of life assurance contracts and appears as an incentive for entering into such contracts. Relief for payment of life assurance premiums has existed in one form or another since the very early days of income tax, and is likely to continue despite the resultant discrimination against other ways in which the taxpayer could provide for his retirement and old age or for his dependents.

Tax on the income of companies

The selection of method for the taxation of companies has been associated with three major controversies in recent years: one concerned with the fairest way of measuring the taxable income of companies when price levels are changing, one concerned with the best method of providing

"He was a successful chartered accountant until they got him for an income tax offence — he shot the tax inspector."

incentives for investment by companies, and an overriding controversy concerned with the very nature of companies and the relationship between a company and its shareholders. Consider first, the overriding controversy. Some people take the 'proprietorial' view that a company is merely a convenient way for a number of people to combine their resources and to share the resultant profits (or limited losses). They would argue that a company is nothing more than a partnership, and that the profits of a company, like those of the partnership should be fully allocated to individuals for the purpose of ascertaining taxes on income. Other people take the 'entity' view of companies which emphasises the legal position that the company is independent of its shareholders. Their argument, at its extreme, is that the company has taxable income in its own right, and that when the company distributes part or all of such income to its shareholders it thereby creates a new taxable income in the hands of those shareholders. In 1965, the British tax system made a major move towards the entity viewpoint. In that year, a new tax on company income was introduced called Corporation Tax, and all distributions of dividends by companies were additionally taxed as income in the hands of shareholders. Proprietorialists objected to this 'classical' system of Corporation Tax on the grounds that 'a single income was being taxed twice', and economists seemed to agree because the phenomenon is known as 'economic double taxation'.

An intermediate position between the proprietorialists and that of the supporters of the classical system of Corporation Tax was reached in 1973 when the imputation system of Corporation Tax was introduced. The imputation system differed from the classical system in that dividend distributions by companies were now to be treated as having borne income tax at the basic rate on the 'grossed-up' equivalent of the net cash amount actually paid. From the shareholder's viewpoint, the imputed tax on his dividend comes to him as a tax credit which is set against his personal tax liability (and may be reclaimed by him if his tax credits exceed his liability). In our example (see above), Mr Tumbril received cash dividends of £3,250 and the associated tax credit was calculated as £1,750 to give a grossed-up amount of £5,000. The tax credit appeared again as a deduction in the calculation of tax payable.

For administrative reasons, and to avoid loss of revenue, the company actually pays to the tax authorities, tax equal to the tax credits on the dividends. The payment is made shortly after the payment of the dividend, but it is treated not as extra income tax (as would have been the case under the classical system) but as a prepayment of the Corporation Tax which will eventually be payable on the company's profits. The prepayment is known as 'Advance Corporation

Table 1   Impact of corporate taxation on retained earnings

	A *High pay-out ratio*	B *Medium pay-out ratio*	C *Low pay-out ratio*
Classical sytem			
Taxable profits (thousands)	1000	1000	1000
Corporation tax (40%)	400	400	400
Net earnings	600	600	600
Gross taxable dividend	450	285.7	200
Retained profit	150	314.3	400
Imputation system			
Taxable profits (thousands)	1000	1000	1000
Corporation tax (50%)	500	500	500
Net earnings on basis of nil distribution	500	500	500
Net dividend	292.5	185.7	140
Retained profit	207.5	314.3	360
Both systems			
Net dividend received by shareholders	292.5	185.7	130
Income tax (classical system) or Tax credit (imputation system)	157.5	100	70
Gross taxable dividend	450	285.7	200

Tax' and is said to be paid on account of the 'main-stream Corporation Tax liability'. Thus, under the imputation system of Corporation Tax, there is an element of compromise by which all company profits are subject to Corporation Tax, whether they are distributed or not (as if the company were an entity) but at the same time part of the Corporation Tax is made available to the shareholder as a tax credit for basic-rate income tax in respect of his dividends. The introduction of the tax credit was an important concession to the proprietary view of the nature of companies (which sees companies as transparent instruments of their shareholders) and it alleviated the 'discrimination' against companies with high pay-out ratios which had been a feature of the economic double taxation associated with the classical system of Corporation Tax.

Table 1 illustrates the possible impact on retained earnings when levels of gross dividend per million pounds of pre-tax profits are held constant for either system of Corporation Tax.

We have assumed for the purpose of the table, that the rate of Corporation Tax under the imputation system would be set higher than that under the classical system, in order to compensate for the revenue lost by the granting of tax credits. Comparison of the levels of retained profit under each of the systems illustrated in the table shows that a company with a relatively high pay-out ratio (see column A) has more retained profit per million pounds of taxable profits under the imputation system than under the classical system, whereas the reverse is true for a company with a relatively low pay-out ratio (see column C).

Incentives for investment

One of the major motivations for the change to the imputation system in 1973 appears to derive from beliefs concerning the second of the controversies mentioned at the start of the section on tax on the income of companies — namely the controversy concerned with the best method of providing incentives for investment by companies. In this respect, the classical system gives relative advantage to companies which retain a high proportion of their taxable income (those with a low pay-out ratio) and thereby discourages dividends. It was the stated belief of those who introduced the classical system into Britain in 1965, that the additional retained profits would be used for additional industrial investment. Opponents of the system argued that industrial investment would only be optimally directed when funds were raised through the capital market, that the classical system did nothing to match available funds with investment opportunities, and that any investment it did encourage (as distinct from the mere retention of profits) would be unlikely to have stood the test of profitability.

By removing 'economic double taxation', the introduction of the imputation system restored neutrality (from the viewpoint of shareholders with a marginal income tax rate equal to the basic rate) in the tax treatment of the taxable income of companies with differing pay-out ratios. It is interesting to note, however, that the removal of fiscal restraint upon dividend increases was followed almost immediately by the imposition of other kinds of dividend restraints associated with attempts to control inflation. It is paradoxical that companies which had accepted the incentives provided by the classical system were to be prevented from readjusting their pay-out ratios in accordance with their own self interest and the logic of the new fiscal policy. The attempt to reintroduce profitability as the prime arbiter of investment was frustrated by action in support of the conflicting objective of restraining inflation. It is not unusual in matters concerned with taxation to find that conflicts between objectives are resolved by circumstance rather than intention, and it is a common plea that a coordinated strategy for public policies should be devised.

Equitable measurement of the taxable income of companies

Not even a brief review of controversial issues in taxation would be complete without reference to the problem of finding the fairest way of measuring the taxable income of companies. Comparability of the results of income measurement is an essential feature of providing fairness. The problem of achieving fairness in income measurement is alleviated, but not resolved, by the practice of standardising the form of allowance for capital expenditure, so that a company's choice of depreciation method is irrelevant to its tax liability. Unfortunately, present methods for the financial reporting of tax matters by companies do not always make it easy to confirm that the impact of tax on companies is fair. Thus any reference to an 'effective rate of tax' on a company's profits, is a reference to an average rate and will have failed to distinguish the two main components of the tax bill, namely the payment derived from application of the tax rate to a fair measure of a company's taxable income and the receipt (or deduction from the tax bill) which results from the special tax incentives given to companies for behaving in ways considered by the tax authorities to be socially desirable (e.g. for investing in particular things, at particular places or at particular times or for financing such investments in particular ways).

The difficult problem of income measurement when price levels are changing has yet to be resolved for taxation purposes no less than for financial reporting generally. In this respect, we can go no further, in our introductory discussion, than to say that the method of income measurement which is selected for the preparation of reports to shareholders need not necessarily be identical to that which is conducive to the achievement of horizontal equity in taxation — the equal treatment of companies with similar taxable capacities.

Conclusion

Our survey of tax problems has revealed a number of controversial issues in the field of personal taxation including those derived from the lack of agreement on the conceptual relationship between shareholders and the income of companies in which they hold shares. It seems that objectives of achieving horizontal and vertical equity will be with us for many years, but that the perceptions of equity will change with political, social and economic circumstances, and interim solutions to the basic problems of personal and corporate taxation will continue to evolve.

11

Accounting for nationalised industries

MICHAEL SHERER and ALAN SOUTHWORTH

Lecturers in Accounting, University of Manchester

Introduction

Most of you, at some time, perhaps after a few drinks in the Union bar, have probably voiced an opinion about the performance of the 'nationalised industries'. Your opinion may vary from 'the first step on the road to Utopia' to 'one of the reasons why this country is in such a mess'. Not only is the subject of nationalised industries controversial, but also, as the newspaper headlines in figure 1 aptly illustrate, it is very topical. But what is the information upon which your judgements and those of the Press are based; how relevant is it in assessing the performance of nationalised industries? More important, what kind of information is used by those who make decisions concerning nationalised industries and to what extent is it relevant for those decisions? These are some of the questions which we intend to discuss in this chapter.

From the very beginning we wish to make our position clear: we do not think that accounting for nationalised industries is more important than accounting for private sector companies, but we do think that accounting for nationalised industries emphasises issues and problems which are not covered elsewhere in this book. Hence the need for a separate chapter which will have the following scheme.

172

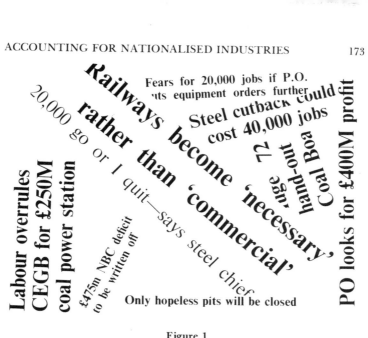

Figure 1

We shall describe what we mean by nationalised industries and identify those enterprises which are encompassed by our description. We shall also present our understanding of the accounting process and in particular show how published accounting reports may be used for prediction and control.

Our model of the accounting process reduces to three main parts: the originator or reporter and the events he chooses to report; the user or decision-maker; and the message or accounting report which links these two together. Beginning with the reporter, in this case the nationalised industries themselves, we shall describe those characteristics and activities of nationalised industries which differentiate them from private sector companies. Secondly, we shall describe the objectives which have been attributed to nationalised industries and which become the control criterion for the decision-makers. Then follows an examination of the various decision-making groups, the associated institutional arrangements and the kind of information currently available to the decision-makers. The last section, which also serves as the conclusion, considers the implications of the preceding discussion for the 'message', i.e. the type of accounting report which is needed for nationalised industries.

We should like to stress a final point in this introduction. We cannot offer solutions to all of the questions we pose — much research is required before such a stage is reached. Nevertheless we hope we shall have introduced you to an important and exciting subject area and provided you with a viable framework within which you can discuss the problems of accounting for nationalised industries.

Which are the nationalised industries?

The answer to this question is fairly obvious: we simply take the official government definition of a nationalised industry and list those corporations which are are so classified by the government. However, those industries which are 'treated' as 'nationalised' by the government do not coincide precisely with any official definition. So we must find our own way there.

At the outset let us state that we are interested only in those enterprises which are primarily engaged in industrial or other commercial activities, and therefore we can eliminate the health and education services provided by the government. Further, we are only interested in those industries which are able to manage their affairs without detailed control by any elected body, and in particular those industries which are able to retain any surpluses they generate and so maintain their own reserves. Thus, all local authority trading undertakings are excluded from our area of interest on both counts. Finally, the enterprise must be wholly owned by the state. This eliminates those companies in which the government is only one of several shareholders, e.g. British Petroleum and the less well known Anglo-Venezuelan Railway Company (we wonder whether the plan is for a bridge or a tunnel!).

Thus far we have defined a nationalised industry as an industrial or commercial enterprise, wholly owned by the state and yet with freedom from detailed control. To arrive at a manageable and familiar list we shall add two further characteristics: the enterprise should have a dominant, if not 100%, share in its particular industry and it should employ more than 50,000 people. We have now emerged with the eight major corporations which are popularly called 'the nationalised industries' — British Airways Board; British Gas Corporation; British Railways Board; British Steel Corporation; Electricity industry in England and Wales; National Bus Company; National Coal Board; and the Post Office.

The accounting process and published reports

It is generally accepted that companies in the private sector should provide information which is relevant to the decision models of particular user groups. In 1966 the American Accounting Association defined accounting 'as the process of identifying, measuring and communicating economic information to permit informed judgements and decisions by users of the information'.

This definition was echoed in the UK in 1975 with the publication of the Accounting Standards Committee's *The Corporate Report* which stated that the main purpose of accounting reports 'is to communicate economic measurements of and information about the resources and performance of the reporting entity useful to those having reasonable rights to such information'.

Both definitions suggest that accounting is concerned with effective communication and that the information to be communicated should be useful for decision making. Put another way, the receipt of accounting information should induce better decisions. Thus, an effective accounting system requires that the reporter of the event or activity is aware not only of the identity of the decision makers but also of the nature of their decisions and the decision models they use. Only then can the reporter transmit the information which the decision makers require. Moreover, there exist feedback loops in the accounting process by which the action of the decision makers may determine the future activities of the enterprise (e.g. new investment projects) or the information the enterprise selects to report (e.g. non-financial indicators) or even the method the reporter uses to encode the message (e.g. the level of aggregation in the accounts).

Thus, the accounting process enables decision makers to

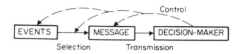

Figure 2   The accounting process

monitor the performance of the enterprise for the purposes of prediction and control, and the accounting report is a vehicle for the transmission of information (the message) from those who have it to those who want it (figure 2).

From this generalised description of the accounting process we can now identify the role of accounting reports for nationalised industries. Various decision-makers, or groups of controllers, want information about the performance of nationalised industries as input for their decision and control models. For example, a minister may require information on performance in order to enable him to evaluate the justification for a proposed price increase.

However, although the accounting process delineated above may be applied to both private sector companies and nationalised industries, the type of information conveyed, the message, need not be similar and in fact is unlikely to be so. While it may be possible to deduce an optimal reporting method for companies in the private sector based upon a normative model of shareholder decision making, it does not follow that such a reporting method should necessarily be used as the basis of external reporting for nationalised industries. Yet, this assumption is implied in the current reporting practices of nationalised industries, for it is customary for their accounts to follow closely the 'best commercial accounting practices' of the private sector, even to the extent of complying wherever possible with the provisions of the Companies Acts and the latest recommendations of the professional accountancy bodies.

But why? Why should the accounts of the nationalised industries adopt reporting methods almost identical to those adopted in the private sector? The responsibility for the format and content of the accounts of nationalised industries belongs to the minister in the appropriate sponsor department. We might hypothesise, *ex post*, that his objective with regard to accounting reports is to secure as much comparability as possible with the accounting reports of companies in the private sector. This would be a rational criterion if the characteristics, and objectives, of nationalised industries were comparable with those of the private sector. However, even the most casual of observations contradict this view. For example, nationalised industries are certainly not observed to maximise the expected future net cash flows to the entity, which may be a reasonable operational objective to be deduced from an observation of the behaviour of companies in the private sector.

Therefore, when discussing relevant accounting information, we cannot assume that what is 'good' for companies in the private sector is equally 'good' for the nationalised industries. And in order to arrive at some notion of what is relevant accounting information for the control of nationalised industries, we must look more closely at the accounting process as it applies to these industries, i.e. we must examine in detail the boxes in figure 2 and ask the following questions:

1 Are the characteristics and hence the objectives of nationalised industries different from those of private sector companies?

2 Are the decision-makers, and their processes of decision making different from those in private sector companies?

3 Are the actual decisions concerning nationalised industries of a different nature from those in the private sector?

If any of these differences exist and are significant, then nationalised industry accounts produced in a similar manner to private sector accounts are unlikely to satisfy the requirements for effective communication and control. Consequently, if we discover that the various decision-makers do require different messages from nationalised industries we must ascertain whether the solution is simply to include the relevant information within the traditional framework of published accounts, or whether the differences are so fundamental as to require a message of a completely different nature.

The main characteristics of the nationalised industries

In this section we shall describe those characteristics which distinguish nationalised industries from companies in the private sector. This should enable us to identify those events and activities which decision-makers wish to control, and hence give us a preliminary indication of the information which needs to be included in the message, the accounting report.

The first distinguishing characteristic is their role as economic regulators. The government is able to direct the activities of the nationalised industries for the purpose of managing the economy with more effect than it can influence the private sector. The government, either through the sponsor department, or occasionally through the Treasury, may oblige a particular industry to bring forward its investment plans to stimulate effective demand and/or reduce unemployment. Similarly, the initial price restraint imposed on nationalised industries in the 1960's was an attempt to reduce inflation and was achieved only because of the corporations' direct relationship with the government.

This role of the nationalised industries as a tool of demand management is a direct result of their strategic importance in the economy. They dominate four key areas of economic activity in the UK, namely communications, energy, iron and steel manufacture, and public transport, and in 1975 all the public corporations contributed 11% of UK gross domestic product, employed 8% of the labour force and accounted for 19% of total fixed investment. Of these, (as shown by table 1) the eight industries we selected previously accounted for approximately 80% of the output and employment, and 70% of the fixed investment. In addition, the importance of particular industries as suppliers to and customers of the private sector (e.g. the electricity industry is the sole distributor of public electricity in the UK, and British Gas has a monopoly of gas supply) means that the

Table 1   UK Nationalised Industries, Shares in the Economy 1975
(percentages of UK total)

	Output	Employment	Fixed investment
British Airways Board	0.3	0.2	0.4
British Gas Corporation	0.8	0.4	1.7
British Railways Board	1.2	1.0	1.0
British Steel Corporation	0.8	0.9	2.0
Electricity Industry	1.5	0.7	2.9
National Coal Board	1.5	1.2	0.9
Post Office	2.8	1.8	4.5
National Bus Company	0.2	0.3	0.1
	9.1	6.5	13.5
Other Nationalised Industries and Public Corporations	1.9	1.5	5.5
All Nationalised Industries and Public Corporations	11.0	8.0	19.0

Source: NEDO, A Study of UK Nationalised Industries: Background
Paper 1: Financial Analysis, HMSO 1976.

government can also influence, indirectly, the behaviour of
companies in the private sector by changing the level or
direction of activities in the nationalised industries.
    Related to the strategic importance of the nationalised
industries in the economy is the monopoly characteristic of
most of the goods and services they provide. Some of these
are natural monopolies such as electricity and telephone
communication and were provided by only a small number
of private firms before coming into public ownership.
However, whereas such private sector companies would be
prevented from exploiting their monopoly position by the
threat of the intervention of the Monopolies Commission,
and even of nationalisation itself, neither of these are
effective restrictions upon the activities of nationalised
industries. Information is therefore required to measure the
extent of any exploitation of monopoly position,
particularly in terms of pricing and quality of service.
    On the other hand, there are few pure monopolies in the

real world. Substitutes or alternatives exist for most goods and services and most nationalised industries face competition in this way. For example, the electricity industry competes directly with the coal and gas industries in certain products and services, and all three face competition from the predominantly privately owned oil companies. However, they cannot react to this competitive situation in the same manner as can private sector companies. A nationalised industry may be unable to alter its prices owing to direct controls on its pricing policy, or it may be required to use uneconomic inputs as part of an overall government strategy (e.g. the electricity industry is now the major customer of the NCB).

Several other market forces exist which, although of considerable importance in the private sector, are irrelevant in the context of the nationalised industries. Many stem from the fact that the industries are state-owned, with no private equity capital which could be traded by the general public on the stock market. One consequence of this situation is that nationalised industries effectively face an indefinite life with no fear of disenchanted shareholders demanding the liquidation of the business. However, the absence of any share price for the public enterprises does mean the absence of a major indicator of successful past performance and future expectations, and hence the loss of a significant control mechanism that exists in the private sector. A private sector company whose performance does not match its potential may find that its low share price makes it a suitable subject for a takeover bid.

There is little market pressure either from long-term creditors, for although loan finance has been raised on the capital markets both in the UK and abroad, the payment of interest and the eventual repayment of the loan has always been guaranteed by the Treasury.

The above suggests that market mechanisms are unable to control the behaviour of nationalised industries in the way they control companies in the private sector. Thus in the absence of a single share price reflecting a consensus of opinion amongst a multitude of investors and City analysts, one must substitute an administrative management. In this context, the provision of relevant information for prediction and control is even more important than it is for companies in the private sector.

Such information relevant to the prediction and control of the performance of nationalised industries can only be ascertained after a clear specification of the objectives of that system. Consequently, in the next section, we turn to an examination of the objectives of the nationalised industries.

Objectives of the nationalised industries

In contrast to companies in the private sector, the objectives of nationalised industries are stated explicitly in Acts of Parliament. Indeed, the nationalising legislation imposes a wide range of duties upon the boards of nationalised industries and these duties are in effect the criteria by which the performance of nationalised industries are judged.

Although each Nationalisation Act lays down obligations specific to the particular industry — for example, the Electricity Act of 1947 requires the Board to extend supplies to rural areas — three basic objectives are common to all industries:

1 to provide on a continuing basis a particular product or service, e.g. the Post Office is obliged to deliver mail to all parts of the country;

2 to break-even taking one year with another (this has since been modified — see below); and

3 to take into account the public interest, especially with regard to employees and the local community.

The multiple nature of these objectives can and does produce internal conflicts. For example the closure of a branch railway line in pursuit of the financial objective conflicts directly with the duty to provide a continuing service and may conflict with the public interest if it results in immediate redundancies or if the local community is without alternative transport facilities. This inherent conflict between objectives does not necessarily make them non-operational for control purposes, since goal programming may be used to ascertain the sensitivity of each objective against the others for given management decisions. What does make them difficult to transform into criteria for the purpose of assessment is the vagueness and ambiguity of the language.

Because of this it is often left to the corporation, rather than the sponsor department, to make its own assessment of what is in the public interest, and as a result it is only when resistance is met to a particular decision (e.g. the removal of a service) that the social issues are judged in a wider context. Equally as difficult is the pursuit of a financial objective which takes into account the maintenence of employment.

"Apparently it's an attempt to formulate their objectives—they don't know whether they're coming or going."

The government has faced this dilemma (for example, upon nationalising certain labour-intensive industries such as coal, railways, and steel) of whether to increase efficiency by pruning the labour force, or to instruct the corporation to modify their investments so as to protect jobs (figure 1). In the context of the government's overall responsibility for the economy it may be considered justifiable to maintain a higher level of employment at the expense of a possible degree of inefficiency. Moreover, there is a case for believing that a nationalised industry should offer greater job security than its private sector counterpart.

What is clear from the above is that it is not possible to determine whether the policies of a nationalised industry are taking into account the public interest unless precise standards of performance are given with respect to employees or the local community. It should also be obvious that the lack of clear social objectives must affect the nationalised industries' pursuit of financial objectives. The original objective of breaking-even has caused two problems. First, because of their monopoly situation, those industries which could have made huge commercial profits have been forced to reduce their prices to an artificially low level in order only to break even. (In the electricity industry, this led to a demand which far exceeded capacity. As a result the industry requested more capital from the government for new investment, and threatened to damage the government's wider economic strategy.) Second, at the other extreme, corporations that took over unprofitable industries, e.g. British Rail, could not manage even a zero profit. So, from 1962/3 onwards, it was recognised that each industry was to be treated separately and was to be given some financial objective, usually in the form of a return on net assets. This has varied from a rate of 12.5% p.a. required from the British Airways Board, to the requirement that British Rail should simply reduce its deficit and break even as quickly as possible. (For other examples, see figure 3.)

By the late 1960's, therefore, the nationalised industries appeared to have been placed on a commercial footing, with clear target rates of return against which their performance could be assessed — or had they? Government policy has never made it clear what should be the general objectives of the boards in terms of commercial policy. We have already mentioned the limitations on the commercial freedom of nationalised industries. A company in the private sector can expand and improve its return by moving into associated industries, taking over competitors, etc., and a company in a declining industry can run down one particular interest whilst diversifying into other areas. No such opportunity is available to the nationalised industry. The NCB is essentially restricted to the (uneconomic) mining of coal, and far from the Post Office expanding into new areas there

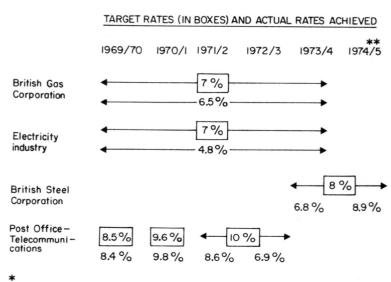

TARGET RATES (IN BOXES) AND ACTUAL RATES ACHIEVED

Figure 3   Return on net assets*

is a constant debate as to whether its profitable sector (tele-communications) should be 'hived off' to the private sector.

Perhaps the answer is that the corporations are expected to achieve their commercial return, within the framework of certain economic and social obligations as presented by the Government. Thus, the Post Office was set a separate target for its telecommunications business of 10% in 1972/3, while the target for its posts business was only 2% on revenue expenditure. The aim here appears to be to separate the two areas of business and so prevent the profits of one covering the losses of the other. And yet conversely we have already noted that there is pressure on the electricity industry to continue buying coal from the NCB, resulting in just such a cross subsidy.

What emerges from this examination of financial targets is that they can only begin to make sense if we examine them in the light of the government's social and economic policies as applied to each separate industry. Only then can we ascertain the constraints imposed upon the individual corporation's ability to meet its financial objective.

The decision-makers

We here consider the institutional arrangements for control and identify those groups who are the users of accounting reports. We shall describe the kinds of decisions that are made by these groups with respect to nationalised industries and the information currently available to them. The final section will then compare currently available information with the relevant information as implied by the characteristics and objectives of nationalised industries.

In common with companies in the private sector, a number of different groups can be identified as users of the accounting reports of nationalised industries. However, some of these groups, notably employees and society, are dealt with elsewhere in this book and there is no *a priori* reason why their informational needs should be different for different types of entity. In addition, some of the user groups of private sector accounting information are not relevant in the context of nationalised industries e.g. shareholders, although, as we shall see, some of the decisions made by such groups are similar to the decisions made by the main user groups of nationalised industries. We are left with a number of groups of decision-makers who are either instruments of the state or agents on behalf of the public interest, namely: the minister and the civil servants within the sponsor department; the Treasury and other interested departments, e.g. Employment; Parliament, including the Select Committee on Nationalised Industries; the consumers as represented by the Consultative Consumer Councils and Department of Prices and Consumer Protection.

The sponsor department. The Boards of the electricity, gas and coal industries are appointed by and are responsible to the Secretary of State at the Department of Energy. For the decision whether to re-appoint members of the Board, information is required about the effectiveness of past managerial performance in the light of the objectives set for the industry concerned. Hence there is some parallel with private sector rights of shareholders. The main source of this information is the published accounts and in particular the accounting profit or loss for the year.

The Secretary of State, together with his civil servants, also has responsibility for approving the investment proposals and the corresponding financial requirements of particular nationalised industries. Therefore, the sponsor department makes decisions as to whether a new project should be implemented. The information available to the department, provided by the appropriate nationalised industry, is in the form of a project appraisal, showing whether the new investment is expected to achieve a positive net present value when the cash flows are discounted using a predetermined discount rate. This rate is currently set at 10%, and is supposed to be comparable with discount rates used in the private sector for low risk projects.

The acceptance of a new investment project effectively pre-empts the borrowing decision, and therefore subject to Treasury approval, the provision of the requisite finance is automatic. The reduced importance of the borrowing decision has been reinforced by a recent policy change by the Government, which requires the nationalised industries to become more self-financing, i.e. to provide for investment funds out of their current operating profit. This policy has necessitated most nationalised industries raising the prices of their goods and services, approval for which has usually been based upon the level of accounting profit or loss for the previous year, e.g. the Post Office announced that following reported profits of £155 million from its telephone operations during 1975/76 there would be no increase in telephone charges until July 1977.

The Treasury and other departments. As mentioned above, the Treasury's main concern has been to approve increases in borrowings for new investments, and its main criterion in recent times has been the effect on the level of the public sector borrowing requirement. Thus in the 1960's the nationalised industries were encouraged to raise loans from abroad instead of from the UK capital market.

The Department of Employment on the other hand, is concerned with the effect on employment levels of particular decisions taken in the sponsor department and the nationalised industry itself, for example the social and economic costs of unemployment arising from the closure of an 'uneconomic' steel plant. Such information, however, is not available in published accounts and is probably derived from Treasury economists.

Finally, the Department of Prices and Consumer Protection has an interest in the impact of increases in the prices of goods and services and cooperates closely with the consultative consumer councils (see below).

Parliament. The main concern of Parliament has been the overall performance of nationalised industries. The need for relevant information on the efficiency or otherwise of nationalised industries was reinforced by the large deficits incurred in the early 70's. Originally, Members of Parliament were only able to question ministers on general policy matters, since in theory ministers were only responsible for policy decisions. However, the increased participation by government in the day-to-day management of nationalised industries required a more effective monitoring mechanism. As a result, the Select Committee on Nationalised Industries, comprising back bench MP's of all parties, is now the main instrument by which Parliament, on behalf of the taxpayers and the electorate, evaluates the performance of the nationalised industries in the light of their objectives. This Committee performs a detailed review of each nationalised industry at least once every seven years, and has recently conducted brief annual reviews based on the published accounts.

Consultative consumer councils. These have been established for many of the nationalised industries, and although they can do no more than make representations to the Board, they do provide a focal point for consumer views on the reasonableness of prices and the quality of goods and services. At the present time, they obtain some information directly from the nationalised industries, although reliance is also placed upon the published accounts and information provided by the Department of Prices and Consumer Protection.

From this brief review of the main user groups and the kinds of decisions they are concerned with, we now turn to the final section in which we outline the type of information which might be relevant to those decisons.

The message

In the last section we saw that accounting information, whether or not in the form of published accounts, is used by all the main user groups concerned with nationalised industries. The fundamental question now is to what extent does this information relate the needs of the decision makers to the characteristics and objectives of nationalised industries?

We may summarise the kind of information that would be useful to the various user groups. They would like measures of economic and financial performance to assess whether the nationalised industries are breaking even taking one year with another, whether target rates of return are being achieved and whether the enterprise is being managed efficiently for the benefit of society as a whole. But they also want measures of social performance to assess whether the public interest is being served, and whether the nationalised industries are abusing their monopoly position in terms of the prices they charge and the quality of goods and services they provide.

The press, television, Parliament and the public implicitly assume that the progress towards economic and financial objectives is adequately measured by the published accounts, or equivalent accounting information. But the economic and financial objectives, whether to break even or achieve a positive rate of profit on net assets, are imprecise because of the extent of the flexibility allowed by the use of current accounting conventions. Indeed, any accounting method allows management considerable, and often undisclosed, freedom in determining both asset values and the appropriate rate of capital maintenance. For example, the Post Office is one of the few corporations we listed which depreciates on a replacement cost basis, yet this is seldom taken into account when comparisons of accounting performance are made. Moreover, this flexibility may enable the nationalised industries to exhibit short-term surpluses, at the expense of long-term efficiency, a practice which is encouraged by the greater scrutiny given to loss-making industries than to profit-making ones. Indeed, past accounting profit appears to be the main criterion in determining the level of capital expenditure above which ministerial approval is required. Thus British Rail with an accumulated deficit of over £1000 million for the period 1963-74, must submit all proposals with an outlay exceeding £2m; British Steel with losses of only £25m for the period 1967-74 can undertake investments with an outlay of up to £50m without ministerial approval; and the Post Office, with the largest expenditure on fixed investment, does not have to submit any of its proposals. This could be because 90% of its investments are concentrated in telecommunications, which amassed surpluses of over £450m during the period 1963-74.

We noted in the previous section that the use of discounted cash flow techniques has placed the appraisal of projects on a scientific basis, yet it might also have had the unintentional effect of producing automatic approval for any project which satisfies the test discount rate. Does the Post Office, for instance, take into account the wider economic and social implications of its capital investments? Further, the lack of expertise and time available in the sponsor department might also result in an inadequate monitoring of new projects once they have been initiated. Having approved an investment on the basis of a corporation's estimates of future cash flows it would seem imperative that the sponsor department should require evidence of actual cash flows as they arise in order to compare them with the estimates. There is no indication that this occurs, and the published accounts do not help in this respect since not only do they report revenue and expenditure on an accruals basis rather than on a cash flow basis, but they also fail to analyse performance on a project by project basis. Instead the accounts show revenues and expenditures for the industry as a whole, or at best break down information into specific divisions within the industry.

We noted earlier that parliament's concern, on behalf of the taxpayer and the electorate as a whole, should be with whether the nationalised industries are operating in an efficient manner and whether the funds provided as subsidies are justified either on economic or on social grounds. For this purpose Parliament would need information which measures the external effects of any particular policy upon other sectors of society. For example, the closure of a steel plant would result in increased unemployment benefits, and a reduction in spending power in that community affecting other local businesses; and might result in long-term unemployment for some workers, thereby raising the possibility of various social costs (including the break up of the local community.)

As the minister, the sponsor department, the Treasury, and the Department of Employment also require this information for their decision models, the same information provided to Parliament should allow MP's to assess and evaluate the decisions of the ministers involved. Again, the monitoring of events after the decision has been taken is essential for an assessment of the decision makers' ability in forecasting future events.

It is apparent that nationalised industries do not operate to achieve only commercial and financial objectives. They are obliged to pursue policies which may provide social benefits to society, but which would not be undertaken by companies in the private sector applying strict economic criteria. Consequently, it is inappropriate to evaluate the economic performance of a nationalised industry using accounting measures which assume either that all the variables are controllable by management, or at least that management has the freedom to adapt to changing economic conditions.

Ideally, then, the nationalised industries should provide measures of their progress towards social goals, such as security of employment, the quality of goods and services produced, benefits to local communities, etc., which can be compared with predetermined standards of performance mutually agreed by the corporation and the various user groups. But, at the very least, the effects of pursuing 'uneconomic' policies should be shown separately in the accounts so that the cost of those policies may be known and the benefits evaluated accordingly.

We conclude that the far-reaching consequences of decisions based upon the accounts of nationalised industries demand that we should query whether these accounts, biased as they are towards the requirements of the private sector, provide the relevant information to decision makers. As we have seen, the nationalised industries are more than just commercial enterprises and therefore to ensure effective control they must transmit messages which measure their success in achieving both economic and social objectives.

Suggested further reading

D. L. Coombes, *State Enterprise: Business or Politics?*, Allen & Unwin 1971.

C. D. Foster, *Politics, Finance and the Role of Economics*, Allen & Unwin, 1971.

National Economic Development Office (NEDO) *A Study of UK Nationalised Industries*, 1976.

Nationalised Industries: A Review of Economic and Financial Objectives, Cmnd 3437, HMSO 1967.

A. Nove, *Efficiency Criteria for Nationalised Industries*, Allen & Unwin 1973

M. H. Peston, 'The nationalised industries' in R. M. Grant and G. K. Shaw (eds), *Current Issues in Economic Policy*, Philip Allan 1975.

R. E. Thomas, *The Government of Business*, Philip Allan 1976.

12
Accounting and economics

GEOFFREY WHITTINGTON
Professor of Accounting, University of Bristol

Introduction

Accounting is concerned with the provision of data relating to economic activity. Economic analysis should therefore clarify the questions which the accountant is trying to answer. Furthermore, the accountant's answers to these questions should provide important data for the economist who is concerned to test his theories against events in the real world. Accounting and economics are therefore complementary disciplines. Thus a distinguished economist has written 'business accounts constitute the single most important source of information about the economic activity of a nation'[1], whilst an eminent academic accountant writes '. . . there cannot be any conflict between economic and accounting concepts . . . whenever an accounting concept seems to be at variance with the precepts of economics, it must be regarded as suspect, and on close examination it will usually be found to be flawed.'[2]

However, the relationship between accounting and economics has not always been one of harmonious cooperation. The same distinguished economist goes on to comment: 'Unfortunately, the contacts between economic theory and accounting theory and practice are far thinner than one would like and have reason to expect. As a result, both have suffered.'[3] Equally, our eminent academic accountant, writing much later and in the context of education rather than research, is distinctly less enthusiastic about the contribution of economics to accounting: '. . . accounting studies have suffered from a position of tutelage in departments of economics . . . from which they are only now emerging.'[4] 'This is not to say that close relations between accounting and economics should not be maintained. But until accounting has an identity of its own in the universities, it cannot flourish. Its position hitherto — and in a few universities still — can be understood by imagining what would have happened to engineering education if engineering had remained as a branch of applied mathematics, dependent on mathematicians to speak for it when its voice needed to be heard.'[5]

The latter quotation states the essential nature of the tension which exists between accounting and economics. The two disciplines are complemetary because they study the same material from different points of view. These differing points of view lead to difficulties of communication and to conflicts of interest. Kenneth Boulding has neatly characterised the situation by describing economics and accounting as 'the uncongenial twins.'[6] However, in recent years, developments in both economics and accounting have brought the two subjects closer together, so that the following account of their historical differences should not be taken as an indication of their likely future relationship. It should also be emphasised that the two disciplines have contributed a great deal to one another in the past : a little tension may even be creative.

Historical differences between accounting and economics

Both accounting and economics have long histories, which is not surprising since they both relate to economic activity which is itself as old as society (indeed, older, if we consider the 'Robinson Crusoe' one-man economy which is still a popular model for economic theorists). The two disciplines have developed in different ways because accounting arose out of a practical need to report the results of economic activity, whereas economics arose out of a desire to understand the workings of the economy. This led to a

number of differences of emphasis, of which the following
are perhaps the most important.

The backward-looking accountant and the forward-looking economist. The earliest function of the accountant
was stewardship, i.e. rendering a factual account of past
transactions in order to settle indebtedness between the
steward and his principal. This function was later extended
to partnerships (the division of profits between partners
being the primary consideration) and to companies (the
directors now being the stewards and the shareholders being
the principals), and it is still one important purpose of
financial reports. This led accountants to record events *ex
post* rather than anticipating the future and, since honesty
was usually seen as the most desirable attribute of a steward,
there was a strong preference for objective measures. The
pursuit of objectivity led again to a preference for
accounting practices based upon observable (i.e. past)
events, such as the valuation of assets at historic cost.

The economist, on the other hand, has always been
interested in the motivation of economic agents, rather than
merely reporting the results of their activities. He has therefore concentrated upon the process of decision-making by
the individual entrepreneur or the firm. Since a decision
necessarily precedes its consequences, the economist has
tended to regard *ex ante* estimates of the future consequences of a decision as being crucial. He has therefore
tended to regard the accountant an an unimaginative and
excessively cautious provider of irrelevant information.
The accountant, on the other hand, has tended to regard the
economist as an unrealistic theorist, unaware of the
practical dangers of putting subjective estimates into
accounts.

In recent years, accountants have moved closer to
economists in this respect. They have increasingly become
aware that good stewardship, in heavily capitalised
companies, cannot be merely a matter of reporting past
events,[7] particularly in periods of rapid inflation which
tends to increase the disparity between historic cost and
current value. Objective information which is also irrelevant can mislead the reader of accounts just as effectively as
subjective information which is relevant but incorrect. The

recent adoption by the accountancy profession of current cost accounting[8] is the culmination of this change of heart by accountants. Current cost accounting implies that the published accounts of companies will show assets valued on the basis of current values rather than historic costs, and the choice of current values will involve the estimation of possible future returns[9] rather than the recording of realised historic costs.

Other differences between the reporting accountant and the enquiring economist. Although the backward-looking attitude of the accountant as contrasted with the forward-looking attitude of the economist is the most obvious difference between the approaches of the two disciplines, there are several other important differences arising from the different functions of the accountant and the economist.

Firstly, the economist has always concerned himself to a significant extent with normative questions, i.e. how *ought* the economy to run? This is most obvious in the field of welfare economics. The accountant, on the other hand, has rarely questioned his assumed norms of profit maximisation or cost minimisation. Secondly, the accountant has traditionally confined his attention to the individual firm whose activities he reports upon, whereas the economist has dealt with the economy on a variety of levels of aggregation and has usually had in mind the ultimate objective of achieving a better understanding of the working of the economy as a whole. For example, Adam Smith, who has as good a claim as any to be the father of modern economics, entitled his great work 'An Enquiry into the Nature and Causes of the Wealth of Nations', thus emphasising that he was concerned with the workings of the economy as a whole, despite the fact that the microeconomic foundations of his work are full of insights into the workings of the individual firm, such as his famous example of the pin factory which was used to illustrate the benefits of the division of labour. Thirdly, the accountant has traditionally developed practices in response to practical needs and accounting theory has emerged as a generalisation of such practices, whereas the economist has tended to make assumptions, of varying degrees of realism, and to deduce theoretical results from them, confronting theoretical predictions with the facts only at the final stage of his work, and not always then. In other words, the accountant has traditionally been inductive in his approach, whereas the economist has been deductive.

The above differences of approach are, of course, matters of emphasis rather than of strict difference and have, as with the backward-looking/ forward-looking distinction, been blurred by recent developments. For example, accountants are, as a result of the changing economic, social and political environment, becoming involved in normative questions. Practising accountants become involved in cost-benefit studies, and there is increasing pressure for companies to extend their reports to deal with their 'social performance'[10] which covers a wide range of matters outside the scope of the traditional field of reporting economic performance to the proprietors of a profit-maximising business. Also, the increasing scale and interdependence of business enterprise is broadening the accountant's horizon to include an interest in macroeconomic matters. For example, any accountant involved in budgeting will benefit from a forecast of the future macroeconomic environment in which his firm will operate, and which will be 'an important determinant of such important variables as sales and the availability of outside finance. Finally, induction and deduction are, in practice, complementary aspects of the development of knowledge. Accounting is certainly not void of deductive content; for example, Ijiri[11] has provided a theoretical derivation of the historic cost valuation rules, by a process of logical deduction from three basic axioms. Equally, many economists are at pains to emphasise the complementarity of induction and deduction in the development of economic thought.[12]

Some contributions of economics to accounting

In spite of, or perhaps because of, the differences of approach outlined above, economics has contributed a great deal to accounting. In order to illustrate this, we shall concentrate on three topics, each of which is of vital interest to the accountant: costing, income measurement, and investment appraisal.

Costs for decision-making. The management accountant is

concerned with the provision of accounting information to management. Since one important function of management is to make day-to-day decisions about the allocation of the firm's resources, it is not surprising that economic theory should have something to say about how such decisions should be made, and what accounting information would be required in the process. It is, however, surprising that in fact economic theory made relatively little impact on cost accounting[13] until the nineteen-fifties and sixties. Until that time, the cost accountant was largely preoccupied with applying his objective historic cost measurements originally conceived for the purpose of stewardship rather than management decision making. This led to the provision of cost figures which did not necessarily reflect the consequences of the alternative choices open to management. Furthermore, when faced by overhead expenses, joint costs or joint products, the accountant's tidy mind usually required that these expenses be 'absorbed' by being allocated to particular activities.[14] This led to allocation of costs by arbitrary rules of thumb which served further to mask the relative costs of making alternative decisions. This attitude was partly due to the historical development of accounting and the limitations of the accountant's training at the time, but part of the blame must be laid at the feet of the economists, who made little attempt to spell out the implications of their results for practical decision making.[15] This was, no doubt, because of the economists' preoccupation with the larger theme of how economic systems function: 'managerial economics' did not become a fashionable and respected academic subject until after the Second World War.[16]

The economist's message to practising cost accountants was first spelled out in a pioneering book by J. M. Clark[17] in 1923 and in a series of articles by various authors, published in the late 1930's,[18] but there was a long time-lag in its adoption. The essence of the message was 'different costs for different purposes', i.e. for decision-making purposes, the relevant costs are those which reflect the incremental burden of each alternative choice. These costs are likely to be different for different types of decision. Behind this apparently simple statement are a number of ideas derived from economic analysis.

Firstly, there is the idea of *marginality*: in making a decision about an incremental activity, only the incremental costs and revenues are relevant. Costs which have already been incurred or which will be incurred irrespective of the incremental activity should be ignored.

Secondly, there is the idea of the *time horizon*: different costs and revenues will be variable over different time horizons, and all costs will be variable in the long-run (e.g. a firm may dispose of its fixed assets or change its activity), so that different costs may be relevant to the same decision made for different time periods.

Thirdly, there is the idea of *opportunity cost*: the cost of making one choice rather than any other out of all the opportunities available is the net revenue[19] foregone by failing to make the most profitable alternative choice. There is some controversy as to whether opportunity cost, strictly defined, is a useful concept for decision-making purposes, since its calculation presupposes knowledge of which is the next best alternative, i.e. it assumes that all the information necessary to make the decision is already available when opportunity cost is calculated.[20] However, there is little doubt that the information necessary to calculate opportunity cost, the evaluation of the costs and returns associated with alternative plans, is the relevant information for exercising choice, and in this way the idea of opportunity cost has helped accountants in defining relevant costs.

The basic ideas outlined above are now ingredients of the discussion of relevant costs for decision-making[21] in any good textbook, at even the most elementary level. The contribution of economics to costing has not stopped there, and economics has also made important contributions to other areas of management accounting, such as investment appraisal, which is discussed below. Mention should be made of the application of linear programming techniques to management accounting problems,[22] and of the opportunity cost interpretation of the dual prices of a linear programming solution. The linear programme produces an optimal plan (usually profit-maximising and cost-minimising, depending upon the nature of the objective function which is maximised or minimised) for allocating scarce resources. In the process it produces dual values or shadow prices which value marginal units of the scarce resources in terms of the incremental contribution which they make to the objective function (i.e. usually, to net revenue). These shadow prices have the properties of opportunity costs, described earlier, and they are open to precisely the same objection as opportunity costs from a decision-making point of view, i.e. the process of calculating them (solving the linear programming problem) provides a solution to the decision, the optimal plan, so that when the shadow prices emerge, they are no longer required.

Another relatively recent application to cost accounting of techniques used by economists is in the area of statistical cost analysis. Cost accountants are becoming increasingly aware that the naive assumption of constant marginal costs which was implicit in the traditional break-even chart is, at best, a rough approximation to reality. Economics, using the analytical model of a production function (the functional relationship between output and various inputs) and the estimation techniques of econometrics (traditionally regression analysis) have adopted a more sophisticated approach to estimating the relationship between costs and output. The economist's method has now been adopted by the more up-to-date management accounting textbooks, as well as being used increasingly in practice, although this is an area in which much more work needs to be done, both in refining techniques and in persuading practical men to adopt them.[23]

Enough has been said to indicate that economics has made an important contribution to the accountant's measurement of cost, a crucial component of management accounting. We shall now turn to an equally crucial component of financial accounting,[24] the measurement of income.

Income Measurement. A figure for net income has long been an important element in financial accounts. The net income, or profit, of an accounting entity for a period is taken as being an indication of the success of a firm in generating a surplus over its initial capital. A figure of this type has long been used to determine the amount of dividend a company can legally distribute, the amount of tax it should pay, and how successful its management has been. This variety of uses suggests that a great deal is expected of the measurement of profit and it is not surprising that no single measure has been found to satisfy all of these needs. Indeed, it can reasonably be argued that no single profit measure has been found which will satisfy any one of these needs.

The essential problem of measuring income lies in the deceptively simple phrase of the last paragraph 'a surplus over its initial capital'. In order to measure such a surplus we need two important ingredients, a measure of initial capital and a measure of the economic resources of the entity at the end of the period.[25] Both of these involve valuation and it is the valuation basis of income measurement which has given rise to the greatest difficulty and which has led to the sharpest contrast between the approaches of the economist and the traditional accountant. This controversy provides an excellent illustration of the backward-looking accountant opposing the forward-looking economist. The accountant traditionally has clung to an historic valuation basis for measuring profit. He has preferred to report only profits which have been realised in past transactions and to ignore 'holding gains', i.e. increases in the value of assets which are owned by the entity and have not yet been sold. In order to implement this system, the accountant has erected a series of rules such as the realisation principle, the matching principle, and the doctrine of conservatism, which will be found in any book on accounting theory.

The economist, on the other hand, regards bygones as bygones and is inclined to look on income as an accretion to the current value of wealth, and he therefore regards either current market value or current value in use (i.e. discounted present value of the future returns anticipated from using an asset) as the appropriate valuation base. In a world of changing prices, historic cost can be a very poor proxy indeed for current value. Perhaps because changing prices have recently been a marked feature of the economic environment, it appears that the economists' views have triumphed over those of the traditional accountants, and current values are likely to become the normal basis for financial reporting under the current cost accounting system proposed for the United Kingdom. Similar reforms are under consideration in other countries.

A measure of the contribution of economists to the clarification of our understanding of the theory of income measurement is the overwhelming predominance of economists amongst the contributors to Parker and Harcourt's classic collection of *Readings in the Concept and Measurement of Income,*[26] which contains many of the important contributions made to the subject in the twentieth century. The fundamental contribution to the subject was made by Irving Fisher, an outstanding economic theorist, who was fascinated, almost to the point of obsession, by double-entry accounting.[27] Fisher defined income fundamentally as psychic satisfaction (i.e. the only true income is personal and subjective) but used consumption as his economic proxy for measuring this. He segregated capital strictly from income, measuring capital as the discounted present value of future consumption. He excluded capital gains from his 'income' on the ground that, since capital was discounted future consumption, to include it in present income would lead to double counting. For Fisher's purposes of examining the individual's saving and consumption decisions over his life-time, this was an important distinction to make and his definition of income as consumption was perfectly logical.[28] However, for the purpose of reporting the success of a business, we prefer to define income as potential consumption as in Hicks' classic definition 'we ought to define a man's income as the maximum value a man can consume during a week, and still expect to be as well off at the end of the week as he was at the beginning'.[29] This definition is nearer to what Fisher described as 'earnings'[30]; but otherwise Hicks' approach is similar to that of Fisher in its emphasis on capital values as the outcome of a forward-looking discounting approach.

Thus, Irving Fisher was the founder of modern income theory, although others have polished his ideas and adapted them to the business firm rather than the individual. Fisher was also responsible, indirectly, for the first systematic evaluation of accounting practice in terms of economic theory, for its author, J. B. Canning, was a pupil of Fisher, and made extensive reference to Fisher's ideas.[31] This remarkable book anticipated many of the developments in accounting which have taken place since it was published and raised a number of issues which are still unresolved.

Another aspect of Fisher's work was that he was a pioneer of inflation accounting in the strictest sense, i.e. adjusting monetary values to a unit of constant purchasing power (known popularly as the CPP approach). In his book, *The Purchasing Power of Money*,[32] published in 1911, he advocated the indexation of monetary contracts as a means of dealing with inflation (i.e. relating the monetary amount payable to changes in an index of the purchasing power of money). This idea has recently been revived by Professor Friedman and others,[33] and the adjustment of monetary quantities in accounts by reference to a general index (CPP accounting) can be viewed as a specific application of these ideas.

Finally, Fisher can also be regarded as the father of cash flow reporting: the idea that accountants should abandon their concentration on income measurement, with its attendant problems of valuing accrued assets, in favour of reporting past cash flows (which, being based on past transactions, are entirely objective) and anticipated future cash flows (which, although subjective, are ingredients of a net present value calculation and may therefore allow the user of accounts to make his own 'do-it-yourself' estimate of net present value). This idea has gained considerable support in recent years,[34] although its practical difficulties are considerable.[35] It is essentially an attempt to apply Fisher's 'income as consumption', since the 'consumption' by a firm is measured by its net cash outflow to its proprietors.

The more practical system of forward-looking 'economic' accounting is current value accounting, and here economists have made an important contribution towards the practical application of their ideas. The national income accounts, which were designed by economists[36], have always used a replacement cost method of assessing depreciation and stock appreciation, a procedure very similar to that used in current cost accounting; and it was two economists, E. O. Edwards and P. W. Bell, who produced the most comprehensive analysis of alternative current value accounting systems.[37] Income measurement is still a developing and controversial field, but the economists have provided the essential theoretical framework within which the practical art of income measurement is likely to develop.

Investment appraisal. Every student of accounting now learns the elements of compound interest and discounted cash flow. The idea of the rate of interest as the connection between future value and present value originated not in enonomic theory but in actuarial science and in the analysis of loan repayments by the early mathematician/book-keepers.[38] The application of this technique to the evaluation of investment projects was first made by engineering economists, who were concerned with the evaluation of major capital projects such as mines and railways, which involve the investment of large sums for long periods and in which the correct treatment of the rate of interest (the charge for the use of funds through time) is therefore most important. However, it was economists, around the turn of the twentieth century, who produced the theoretical framework which lent coherence to individual applications of discounting techniques.

The most prominent economist in this field, as in the field of income measurement, was Irving Fisher, who propounded a set of general rules for the appraisal of investment by what we would now call discounted cash flow methods[39]; and integrated these rules with the rest of economic theory by relating the investment decision, through the rate of interest, to the savings and consumption decision. Fisher's contribution was summarised elegantly in a classic paper by Hirshleifer,[40] which also brings together some of the refinements which other economists have introduced into Fisher's analysis, including imperfect markets, capital rationing, and the evaluation of the relative merits of the two alternative discounted cash flow methods, the internal rate of return method (which involves comparing the rate of interest with the implicit rate of return on investment) and the present value method (which involves comparing the cost of an investment with the discounted present value of its future net returns).

Since the time of Hirshleifer's paper, work by both economists and accountants has sought to refine further the techniques of investment appraisal. For example, the methods of dealing with capital rationing have been extended by the application of mathematical programming techniques, following the work of Weingartner,[41] and new insights into the nature and treatment of risk have been obtained by the application of portfolio analysis, following the work of Markowitz[42] and Sharpe.[43] The selection of the appropriate rate of discount to use in investment appraisal is a difficult problem, our understanding of which has been advanced by recent work in the area of finance,[44] which is the subject of another chapter in this book, and this is one area in which economics probably has a good deal more to offer to accounting.

The application of discounted cash flow techniques has lagged considerably behind the theory, and accountants must take much of the blame for this:[45] their doctrine of conservatism and reluctance to forecast beyond the immediate future, led to their clinging to rules of thumb like the payback period, long after they had been shown to be theoretically unsound. Economists were the chief propagandists for discounted cash flow techniques. In the United States, managerial economists in business schools, such as Joel Dean,[46] were very influential in disseminating knowledge of these techniques in the nineteen-fifties. In the United Kingdom, events moved rather more slowly, but discounted cash flow techniques became much more widespread in the nineteen-sixties, thanks to the economists at the National Economic Development Office[47] and to the pioneering work of Merrett and Sykes[48] (an economist and an accountant trained in economics, respectively). It is, however, still true that practice lags notably behind theory in this field. A recent survey of investment appraisal methods currently in use in the United Kingdom showed that discounted cash flow techniques are by no means universally applied, and when they are applied they typically deal with inflation in an inconsistent manner.[49]

The contribution of accounting to economics

The contribution of accounting to economics has been largely in providing data rather than theoretical ideas. This is an unspectacular but vital function and it is so pervasive that it is impossible to give even a superficial survey here. It must suffice to point out that a significant proportion of the data used in the preparation of the national income accounts comes from the published accounts of companies, and that there is a vast number of econometric and statistical studies of individual firms which are also based upon accounting data. It must be admitted that the use of accounting data by economists has sometimes shown ignorance of or disregard for the limitations of the data, and this is one area in which more inter-disciplinary work could and should have been done. The use of accounting data in applied economic research has been facilitated by the development of computers which has enabled vast quantities of data to be subjected to statistical analysis quickly and easily. In the United States, this has been further helped by the preparation of the COMPUSTAT data bank of company accounts, and the present author has helped in the preparation of a similar data bank for the accounts of United Kingdom quoted companies.[50] The variety of topics which has recently been investigated using the latter data bank should illustrate the wide potentiality of the data for applied economics: these topics include studies of the process of industrial concentration,[51] the relationships between directors' remuneration and company performance,[52] the use of accounting ratios in selecting high yielding equity portfolios,[53] the response of net trade credit movements to monetary policy,[54] the profitability of retained earnings,[55] the post-merger performance of merged companies,[56] the relationship between dividend policy and the pattern of financing quoted companies,[57] and the determinants of takeovers.[58] The variety of topics which could (and, hopefully, will) be investigated is much greater.

The accountant's contribution to economics is not, however, confined to the provision of data. He is also in a position to play an important role in the process of induction described earlier: his experience of the economic world and how it operates should enable him to help the economist in the selection of appropriate assumptions for model-building. We have already seen that Irving Fisher contributed enormously to the theoretical background of accounting: it is also apparent in his writing that his understanding of the accounting process also helped him a great deal in his construction of monetary theory. There are a number of other instances of economists using their knowledge of accounting processes in theoretical work, for example, the assumption of cost-plus pricing which has played an important part in macroeconomic studies of the price level[59] was originally derived from an influential study of business practice by a group of Oxford economists.[60] Accountants have not always played a merely passive role in this respect: they have often worked individually on economic problems or in teams with economists. An excellent example of the first type is Professor Baxter's article on the accountant's contribution to the trade cycle,[61] which demonstrated how the misleading information contained in the historic cost data of conventional accounts could serve to exaggerate cycles in the level of investment. A good recent example of team work is the collaboration of Sandford, Willis and Ironside (an economist, a tax administrator, and an accountant) in the area of taxation.[62] It is also notable that a number of professional economists, some in areas of economics which have no obvious direct relationship to accounting, have been trained as accountants. This is little more than an anecdotal account of a few instances in which accountants have contributed to economics, but it is hoped that it has at least demonstrated that there have been contributions in both directions.

Finally, and perhaps most important of all, accounting and economics are converging in a number of areas, so that it is not possible to say what is economics and what is accounting. Business finance is one area in which this is obviously happening. Another area is in the empirical investigation of the utility of accounting data. Academic accountants are now testing the value of accounting data by looking at the impact on share prices of the publication of accounts and at such matters as the ability of accounting ratios to predict business failure.[63] Since economists have recently become much more interested in the micro-economic foundations of their subject,[64] and are concerned about such matters as uncertainty and the effect of information on market behaviour, there seems to be a real possibility of a fruitful interaction between economics and accounting in this field.

Retrospect and prospect

The broad picture which has emerged is that much of the progress made in accounting during the twentieth century has been due to accountants accepting and adapting the theoretical framework given to them by economists. It also appears that accountants have contributed to economics both by providing data and by providing knowledge of institutional and behavioural constraints operating in the economy. It is not, however, claimed that the interaction between the two disciplines has been as fruitful as it could or should have been: accountants have tended to resist economists' ideas and economists have tended to ignore the practical knowledge and experience of accountants.

Neither is it claimed that accounting derives its theoretical ideas solely from economics. Accountants *are* capable of thinking for themselves,[65] and they have also, particularly in the last two decades, drawn heavily on other disciplines such as operational research, psychology and computer science, which are the subjects of subsequent chapters in this book. This suggests that, in the future, accounting will tend to be more like economics in at least one respect: that it will have many specialisms within it. Already, the practice of accounting has divided into certain clearly defined activities (such as auditing, taxation, and management accounting) and the academic study of the subject is now dividing into further specialisms (such as behavioural accounting and computer systems) which are analogous to those into which the study of economics has long been divided (such as welfare economics, public finance, and international economics). This process of specialisation could actually aid communication between accounting and related disciplines, such as economics, but it also raises the attendant difficulty that it may reduce the communication amongst accountants, e.g. the business finance specialist may find that he communicates more easily with economists than with behavioural accounting specialists.

Whatever the outcome of this process of specialisation, the message of this chapter is that there is great scope for future cooperation between accountants and economists:

there are plenty of unresolved problems in all the work described here. Economics is certainly not the only discipline which has something to offer accounting but, in this author's opinion, it has more to offer accounting than any other. It is to be hoped that the 'uncongenial twins' will, in future, live together in a spirit of healthy competition rather than mutual suspicion and envy.

Notes and references

1 Oskar Morgenstern, *On the Accuracy of Economic Observations*, Princeton University Press, 1963, p. 70.

2 David Solomons, 'Economic and accounting concepts of cost and value', p. 117, in Morton Backer (ed.), *Modern Accounting Theory*, Prentice-Hall, 1966.

3 Morgenstern, *op. cit.*, pp. 70-71.

4 David Solomons (with T. M. Berridge), *Prospectus for a Profession*, Advisory Board of Accountancy Education 1974, p. 39.

5 Solomons, *op. cit.*, p. 40.

6 K. E. Boulding, 'Economics and accounting: the uncongenial twins', in W. T. Baxter and Sidney Davidson *(eds)*, *Studies in Accounting Theory*, Irwin 1962, pp. 44-55. The same author once confided to the present author that 'there are only about sixteen lectures on accounting worth giving, but every economist should go to them.' This was a light-hearted remark, but it conveys vividly the mixture of respect and contempt with which economists often regard accounting.

7 See, for example, Accounting Standards Steering Committee, *The Corporate Report*, Institute of Chartered Accountants in England and Wales, 1975, particularly Section 7.

8 Accounting Standards Steering Committee, Exposure Draft 18: *Current Cost Accounting*, Institute of Chartered Accountants in England and Wales 1976.

9 The valuation rules used in current cost accounting were first set out in precise form by David Solomons in the paper quoted in note 2 above.

10 See, for example, *The Corporate Report, op. cit.*, and D. Solomons, 'Corporate social performance: a new dimension in accounting reports?', in Harold Edey and B. S. Yamey, *Debits, Credits, Finance and Profits*, Sweet and Maxwell 1974.

11 Yuji Ijiri, *The Foundations of Accounting Measurement*, Prentice-Hall 1967, Chapter 4.

12 For example: Alfred Marshall, *Principles of Economics*, Ninth (Variorum) Edition, C. W. Guillebaud (ed.), Macmillan 1961, Vol. 1. Appendix C, 'The Scope and Method of Economics', and Richard Stone, 'The *a priori* and the empirical in economics', Chapter 2 of *Mathematics in the Social Sciences and Other Essays*, Chapman and Hall 1966.

13 Cost accounting being one of a number of techniques which are usually gathered together under the general title, management accounting.

14 This is, of course, a very broad description of accountants' attitudes and therefore unfair to certain individuals. Solomons, writing in 1952 (p. 52 of D. Solomons (ed.), *Studies in Costing*, Sweet and Maxwell 1952) concluded a thorough survey of the history of costing with the statement that '. . . there is remarkably little in modern costing that our fathers did not know about', but he concedes that these ideas did not find general acceptance. Economic analysis provided a coherent and persuasive framework w thin which individual insights could be systematised and evaluated.

15 An excellent account of the evolution of cost accounting and the contribution of economics to it will be found in Chapter 2 of R. H. Parker, *Management Accounting, An Historical Perspective*, Macmillan 1969.

16 Joel Dean, *Managerial Economics*, Prentice-Hall 1951, was one of the pioneering textbooks which attempted to spell out the implications of economic theory for business decisions. There is now a very large number of such books.

17 J. M. Clark, *Studies in the Economics of Overhead Costs*, University of Chicago Press 1923.

18 Several of these were included in David Solomons (ed.), *Studies in Costing, op. cit.*

19 Gross revenue less variable costs associated with the particular project whose contribution is being considered.

20 For an account of this controversy and an authoritative account of the impact on accounting of the economist's idea of opportunity cost, see J. R. Gould, 'Opportunity cost: the London tradition' in Edey and Yamey (eds), *op. cit.*

21 It must be emphasised that management accounting in general and cost accounting in particular are concerned with matters of administrative control as well as with decision-making, and the tidy, if unimaginative, methods of the traditional 'stewardship' accountant have much to commend themselves in the former activity.

22 The application of linear programming to accounting, with special emphasis on costing implications, is discussed very clearly and non-mathematically in Bryan Carsberg, *An Introduction to Mathematical Programming for Accountants*, George Allen and Unwin 1969. An excellent exposition of basic economic theory in linear programming terms will be found in W. J. Baumol, *Economic Theory and Operations Analysis*, Prentice-Hall 1961 (and later editions).

23 Good examples of an enlightened modern textbook approach to this subject are in Harold Bierman and Thomas R. Dyckman, *Managerial Cost Accounting*, Macmillan New York, 1971, Chapter 3, and in Bryan Carsberg, *Economics of Business Decisions*, Penguin 1976, Chapter 7.

24 By financial accounting we usually mean reporting to the providers of finance, who include proprietors when, as in a joint stock

company, the proprietors (shareholders) are distinct from management.

25   We also need a measure of capital withdrawn or introduced, but this usually presents less problems.

26   R. H. Parker and G. C. Harcourt (ed.), *Readings in the Concept and Measurement of Income*, Cambridge University Press 1969.

27   For example, his text book *Elementary Principles of Economics* (Macmillan, New York 1912) starts with seven chapters on the measurement of capital and income which would now be regarded as being more appropriate to a textbook on accounting.

28   Students of finance will know that the same distinction is necessary in the dividend valuation model: in valuing a share we must not take account both of retained profits *and* the dividends to which they give rise.

29   J. R. Hicks, *Value and Capital*, Clarendon Press 1946, reprinted in Parker and Harcourt, *op. cit.*, p. 75.

30   Irving Fisher, *The Nature of Capital and Income*, Macmillan, New York, 1906, Chapter IV. This gives a very clear account of Fisher's reasons for confining his definition to consumption. A more popular and accessible summary of Fisher's views is given in the first chapter of his *The Theory of Interest* (Macmillan, New York, 1930) which is reprinted in Parker and Harcourt, *op. cit.*, but Fisher would be better understood if the original work were more widely read.

31   J. B. Canning, *The Economics of Accountancy*, The Ronald Press, New York 1929.

32   Macmillan, New York 1911.

33   For a survey of some of this work, see G. Whittington, 'Indexation: a review article', *Accounting and Business Research*, No.23, Summer 1976, pp. 171-176.

34   David Solomons, for example, concluded his well-known paper on 'Economic and accounting concepts of income' (originally published in *The Accounting Review*, 1961, and reprinted in Parker and Harcourt, *op. cit.*) with the statement that 'we may now be de-emphasising the income statement in favour of a statement of fund flows or cash flows' . . . 'the next twenty-five years may subsequently be seen to have been the twilight of income measurement.').

     A very clear and practical illustration of how a cash flow reporting system might be presented is given in T. A. Lee, 'A case for cash flow reporting', *The Journal of Business Finance*, Summer 1972, pp. 27-36.

35   Historic cash flows could be very misleading without knowledge of futre cash flows, but future cash flows are extremely difficult to forecast.

36   See J. E. Meade and J. R. N. Stone, 'The construction of tables of national income, expenditure, savings and investment', *The Economic Journal*, 1941, reprinted in Parker and Harcourt, *op. cit.*

37   Edgar O. Edwards and Philip W. Bell, *The Theory and Measurement of Business Income*, University of California Press, 1961.

38   A thorough account of the history of discounted cash flow will be found in R. H. Parker, *op. cit.*, Chapter 3.

39 In this field also, *The Nature of Capital and Income* (*op. cit.*), 1906, was his seminal piece of work, Chapter 13 being of particular relevance, and his subsequent work was a development of these basic ideas.

40 J. Hirshleifer, 'On the theory of the optimal investment decision', *Journal of Political Economy*, Vol. 66, 1958, pp. 329-72.

41 H. M. Weingartner, *Mathematical Programming and the Analysis of Capital Budgeting Problems*, Prentice-Hall 1964.

42 H. M. Markowitz, 'Portfolio selection', *Journal of Finance*, March 1952, pp. 77-91.

43 W. G. Sharpe, 'Capital asset prices: a theory of market equilibrium under conditions of risk', *Journal of Finance*, Sept. 1964, pp. 425-442.

44 See, for example, Bryan Carsberg, 'The role of the valuation model in the analysis of investment decisions', in Edey and Yamey, *op. cit.*

45 For a fuller account of the adoption of DCF techniques, see R. H. Parker, *op. cit.*, pp. 49-58.

46 Joel Dean, *Capital Budgeting*, Columbia University Press 1951, and *Managerial Economics, op. cit.*

47 National Economic Development Council, *Investment Appraisal*, HMSO, London, first edition 1965.

48 A. J. Merrett and Allen Sykes, *The Finance and Analysis of Capital Projects*, Longmans, first edition 1963.

49. Bryan Carsberg and Anthony Hope, *Capital Investment Decisions under Inflation*, The Institute of Chartered Accountants in England and Wales 1976.

50 Described in A. Singh and G. Whittington, *Growth, Profitability and Valuation*, Cambridge University Press 1968. More recent work is described in G. Meeks and G. Whittington, 'Giant companies in the United Kingdom 1948-69', *The Economic Journal*, Vol. 85, Dec. 1975, pp. 824-843.

51 A. Singh and G. Whittington, 'The size and growth of firms', *The Review of Economic Studies*, January 1975, pp. 15-26.

52 G. Meeks and G. Whittington, 'Directors' pay, growth, and profitability', *Journal of Industrial Economics*, Sept. 1975, pp. 1-14.

53 C. J. Jones, D. P. Tweedie and G. Whittington, 'The regression portfolio: a statistical investigation of a relative decline model', *Journal of Business Finance and Accounting*, Summer 1976, pp. 71-92.

54 G. Whittington, *The Prediction of Profitability, and Other Studies of Company Behaviour*, Cambridge University Press 1971.

55 G. Whittington, 'The profitability of retained earnings', *The Review of Economics and Statistics*, May 1972, pp. 152-160.

56 G. Meeks, Ph.D thesis, University of Edinburgh, 1975 and a book to be published by Cambridge University Press in 1977.

57 G. Meeks and G. Whittington, *The Financing of Quoted Companies in the United Kingdom*, Royal Commission on the Distribution of Income and Wealth, HMSO, 1976.

58 A. Singh, *Takeovers*, Cambridge University Press 1971.

59 See, for example, W. A. H. Godley and W. D. Nordhaus, 'Pricing in the trade cycle', *The Economic Journal*, Sept. 1972, pp. 853-882.

60 T. Wilson and P. W. S. Andrews (ed.), *Oxford Studies in the Price*

Mechanism, Clarendon Press 1951. The paper by R. C. Hall and C. J. Hitch (originally published in 1939) deals with pricing policy.

61 W. T. Baxter, 'The accountant's contribution to the trade cycle', *Economica*, 1955, pp. 99-112, revised and reprinted in Parker and Harcourt, *op. cit.*

62 C. T. Sandford, J. R. M. Willis and D. J. Ironside, *An Accessions Tax*, Institute for Fiscal Studies 1973, and *An Annual Wealth Tax*, Heinemann 1975.

63 A poineer in this field was W. H. Beaver in his papers 'The information content of annual earnings announcements', *Empirical Research in Accounting: Selected Studies, 1968* a supplement to *The Journal of Accounting Research*; and 'Financial ratios as predictors of failure', *Empirical Research in Accounting: Selected Studies; 1966.*

64 Partly because general equilibrium analysis has broken down the traditional concept of macroeconomics as distinct from micro-economics.

65 See, for example, Ijiri, *op. cit.*, or R. J. Chambers, *Accounting Evaluation and Economic Behavior*, Prentice-Hall 1966.

13
Accounting and finance

J M SAMUELS
Professor of Business Policy, University of Birmingham

and

R E V GROVES
Professor of Accounting, UWIST

Introduction

Finance is the meeting place of accounting and economics. For many years accounting was able to develop as a pragmatic subject, attaching little importance to what was happening in other related fields of study. Accountants within companies were involved in financial decisions using techniques of analysis which ignored economic principles. Accountants did not engage in empirical research to ascertain the impact of their work, for example the effect of annual financial reports on the stock market, nor were they particularly concerned with the needs of the users of the reports. Economists, on the other hand, were concerned with the process by which the prices of securities were determined in the stock market, but did not know very much about the production of the corporate profit figures; they developed techniques to help in decision making, but were not in positions within companies to try to put these ideas into practice.

The work of Irving Fisher represented an early contribution to the development of a theory of finance. He emphasised the need to value financial assets on the basis of the discounted sum of their future cash flows; he identified the nominal rate of interest as equal to the real rate of

213

interest adjusted by the expected rate of inflation, and developed a model of financial markets.[1] There was earlier work by economists and actuaries, on similar topics, but it was Fisher who brought the ideas together into the subject of finance. It was many years later before accountants, who were actually involved in day-to-day financial decision-making at a corporate and multinational level, began to adopt these techniques.

In the early 1960's, with the wider acceptance of present value techniques, with a developing theory of business finance and the adoption of a systems approach to planning, accountants began to adjust their approach to finance to take into account the theories and practices that were developing around them. Through the 1960's the subject of finance developed at a theoretical, empirical and practical level as an extremely useful tool, one that offered a great deal to the financial manager. It was considered possible to measure the cost of capital with a reasonable degree of accuracy;[2] techniques were developed to assist in making optimal capital investment decisions;[3] financial operators appeared on the scene who were expert at understanding the way in which stock market prices would respond to financial information — 'the gunslingers' as Weston calls them.[4] Planning models were developed for companies where finance was seen as just one of the constituent parts, both in terms of objectives and constraints,[5] and models were developed which offered hope that soon it would be possible to manage portfolios in some kind of optimal manner. Then came the doubts. So many of the academic papers reached conflicting conclusions that an accountant familiar with all the literature would be less than confident when advising companies in the business finance area. The financial environment changed. The heroes of one period became the villains of the next. Were discounting techniques really correct? Or, were perhaps the pay back method and cash flow accounting all that mattered?[6] Could one use the weighted average approach to measure the cost of capital? In any case, what was the cost of equity capital?[7] And, recently, we have been confronted with the problem as to how we should incorporate the impact of inflation into financial analysis. As Lintner states, 'a substantial amount of further work involving empirical investigation, testing and implementation is still required before we will have developed a clear and firm knowledge of the effects of inflation and inflationary expectations on the portfolio decisions of differently situated investor groups, and how these interact to affect the prices and returns on different types of securities.'[8]

Traditionally it has been possible to divide the subject of finance up into three sub-groups, which has been convenient at a theoretical, practical and teaching level. But, as Weston points out, 'the traditional trinity of money and capital markets, business finance, and investment is no longer meaningful at the theoretical level and of questionable use for descriptive and empirical study.'[9] It is not always possible to separate the financing question fro: the investment question, as anybody will know who has faced a decision on whether to lease or buy a particular asset.

In making corporate investment decisions, it is becoming increasingly common, at least at a theoretical level, to take into account the goals and wishes of those who have provided the finance through the money and capital markets. Shareholders' behaviour is now being analysed.[10] The directors of a company are interested in the financial expectations of the shareholders; in how long they are prepared to hold the shares; and in whether institutional holders behave differently from private holders. The trend is in the direction of an increasing proportion of the shares of a company being held by institutions and a declining proportion being held by directors. This divorce of ownership and control has important implications for decision-making.[11] As the subject of finance spreads itself wider and wider, important behavioural factors need to be studied. For example, the capital asset pricing model, which is an attempt to ascertain how prices of company shares and fixed interest securities are determined in the stock market, is now seen as just a part of the theory of consumer choice having a behavioural aspect.[12]

The money and capital markets and the financial intermediaries are of key importance in determining the allocation between competing users of funds for investment. One can even go so far as to say that one cannot study corporate finance at an aggregate level without considering the flow of funds between the sectors of the economy because the savings behaviour of the household sector and the increasing involvement of the public sector help to determine the supply of funds for companies and the terms on which it is made available.[13]

In this essay we will discuss some of the issues raised in the introductory section; we will look at the interrelated areas of the choice and financing of investments, and we will examine what impact, if any, the main accounting document, the annual financial report, has on finance, and in particular on financial markets. This potential impact is important for the company, as it affects the wealth of the owners of the company, the availability of future external funds, and possibly has implications on the future ownership, and hence management, of the company. The objectives of published accounting reports are now under scrutiny. *The Corporate Report* expresses the view that 'the fundamental objective . . . is to communicate economic measurements of, and information about, the resources and performance of the reporting entity useful to those having reasonable rights to such information.'[14] It is clearly important to know whether the information conveyed in the accounting reports affects the decision of actual and potential shareholders.

Capital budgeting

One of the most important decisions a company needs to make is whether or not to undertake a particular investment proposal. The consideration of small items of expenditure probably does not justify a great deal of time and effort, but the success or failure of the business can depend on making the correct decision on major items of expenditure. The company is investing resources now and the returns are expected in the future; the future is uncertain, but a decision needs to be made. In so far as the accountant is concerned with the financial health of the company it is clearly part of his role to be involved in the decision. Unfortunately, the traditional image of the accountant in such situations is one of a person who takes on a pessimistic role, a person who raises doubts about other people's 'favourite' project.

It should not be forgotten that an accountant comes into

the investment decision-making process at a late stage. The first part of the exercise involves a search for suitable projects. This is followed by a certain amount of technical and feasibility work, but it is at the data gathering stage that the accountant is formally brought into the process. It is therefore usual that many people's attitudes towards the merits of a particular proposal will have been formed before the accountant can have his say. It is, therefore, not surprising that the accountant may tread on a few toes. The danger is that the accountant, in his concern to see that the funds of the business are not wasted, may sometimes forget that businesses can come to grief not only from undertaking unwise investments, but also from not having enough new projects to go ahead with when the existing product lines become obsolete. Alternatively, a company can be ruined by using machines which are not as efficient as those of its competitors. The accountant needs to ensure that much information, of both a financial and non-financial nature, is given to the decision-makers when a particular proposal is being considered, and also that the information is presented in a meaningful and informative manner. It is particularly important that any assumptions underlying forecasts of the results of a project are made explicit. We will now examine briefly some important aspects of investment decisions: the time value of money, the treatment of inflation, the treatment of uncertainty and the method of computing the cost of capital.

Time value of money

All the techniques of financial analysis which presently command strong theoretical support involve the discounting of future cash flows to their present value. Discounting is necessary because cash amounts arising in the future are less valuable than equal cash amounts arising at the present time, and the further in the future a given cash sum arises, the less valuable it is in present terms. The easiest way to understand the reason that the value of cash receipts and payments depends upon this timing is by observing that the sooner a cash receipt arises, the sooner it may be used for other purposes, including investment to earn interest. This concept is known as 'the time value of money', and the appropriate discount rate to reflect the value of money to a particular company is termed the cost of capital.

The fact that a study undertaken by Mao[15] in 1970 found that present value techniques were not being widely applied by businessmen was a surprise to many, but it could perhaps be explained by the belief, expressed by Weston,[16] that the practical application of theoretical developments usually occurs some eight years after the publication of the developments.

"I see many men crossing water, ...
a cost of capital of 15 %, ...
and a positive net present value."

Many major companies such as Ford, Rio-Tinto Zinc and the large oil companies actually helped to pioneer the development of quantitative techniques used in investment decisions, but there are many other companies who, although they use discounting exercises in project evaluation, do so only as window dressing; the real decision as to whether to go ahead with a project is based on the strength of the personalities involved in the decision-making process. We might ask if these companies are wrong not to base the decision solely on the accounting reports placed in front of them or alternatively we might ask if there are perhaps so many uncertainties surrounding the available data and the capital investment evaluation procedures themselves that in the end the decision should depend on whether or not one has confidence in the people making the proposal.

A comparatively recent survey of capital budgeting practices in the USA revealed extensive data gathering by companies and sophisticated processing of the data.[17] A study by Carsberg and Hope[18] of the situation in the UK found that industry made considerable use of the discounted cash flow techniques, although the precise method of their use did not conform to the recommendations of accepted theory.

Inflation

The impact of inflation must be consistently allowed for in investment appraisal, both in the forecasting of future costs and prices, and in the calculation of the cost of capital. One can either (i) forecast future cash flows in monetary terms (at actual prices allowing for inflation) and discount them using a monetary cost of capital (an actual interest rate allowing for inflation) or (ii) forecast real cash flows (actual cash flows reduced by an index of inflation) and discount them in real terms (eliminating inflation from the monetary cost of capital). It would be wrong to mix forecasts in real terms with forecasts in monetary terms. To forecast everything in terms of today's prices and costs is to assume that the impact of inflation will be neutral, that is, cost increases can be matched with price increases, and that inflation will affect all items of cost equally. This has not proved to be the case, nor is it likely to be so. The study by Carsberg and Hope revealed that most firms were not allowing for inflation in a conceptually satisfactory way. In fact it was found that the treatment of inflation in the discounting procedures was likely to considerably underestimate the net benefits accruing from a project, and so could lead to a lower level of investment than was justified. This is something that UK industry cannot afford. The available empirical work suggests, therefore, that the appraisal processes used by industry leave something to be desired.

Uncertainty

There are many possible methods of incorporating uncertainty into investment appraisal procedures. These may range from simple probability and sensitivity analyses to more advanced techniques of portfolio analysis (i.e from attempts to attach probabilities to a range of possible project outcomes leaving the analysis of the data in subjective terms, to sophisticated attempts to achieve a balance of projects in which rates of return are weighed against corresponding aggregate levels of risk). The problem of quantifying attitudes to alternative levels of risk is complicated in theory and even more complicated in practice. In fact, whereas there is some evidence to show that companies incorporate probabilities and sensitivity analysis into decision-making procedures, there is little or no evidence to show that the fundamental ideas underlying portfolio theory have been applied at the decision-making level. In addition there may be constraints which limit the number of projects a company can undertake, and the choice of an optimal set of projects subject to a number of constraints leads into mathematical programming.[19]

Cost of capital

A company needs to know the cost of its capital for at least two reasons: first in order to determine which investment proposals should be undertaken, and second to determine whether there are cost advantages in obtaining one form of finance rather than another. With regard to the first of these reasons, it is usual to employ the cost of capital as the cut-off point in investment decisions. If an investment can earn a rate of return greater than the cost of capital, it is worth undertaking, or if the net present value criterion is used, the project should be undertaken if there exists a positive cash surplus when future cash flows have been discounted at the cost of capital. This approach to investment decision-taking assumes that a company can raise all the funds it needs and is not in a capital rationing situation. It also assumes that the supply and cost of the finance is independent of the investment projects to be undertaken.

There is now, however, a great deal of discussion in the literature on whether the investment decision should be dealt with separately from the financing decision.[20] The traditional approach has been to calculate a cost of capital based either on the existing capital of the business or, more correctly, on the cost of the next round of fund raising, and then to use this as a guide to determine whether investments are profitable. However, the limitations of this approach resulting from the possible interdependence of the finance and investment decision is now recognised in the academic literature (i.e. the finance the company is able to obtain may depend on which projects it is to undertake as well as on what projects it has already in progress). The clearest case of interdependence of the finance and investment decision occurs in the lease versus purchase decision, which is one reason why this particular problem is so difficult to handle using simple investment criteria.[21]

A second reason why a company will need to know the cost of its capital is in order to determine its optimal level of gearing. The capital of a company may be divided into two broad categories, equity capital and debt capital and the question arises as to what proportion of the latest funds should be provided by debt capital — i.e. what should be the gearing ratio. If the cost of the one source of finance differs from the other, then a company can vary its average cost of capital by altering its ratio of debt to equity.

An optimal capital structure is one particular balance of equity and debt at which the average cost of capital to the company is at its lowest point, and the wealth of the owners is maximised. The maximisation of owners' wealth is the objective underlying most of the optimisation models in corporate finance. One can raise doubts as to whether this particular objective is appropriate in the latter part of the twentieth century.[22] As a theoretical hypothesis it may be defensible, but it is doubtful whether any of the large public companies can any longer afford to see its objectives quite so clearly. However, even if the managers of a company do not wish to maximise shareholders' wealth they should still wish to achieve an optimal capital structure in order to keep the costs of the business as low as possible.

Debt capital, both with regard to capital repayment and the expectation of an annual return, is less risky to the holder than equity capital. Therefore, the holder of debt capital should expect a lower average annual rate of return on his investment than the holder of an equity share. The cost to the company of debt is less than the cost of equity. The tax system also helps to make debt capital cheaper than equity capital. However, when there is a downturn in the economy an excessive amount of debt capital can leave the company exposed to financial difficulties.[23] The company must therefore balance the gains from debt capital against the possible risks.

At a theoretical level there has been a long debate as to whether an optimal capital structure really exists. Modigliani and Miller[24] have shown that, in the absence of various market imperfections and interferences, there would not be an optimal level of gearing. However, in the real world, market imperfections do exist, and it is likely that there is an optimal capital structure for a company.

The measurement of the cost of equity capital is not easy, and there are conflicting views as to how it should be carried out. The idea is to measure the shareholder's opportunity cost (i.e. what a shareholder could have earned elsewhere in a similar risk class if he had not invested in the company) and then to argue that the company needs to earn at least this rate of return on any new investment in order to justify the use of the shareholder's funds. One approach to this measurement problem is that adopted by Merrett and Sykes. They measured past return to shareholders before and after tax in real and monetary terms, averaged over different periods of time.[28] This approach has been criticised on the grounds that past returns may provide a poor guide to what shareholders expect in the future. With the erratic behaviour of the British stock market in the 1970's, this averaging process has become very dependent on the particular period under consideration. An alternative approach to measuring the cost of equity is to observe the term structure of interest rates.[26] It is possible to ascertain what an investor can earn on, say, a bank deposit account, on a government bond and on a first class company debenture. As one moves through different risk classes of investment one can observe higher rates of return being offered to the investor to compensate for the higher levels of risk. Equities clearly require a premium for risk above the return offered on fixed interest securities. The biggest problem lies in deciding on the premium which needs to be added to compensate for the higher levels of risk on equity investments, as the appropriate premium will vary from company to company.

Having measured the cost of equity capital and the cost of debt capital, the company should be in a position to measure its overall cost of capital. Unfortunately, however, yet another dispute has to be settled at this stage. The traditional approach has been to calculate the *weighted* average cost of capital, the cost of each type of capital being weighted according to the proportions of debt and equity.[27] Some writers argue that the weighting should be based on the published balance sheet values of the debt and equity; the alternative view, better based in theory, is that it should be on the basis of market values.

The many debates concerning both the theoretical validity and the practical application of the concept of the cost of capital seem likely to persist for a long time.

Financial information and the stock markets

Writers in the field of finance have not confined their attention solely to an examination of the theory and practice of internal business decision-making, but have also looked closely at what we might term the 'external' impact of accounting information (i.e. the reporting of the results of the decisions undertaken by company management). We mentioned at the start of this essay that the impact of published accounting information was important for company management in that the reaction of financial markets to accounting information has implications for the availability of future finance, and indeed that it directly affects the wealth of the company's owners as reflected in the market price of the company's shares. We might also stress the use of models used by financial theorists as being a common link between the 'internal' appraisal of worthwhile investments, and the 'external' appraisal of published information concerning the company's activities.

It is possible to detect at least three strands in the literature which afford some indication of the impact of published information on shareholder wealth:

1 the extent to which share prices reflect public financial information,

2 the extent to which investors use financial statements to make investment decisions,

3 the extent to which investors are able to distinguish between real economic changes and the 'cosmetic' effects which can result from changes in accounting methods.

1 Share prices and public information. The theory which underlies the relationship between quoted share prices and published information is often termed the 'efficient capital market hypothesis'. The implications of the hypothesis are important for shareholders' investment decisions, because if capital markets (stock exchanges) are efficient in the sense of the theory, investors cannot expect to make abnormal gains from an analysis of publicly available information. An efficient capital market is defined as one in which the prices of shares always fully reflect all publicly available information concerning the shares, and thus, by implication, prices will adjust immediately and unbiasedly to any piece of new information released to the market.

Research studies of the efficient capital markets hypothesis[28] can be classified as to the 'weak' form of the hypothesis, the 'semi-strong' form and the 'strong' form. The weak form states that current prices fully reflect all the information given to the market regarding historical events, and therefore that the investor, with knowledge of the past sequence of prices and events, can neither abnormally enhance his investment return, nor improve his ability to select shares. Studies of the weak form have mainly dealt with the extent to which successive share price changes are dependent on prior changes. The research has tried to determine whether there is any statistical relationship between daily changes in share prices. Tests have been conducted on stock and commodity prices in the USA,

Britain and France and all the results reveal that, in general, the extent of dependence between successive price changes is negligible, i.e. that the market is efficient in the terms of the weak form of the hypothesis.

Tests of the 'semi-strong' form of the hypothesis have been concerned with whether current share prices reflect all public knowledge about the particular company and also with the speed of price adjustment to the public announcement of information (i.e. researchers have been interested in finding whether it is worth some effort on the part of investors to acquire and analyse this public knowledge in the hope of gaining superior investment results). Generally speaking, the evidence suggests that share price adjustment is speedy and in the right direction, thereby confirming the efficient markets hypothesis.

The final form of test is the 'strong' form. It presupposes that there exists a group of individuals who have access to privileged inside information which is not generally available. If the market fails to exhibit 'strong form efficiency', these individuals can put their privileged information to profitable use[29] (for example, there are specialists who have access to information which is not easily and immediately available to the general public, in the same way that corporate officials have some monopolistic power over information about their company). It is difficult to prove whether either group turns this information to advantage. The only certainty is that it is illegal for corporate officials to do so.

Often, unit trust managements claim better investment performance, in part due to the accessibility of special and private research information concerning company securities. However, when the risk of the portfolio and the costs of transactions are taken into account, the performance of these funds has not produced abnormal returns. So even if the large institutional investors have a better class of information it is not certain that this enables them to produce better results. Implicit in this test is the assumption that access to the information is not fully reflected in share prices, but from the results one can only assume that market reactions are fast enough and in the appropriate direction to amend a share price appropriately when the investment trading pattern of an institutional investor is noticed.

Thus we can conclude, especially in the weak and semi-strong case, that the available evidence generally supports the efficient market hypothesis. We now consider the extent to which investors use financial statements to make investment decisions.

2 Financial statements and investors' decisions. If it proved to be possible to detect a relationship between large movements in share prices and changes in published accounting profits it would afford some evidence that accounting profits were used by investors to help decide whether to increase or reduce the level of their shareholdings (i.e. that accounting profits numbers were useful). An early study by Ball and Brown attempted to answer this question. Using the semi-strong form of the efficient markets hypothesis (i.e. that the market will adjust security prices correctly and quickly upon the availability of information) Ball and Brown hypothesised that 'an observed revision of stock prices associated with the release of the income report would thus provide evidence that the information reflected in income numbers is useful'.[30]

Investors build up expectations about earnings and some portion of the total earnings announced in the accounting report will therefore have been anticipated. This expected part should already have been reflected in the share price. If the market is efficient, only the unexpected part of the total information will be relevant to the market and the market should ensure that the share price reacts quickly and in the appropriate direction. If the actual change in earnings is greater than that forecast this is termed 'good news'; 'bad news' arises when the actual income change is less than expected. The hypothesis tested by Ball and Brown was that if the released information contained 'good news' the stock price would rise, whereas if it contained 'bad news' the stock price would fall, while 'no news' (i.e. actual earnings equalled forecast earnings) should be associated with no effect on share price. A twelve-month period before, followed by a six-month period after, the date of announcement of earnings were investigated, and the portion of change which reflected general price movement in a specific share price was removed. Earnings announcements were classified into 'good news' and 'bad news' by comparing actual earnings with a forecast of earnings derived by statistical analysis of past earnings of the firm and the earnings of other firms. The share prices of the 'good news' companies gradually rose throughout the twelve months before the announcement date. Conversely, 'bad news' companies found that their share price gradually declined before the announcement date. In some cases adjustments still continued for approximately two more months after the announcement.

Ball and Brown found that 50% or more of all the information about an individual firm that becomes available during the year is reflected in the year's accounting profit figure. Most of this information was reflected in the market price before the announcement of earnings and on average only 10%-15% of the price adjustment took place in the announcement month. These results are not very surprising because a substantial part of the accounting information provided on the announcement date will have been made available to the market through formal interim reports, statements by corporate officials or investigations by analysts confirmed by corporate contacts. Nevertheless, they show that the provision of income and accounting data to investors does have some influence on their investment decisions. Knowledge of the direction of the earnings changes would have been worthwhile for investors since the 'good news' companies had a higher stock price appreciation than the general market movement, while the share prices of the 'bad news' companies fell significantly more than would have been expected from the general price movement.

In interpreting the results of the Ball and Brown studies, it is important to keep in mind their limitations: they were *ex post* studies (i.e. they were undertaken after the event) and the prediction model used may have been relevant only to the particular period under study. Investors expectations change over time and their prediction models may also change; it would be preferable to examine the effect of financial data on investor decisions independently of any specific prediction model.

In examining the same issue of the usefulness of accounting information to investors, Beaver[31] took the view that though there may be no change in the overall *market* expectations when new information is released, there may be significant changes in the expectations of *individual* investors. This change in individual expectations would not necessarily be shown up by price tests such as that conducted by Ball and Brown, because if there is no overall change in market expectations the *price* will not change. However, there may be significant trading *volume* changes through shifts in individual investor positions. Beaver, therefore, hypothesised that if the information was relevant (i.e. if it changed an investor's expectations) then there would be a significant change in transactions volume around the announcement date.

Beaver looked at 143 US firms over the period 1961-65. These firms provided 506 earnings announcements. The week which included the date of the announcement of the results in *The Wall Street Journal* was deemed to be 'week O'. The volume of transactions in week O was on average 33% higher than the average volume for any of the eight weeks before or after week O. Beaver concluded on the basis of his tests that the significance of the trading volume in week O showed that the expectations of individual investors are changed by the announcement of profit figures, and that therefore accounting data are used by investors for financial decisions.

3 Impact of changes in accounting methods. A firm may, within limits, report its economic situation in different ways depending on its choice of accounting method. For example, a company choosing to use the accelerated depreciation method would produce a lower profit than if it had used the straight line approach, assuming that the company is expanding and investing regularly in new assets. In an efficient capital market, investors should be able to perceive, analyse and account for the impact of any change in an accounting method (or for differences between methods used by different firms) so that only real economic factors would be taken into account in the investors' decision.

Early research to test investors' perceptions used experimental and simulation studies, beginning with Dyckman's[32] series of studies which used undergraduate accounting students. The students were presented with pairs of financial statements which were identical except for the different stock valuation methods used. The studies did not establish clearly whether the student investor had or had not been able to see that the underlying economic situation was similar for corresponding sets of accounts.

Jensen[33] used security analysts for his subjects, sending questionnaires to try to examine the effects of different depreciation and stock methods on investment decisions. His results suggested that the analysts' decisions were affected by the different accounting methods. Bruns[34] and Barrett[35] likewise conducted behavioural 'laboratory' studies and found that given sufficient information in footnotes, etc., different accounting methods did not confuse the accounting oriented investor. There are, however, problems with this type of experimental study. The subjects are not in a real-world situation (i.e. they are participating as if in a game) and, as in Jensen's case, the subjects are not under the direct control of the researcher.

More sophisticated analyses, studying the impact of accounting techniques on stock market prices, have been used in several more recent studies. A study by Kaplan and Roll,[36] using a sample of 350 firms, examined the effects of alternative accounting methods on stock prices. The results indicated that changes in the accounting method were allowed for by investors after a small delay, during which time firms whose earnings were inflated by an accounting change had seen their shares subject to temporary 'overvaluation'. Reamer, Comiskey and Groves[37] using the same analytical approach showed that the market did award premium valuations to companies which adopted an accounting method of real value. They monitored a change which produced a cash saving of taxation payments.

In this section, we have referred to only a few of the many studies of capital market efficiency. In summary, the evidence suggests that large capital markets are efficient in so far as they reflect all publicly available accounting information; that investors do use financial statements and other accounting information to make their investment decisions; and that, in the main, investors are able to distinguish between real economic changes and the cosmetic effects that can result from changes in accounting methods.

Conclusions

One of the problems now is that the theory of finance has advanced so much with sophisticated mathematical teaching being applied at the academic level, that company management is less able to understand, and is perhaps less interested in, what is going on in the academic institutions. The result is that academic work is becoming removed from practical uses. Solomons[38] in a 1966 article foresaw the way in which the subject was developing and felt that it would become increasingly complex. The accountant, heavily involved in the practical side of business, needs to be aware of many of the developments that are taking place in the financial theory. On the other hand, many academics need to be reminded of the desirability of taking account of the actual problems of practice. The gulf between academics and practitioners has widened, and it would be beneficial if effort were to be directed towards narrowing it again.

Notes and references

1 I. Fisher, *Appreciation and Interest*, American Economics Association, Third series, August 1896.
   1 Fisher — 'The Rate of Interest' . . . 1907
   2 Fisher — 'The Theory of Interest' . . . 1930
2 See, for example, A. A. Robichek and S. C. Myers, *Optimal Financing Decisions*, Prentice Hall 1965, and E. Solomons, *The Theory of Financial Management*, Columbia University Press 1963.
3 See A. J. Merrett and A. Sykes, *The Finance and Analysis of Capital Projects*, Longmans 1963.
4 J. F. Weston, 'New themes in finance', *Journal of Finance*, March 1974.
5 For an early example see B. A. Charnes, W. W. Cooper and M. N. Miller 'Application of linear programming to financial budgeting and costing of funds', *Journal of Business*, January 1959.
6 R. M. Adelson, 'Discounted cash flow, can we discount it?', *Journal of Business Finance*, Summer 1970.
7 R. A. Fawthrop, 'Underlying problems in discounted cash flow appraisal', *Accounting and Business Research*, Summer 1971.
8 J. Lintner, 'Inflation and security returns', *Journal of Finance*, May 1975.
9 *op. cit.* ref. (4).
10 R. J. Briston, 'Fisons stockholder survey', *Journal of Business Policy*, Autumn 1970.
11 G. Donaldson, 'Strategy for financial emergencies', *Harvard Business Review* 1969.

12 M. Keenan, 'Models of equity valuation — the great SERM bubble', *Journal of Finance*, May 1970.

13 J. Stiglitz, 'On the irrelevance of corporate financial policy', *American Economic Review*, December 1974.

14 Accounting Standards Committee, *The Corporate Report*, Institute of Chartered Accountants in England and Wales 1975.

15 J. C. T. Mao, 'Survey of capital budgeting : theory and practice', *Journal of Finance*, May 1970.

16 J. F. Weston — *op. cit.* ref. (4).

17 T. Klammer, 'Empirical evidence on the adoption of sophisticated capital budgeting techniques', *Journal of Business*, July 1972.

18 B. V. Carsberg and A. Hope, *Business Investment Decisions under Inflation*, Institute of Chartered Accountants 1976.

19 See H. M. Weingartner, *Mathematical Programming and the Analysis of Capital Budgeting Problems*, Prentice Hall 1963.

20 S. C. Myers, 'Interaction of corporate financing and investment decisions — implications for capital budgeting', *Journal of Finance*, March 1974.

21 See for example R. W. Johnson and W. Llewellen, 'Analysis of the lease or buy decision', *Journal of Finance*, September 1972.

22 G. Donaldson. *Strategy for Financial Mobility*, Harvard University Press.

23 A. A. Robichek and S. C. Myers, *op. cit.* ref (2).

24 M. H. Modigliani and F. Miller, 'The cost of capital, corporation finance and the theory of investments', *American Economic Review*, June 1958.

25 A. J. Merrett and A. Sykes, 'Return on equities and fixed interest securities 1919-1966', *District Bank Review*, June 1966.

26 R. C. Ibbotson and R. A. Sinquefield, 'Stocks, bonds, bills and inflation: simulation of the future', *Journal of Business*, July 1976.

27 T. J. Nantell and C. R. Carlson, 'The cost of capital as a weighted average', *Journal of Finance*, December 1975.

28 See for example, E. F. Fama, 'Efficient capital markets: a review of theory and empirical work', *The Journal of Finance*, May 1970, p. 387-417. This article provides a comprehensive bibliography of studies up to 1970, including such works by Bachelier, Roberts, Cootner, Osborne, Kendal, Cowles, Moore, Granger and Morgenstern, as well as work by Fama himself.

29 See Fama, ibid, for further description and bibliography of the strong form tests. Friend, Blume, Crockett, Jensen and Sharpe and other individuals who have done work in this area are listed in Fama. Also see J. C. Francis and S. H. Archer, *Portfolio Analysis*, Prentice Hall.

30 R. Ball and P. Brown, 'An empirical evaluation of accounting income numbers', *Journal of Accounting Research*, 6 Autumn 1968, p. 159-78. Quote from page 161. The first stage of this project was reported in R. Ball and P. Brown, 'Some preliminary findings on the association between the earnings of a firm, its industry and the economy,' Empirical Research in Accounting: Selected Studies 1967, Supplement to Vol. 5. *Journal of Accounting Research*, p. 55-77.

31   W. H. Beaver, 'The information content of annual earnings announcements', Empirical Research in Accounting, Selected Studies, 1968, Supplement to Vol. 6, *Journal of Accounting Research* p. 67-92.

32   T. R. Dyckman, 'On the investment decision', *The Accounting Review*, **39**, April 1964, p. 285-295; Dyckman, 'The effects of alternative accounting techniques on certain management decisions', *Journal of Accounting Research*, **2**, Spring 1964, p. 91-107; Dyckman, 'On the effects of earnings-trend, size and investment valuation procedures in evaluating a business firm', R. K. Jaedicke, Y. Ijiri and O. Nielsen (eds.) in *Research in Accounting Measurement*, American Accounting Association 1966.

33   R. E. Jensen, 'An experimental design for study of effects of accounting variations in decision-making', *Journal of Accounting Research*, **4**, Autumn 1966, p. 224-38.

34   W. J. Bruns Jr., 'Inventory valuation and management decisions', *The Accounting Review*, **40**, April 1965, p. 345-57.

35   M. E. Barrett, 'Accounting for intercorporate investments: a behavioural field experiment', Empirical Research in Accounting: Selected Studies, 1971, Supplement to Vol. 9, *Journal of Accounting Research*, p. 50-65.

36   R. S. Kaplan and R. Roll, 'Investor evaluation of accounting information: some empirical evidence', *Journal of Business*, **45**, April 1972, p. 225-57.

37   J. Reamer, E. E. Comiskey and R. E. V. Groves. 'A test of market response to a tax-accounting change', *Journal of Business Research*, **3**. July 1975, p. 211-225.

38   E. Solomons, 'What should we teach in a course on business finance?', *Journal of Finance*, May 1966.

14

Accounting and operations research

CYRIL TOMKINS

Professor of Accounting, University of Bath

It is obviously very difficult to say how old any particular discipline or area of study is, but if forced to place an age on operations research many would plump for 37 years. In 1940 Britain faced as big a problem as it had ever faced with the impending Battle of Britain. She had few planes and skilled pilots in comparison with the enemy and, as everyone knows, those 'few' performed deeds to earn our gratitude and write themselves into history. However, not many are aware of those, even fewer in number, who helped achieve that victory by employing scientific methods in an attempt to find a solution to an apparently unsolvable problem — the distribution of the limited resources in such a way as to achieve victory. Fortunately, this 'scientific approach', together with the valour of 'the few' proved to be successful. Operations analysis (or operations research) had passed its first major test. Following this success, OR continued to be employed throughout the war and soon afterwards spread to the industrial field in the UK, the USA and further afield.

The nature of operations research

While it has been stated that OR tackles problems in a 'scientific' way, it is necessary to be more precise than this if the effect of OR on accounting is to be identified. It is probable that if one asked a sample of non-OR specialists what OR is, by far the majority would immediatley think of a collection of techniques including inventory models, linear programming, queuing theory, network analysis, and so on. However, while these do represent important proposals from OR scientists for the solution of specific types of business problems, OR is much more than a collection of specific mathematical techniques — although one could be misled over this by looking at many introductory OR syllabuses and textbooks. Stated broadly, OR is a scientific approach to solve business problems at any level in the organisation, including problems associated with overall policy faced by the most senior executives. Indeed some OR scientists would say that OR is exclusively concerned with top level corporate policy and this is what distinguishes OR from scientific approaches, operated for many years in, for example, production control. However, it is quite possible for OR applications to cut across the boundaries of functional departments even though not operating at the overall company policy level, and so this author prefers to think of OR as a scientific approach for developing possible solutions to problems where the approach is not necessarily constrained by existing organisational structures. This does not mean that in practical applications one can ignore organisational structures or the types of behaviour which are likely to be shown by various types of persons usually found in different parts of the organisation's network. Far from it; later in this chapter some brief reference is made to the problems created by differences in personal backgrounds and attitudes and the subject of accounting processes and behavioural sciences is examined in much more depth in the following chapter. However, there is a need for businesses to search for solutions to problems in a logical, scientific way cutting across departmental boundaries; otherwise feasible solutions may remain undetected. Some suggested solutions may prove to be unacceptable because organisational factors are too strong, but the likelihood of this can be diminished by organising the OR team properly so that it is inter-disciplinary in character and not composed entirely of mathematicians or physical scientists. It is then quite possible that the use of OR not only produces a greater array of possible solutions to any problem, but also proposes solutions which are more acceptable to all important parts of the organisation than those which would be proposed by individual departments. This is the ideal; it does not follow that this has been achieved by OR teams in practice. Indeed many practical OR studies appear to have failed to achieve this objective, but more on that later.

The definition of the 'scientific approach' is also hard to expound — indeed major controversies have occurred over this question. However, once again it suffices for this paper to define the phrase in general terms. The 'scientific approach' to business problems involves the identification of the problem to be solved, the measurement, behaviour and relationships of variables which affect outcomes in the problem area, the construction of a mathematical model which captures sufficient of reality to enable the problem to be solved, the determination of the parameter values for the model and the calculation of a proposed solution. Although many elementary OR texts give illustrations of applications which end at this stage, such a process is incomplete. A model can never reflect the *total* reality of the business situation. Consequently, one is never 100% sure that the solution proposed (i.e. the values at which to set the business variables under control in order to generate a solution in the real world) will generate the desired solution. Consequently, no OR application is complete until the model has been validated with test data and then, if it passes that first test, with a real-world application. Even then successful application initially should not mean that the process is at an end unless there is strong evidence to suggest that the economic environment which affects this application is stable. Usually the dynamics of real-world markets, technological developments and institutiónal relationships are such that, at the very least, parameters change in scale. In addition, the nature of interactions between variables in the model often change — especially if dealing with problems at overall corporate policy level. In this situation OR should be seen as part of a dynamic problem solving and control system rather than the identification of a particular mathematical technique to solve a single problem. The repeated application of the model needs monitoring and, if necessary, the model itself, rather than just the parameter input values, adapted to reflect changes in business reality. Even where OR decisions result in large capital outlays where specific decisions cannot be easily reversed, monitoring is necessary to judge the efficiency of the decision model and whether it should be relied upon in future.

How can the accountant help in OR studies?

The aim of this chapter is to demonstrate the interaction between accounting and OR. In this section the nature of an 'ideal' OR approach is mapped out in reasonable detail and the part that accountants can play at each stage is considered. This will provide a meaningful basis for evaluating the actual influence which OR has had to date on the activities of accountants and accounting literature.

Figure 1 shows a flow chart of OR when seen as part of a dynamic planning and control process. The key features distinguishing the process from traditional planning and control systems are the overall description of the system associated with the problem area and the prominent part played by the mathematical formulation of the system.

To begin, assume that a problem has been recognised. For example, let it be assumed that a company has to decide what mix of materials to buy each month to produce a given marketable finished product mix where the prices of raw materials vary considerably from month to month. Assume also that the proportions of raw materials used on the production process can be modified, within limits, for each type of finished product. Such a problem might arise in the case of a sausage manufacturer who has to decide what cuts of meat to use given that the price for each cut varies in different proportions from month to month. Initially the decision to buy different quantities of materials may have been made on an intuitive basis by a company official and it

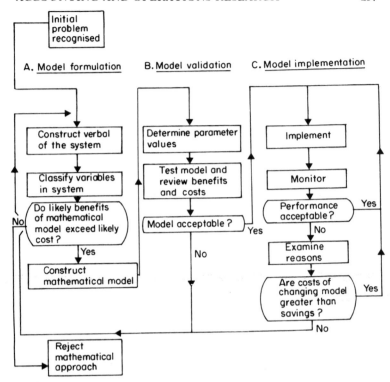

Figure 1 Flow chart of operations research as continuous decision process

has now been decided to ask an OR team to investigate the problem with a view to reducing material costs.

As a first step the team should attempt to describe their problem in words and also the type of procedure needed to solve the problem. This should not be undertaken lightly. In terms of the example, a complete description should be drawn up of the processes involved in acquiring, evaluating and using various cuts of meat together with the effect on the finished products of using different input mixes. If this verbal model is not complete some essential aspect of reality may have been omitted and, if that occurs at this stage, the error will be perpetrated through the whole process and will not be discovered until the model is tested or perhaps not until the practical implementation stage. The accountant can help in formulating the verbal model. In order to construct his existing accounting records he will usually have become familiar with the way in which costs are incurred. He will also have a good idea of the magnitude of the different cost elements involved in the process — the cost concepts used may not be those needed subsequently for the mathematical model, but his existing cost data will probably be useful for an *initial* appraisal of the problem. In the example of the input mix, the accountant would probably be unable to advise on the technical aspects of what mixes of ingredients were permitted or the effects of each mix in finished products. Consequently, the OR team would need technical advice from elsewhere on these matters.

A very important part of the verbal explanation of the system and problem is to identify appropriate 'system boundaries'. The problem to be tackled probably relates to one area of activity (even if cutting across departmental boundaries) in the company. It would be quite possible to focus on this area and arrive at a satisfactory solution but to miss the fact that such a solution has undesirable effects elsewhere in the organisation. In other words, sub-optimisation may not be consisent with optimisation for the whole organisational system. One answer would be to solve every problem in the context of a total corporate model. However, this would usually be far too complex, costly and time-consuming. The OR. analyst is, therefore, forced to define his problem area in such a way that the overlapping effects beyond that area are minimal or easily quantified. The accountant could be of considerable assistance in this type of problem definition. He is one person in the organisation who has an overview of all departmental activities and through his experience in constructing the company's budget (assuming it has one — it almost certainly will if it employs its own 'in-house' OR analysts) he will be familiar with many of the inter-departmental factors which need to be considered. At the very least he should be familiar with the cases where activity by one department affects money costs and revenues of another department in a reasonably direct way, although he may not be aware of more subtle inter-departmental effects due to *behavioural* factors. Nevertheless, at this early stage of the OR project, the accountant can help considerably in identifying the range and scope of the problem area.

Having formulated the problem and the associated system of operation in words, the OR analyst must then identify which of the key variables are controllable and which are not. In terms of the example already given he might ask whether the prices of the product ingredients are given by the market or can special deals be made for bulk purchase in advance at lower or guaranteed prices? The accountant may well be able to help the analyst here if he has been involved in or advised of negotiations with suppliers. From his cost records he may also be able to provide an indication of how purchase prices behave seasonally even if they are not directly controllable. In addition, some system variables may be closely controllable, but an examination of the cost records may indicate that even lax control here does not significantly increase costs. However, the analyst should not fall into the trap of thinking that all key variables which are quantifiable have been captured in the existing accounting system.

The next stage in the model formulation process is often left implicit by OR authors, but it is an important step. After the initial investigation of the problem area the analyst should always question whether the system is well-enough defined to enable a mathematical model to be formed and, in addition, the scale of benefits and costs likely to result from the OR work. At this stage costs and benefits can only be crudely assessed, but some attempt should be made to assess them. The OR exercise itself can be costly in man-hours and computer time and these resources can often be put to alternative use. In addition such estimates, though crude, may play some part in the measurement of long-term efficiency of the OR unit itself — if one exists. One factor always difficult to evaluate is, not surprisingly, the possible indirect benefits resulting from the OR activity. The process of merely questioning departmental managers may itself be productive by getting departments to examine their activities more closely and think about ways in which they may themselves improve their performance. Any likely benefit of this sort will depend very much on the type of OR investigation being made and one cannot generalise in a meaningful way.

The final step in the model formulation is that usually most closely identified with OR — the construction of the mathematical model itself. The accountant has probably very little to offer in the way of mathematical expertise. The analyst will probably consider first whether any of the standard OR models are suitable for the problem at hand and, if not, will formulate a new form of mathematical procedure specifically for the problem. In the case of the ingredient mix problem, he might well choose linear programming as a method to minimise material costs subject to satisfying constraints on the minimum quantities of each material required for each product. He will also need to consider whether the model should be *deterministic* or *stochastic*. In a deterministic system the relationships between variables are clearly established such that, for any given set of input values, the outcome is certain provided that the model accurately reflects the real world deterministic system. On the other hand, in the majority of real-world problems, it is important completely to identify and quantify all variables and their inter-relationships and, consequently, it is impossible to say that for a given set of parameter values any specific outcome will definitely result. The best that one may be able to do is to state the probability attached to different outcomes for different parameter sets. Such a model would be stochastic. While the accountant may not be able to advise on mathematical methods, he may well be able to comment usefully on the appropriate general form of the model.

While the accountant may not be skilled in mathematics, he should be kept closely informed of the type of model being used by the OR analyst if he is to help significantly in testing the model and monitoring its implementation — and this is where the accountant has most to offer. It is arguable that the OR analyst can merely ask the accountant for relevant data in order to determine parameter values and test data in the model validation stages. The OR analyst may even provide precise definitions of the way in which costs and quantities are to be interpreted. However, in practice, this is where the accountant and operations researcher are most likely to confuse each other — perhaps quite unknowingly. The majority of OR analysts have nothing more than an introductory knowledge of cost accounting and its associated terminology or of the problems faced by accountants in designing their cost systems and the objectives that accountants have in mind. Similarly, the majority of accountants have little knowledge of the mathematical models used by OR analysts. Assuming that both sides have a willingness to listen and learn (an assumption made with some hesitation), each should take the trouble to explain to the other the exact nature of the different concepts. The accountant may not need to grasp the mathematical technique by which the model is solved, but he should familiarise himself with the model structure and its input and output characteristics. It is not good enough for him to leave it to the OR analyst to ask for what he wants. The scope for confusion over perceptions of terms like marginal cost, full cost, overheads, direct costs, profit contributions, etc., are considerable and the model will only be reliable if the input data is appropriately specified. Moreover, even if there is no 'language problem', the chances are that the accounting records in use will not yield the precise type of information the OR analyst requires. Liaison with the accountant should be encouraged to see how this information may then be best approximated or collected in the cheapest way.

Once the test data has been applied to the model, an OR analyst will continue developing the model until he is satisfied and then make proposals to the relevant company committee for its implementation. At this stage there should also be an analysis of the costs and benefits attached to alternative (e.g. traditional) methods of taking such a decision and the accountant will obviously want to be involved at this point and to be consulted over the criteria for determining acceptability. Moreover, at this stage of events, if the OR analyst and the accountant have been working in close liaison, the latter should be able to help considerably in explaining and 'selling' the OR method to the senior company officials who are responsible for making the decision. The accountant traditionally occupies a central role in the presentation of information to top level executives and this position could be invaluable in assisting the progress of scientific decision-making within the organisation. Indeed, if the organisation has senior accountants with a 'progressive outlook', a strong argument could be established that the technical OR analysts should be part of the managerial accounting function. Paradoxically perhaps, the successful development of 'scientific decision-making' in companies seems to depend very much on the *personalities* of the OR analysts, accountants and other interested parties.

In major stage C, the operation of the model has to be monitored. This surely is an accounting function and the plain truth is that most current accounting systems are ill-equipped to provide this service. As stated earlier, conventional cost accounting uses concepts which are likely to be different from the strictly marginal figures often required for many OR models. If the models are likely to be in repetitive use, the accounting system must, therefore, be modified to provide data on actual performance which is consistent in concept with that used in the model. Consequently, parameter input values must be compared with actual values; and in order to evaluate the forecasting element of the model, output must be compared with outputs predicted by the model and reasons for differences examined. These reasons are only likely to be identified by investigating key differences and the accountant with his experience of variance accounting is well placed to perform this function — although he will need to be flexible and not adopt a 'blinkered' view, insisting on a conventional standard costing analysis of variances.

Finally, if the model is not performing reasonably, costs and benefits of operating the model must be reviewed again and if necessary the mathematical model will be abandoned or modified by returning to the model formulation stage.

The existing state of OR vs. accounting in practice

The previous section referred to the process of OR and the part that the accountant *should* play in it. The real-world application of OR leaves much to be desired in terms of close liaison with the accounting function — despite the fact that OR can no longer be considered as something new and trendy, which might not persist. In practice, one may levy general criticisms of both OR and accounting. Accountants do not get involved in the detail of OR applications in the way that would considerably increase their usefulness. OR analysts on the other hand are often criticised for concentrating too much upon the mathematical formulation of the model with less regard for problem boundary definition, correct measurement of costs, feasibility in operation and monitoring performance. Evidence for these assertions based on reliable research is scarce, but anyone concerned with this field of study will be aware of discussions with accountants and OR analysts which included comments of this type.

Recommended reading in this topic is an unpublished Ph.D. thesis written by A. Noor at the University of Sheffield[1], which attempted to measure the impact of developments in electronic data processing and OR upon accountants and the effect of accountants on these new disciplines. After a series of case studies, personal interviews and mailed questionnaires collecting the views of over 700 persons in management accounting, data processing and OR, Noor concludes that accountants only tend to use, or get involved in, OR and computer-based models falling within a narrow range of well structured, deterministic models normally confined within the boundaries of functional departments. Noor explains this as due to a lack of mutual understanding between accountants and OR specialists, which in turn is due to the differences in background and training of the two groups, insufficient appreciation by accountants of the beneficial effects of interdisciplinary contributions, and incompatibilities between the two groups in terms of functional procedures, conventions, practices and normal time horizons. Noor wisely stresses that sweeping generalities should be avoided and that one should not assume that all organisations illustrate these features. However, he found sufficient cases to state that these conclusions are observable in many organisations. One the other hand Noor points out that the gloomy picture portrayed by much earlier literature — i.e. that accountants are concerned to maintain their status in organisations and also to block the development of OR, by withholding data or, at least, impeding its extraction — is not well founded. The slow progress made to date in truly inter-disciplinary OR including collaboration with accountants, therefore, appears to be due to educational defects as much as anything. This can be deduced from the results of tests Noor conducted on 174 persons on 60 different behavioural indicators. The tests resulted in the general conclusions outlined above, but also referred to more specific factors such as the 'over-selling' of OR by the OR specialists so that hopes were raised beyond those which could be satisfied, clear indications of inconsistent terminology, the concern of accountants for day-to-day activities and speedy provision of information on current activities, lack of recognition of the part which OR could play in improving accounting practice — i.e. the view that OR has little to offer accountants who are concerned with routine reporting activities. Accountants questioned did not, on the whole, feel jealous of the new discipline nor threatened by it. It seemed clear that accountants were the clear authorities in the company regarding stock exchange regulations, taxation and statutory regulations and reports. Most accountants were not anti-OR but seemed passive towards it — OR does not help them in their specific tasks, so they were not greatly concerned.

Noor's thesis has been referred to at some length because it has taken an important step towards explaining a paradox. An earlier section showed that in order to achieve the full benefits of OR, accountants (amongst others) should be involved. Accounting 'academic literature' in the last two decades has become increasingly mathematical and rigorous in content, such that a visitor from Mars who read nothing but the leading accounting journals would immediately think that practising accountants were not only involved in OR processes, but that accountants were also actively pushing back the frontiers of knowledge in mathematical modelling in accounting and allied fields. However, while certainly considerable practical advances have been made in some fields (in particular, the control of capital expenditures through PERT/Cost, and the recent developments in corporate modelling), most professional accountants (of all types) are *not* playing an active role in such developments. The answer lies, according to Noor, in the different nature of the tasks the accountant is expected to perform compared to the OR analyst — this indicates a lack of top management perception of the OR process, inadequate education of accountants in OR and of OR specialists in accounting. The professional accounting institutes have now introduced aspects of OR into their syllabuses and this is an important step forward — but there is the danger that a brief exposure to a set of OR standard techniques will bore student accountants just as much as routine double-entry procedures. Accountants need to be educated in *the process of decision-making* which OR offers. It is a rational *approach* to decision-making *within which accounting rules of thumb will definitely figure prominently if they are cost effective.* In fact, accounting researchers might gain much by adopting a framework for research into accounting based upon figure 1, except that the relevant accounting model would be inserted. This may or may not be a 'mathematical' one.

The impact of OR on accounting literature

It was concluded above that OR has not contributed significantly to the *general* development of accounting practice so far. However, with appropriate education the situation could change. What would be the results of such changes? The first obvious development would be involvement of accountants in a decision-making process in the way described earlier. However, that has been sufficiently described already. To gain additional insight into what might happen to existing accounting processes, one can look at the leading academic journals. Academics, presumably motivated to a large extent by the acquisition of knowledge for its own sake (certainly not by monetary reward in UK universities!), are free of necessity to persuade people that their schemes should be immediately implemented in order to justify their existence. They are, therefore, more able to spend time devising accounting models with a rigorous mathematical basis. Unfortunately, too high a proportion of them remain untested in practical application, but there is a clear tendency towards a greater advocation of such models. Mattesich[2], writing in 1966, stated that the *Accounting Review*, vol. 34 (1959), contained just two articles which would be described as mathematical; whereas there were 14 in 1964. In the two latest copies of that journal, which happened to be at hand at the time of writing, there are five of the nine in the July 1976 issue and nine out of 14 in the October 1976 issue. While one could easily get involved in arguments over what is a 'mathematical article', it is at least clear that the proportion of such articles has roughly doubled over the last decade and increased from virtually zero percent to now account for the majority of articles published. Other leading accounting journals show a similar trend.

The range of mathematical applications to accounting is rapidly becoming extended. Earlier applications tended to concentrate upon topics such as linear programming and simulation applications to product mix and budget systems, statistical sampling for auditors, differences between full and direct costing systems, matrix methods of cost allocations, developments of break-even analysis, inventory applications, critical path analysis and opportunity costing. These were followed in the later 1960's by more sophisticated developments of standard costing based on linear programming, integrated forecasting and operating evaluation systems, input-output analysis for cost accounting, models for planning and control in divisionalised organisations, corporate models, etc. More recently, the literature of the first half of the 1970's seems to have concerned itself much more with stochastic models, testing the usefulness of accounting reports for prediction purposes (e.g. for insolvency or stock market performance), with examining the part which accounting has to play in efficient stock markets, and with developments of information theory and its relation to accounting, as well as further developments of topics listed above for the 1960's. This list is not comprehensive — it cannot be without listing and classifying the articles in the leading academic journals. Readers can merely glance at a few years copies of *Accounting Review, Journal of Accounting Research, Abacus*, etc., to see the validity of these statements. In short, there is no shortage of ideas emanating from the academic world for the development of more rigorous accounting methods. However, the gap between the academic and the practising world has yet to be effectively bridged. Meanwhile it appears that OR has affected academics operating in the accounting field far more than accounting practitioners. Perhaps this is not surprising. It often takes several decades for developments in the academic world to be sifted and then percolate through to widespread practical application. Nevertheless, there have been various indications recently that professional accountants are gradually becoming more prepared to carry out a fundamental and rigorous reappraisal of their existing priorities. Notable among these have been *Exposure Draft 18* and *The Corporate Report*. It has also been apparent that such fundamental reappraisals can easily give rise to much confusion and many misunderstandings. Given the current trend for fundamental re-thinking of existing practices, perhaps OR offers a basic approach for tackling this area so that debates and controversies can relate clearly to the relevant part of the process involved in coming to a decision regarding the adoption or rejection of new proposals. However, what is more relevant for this paper, students should be warned that few of the mathematical accounting models that they read about in the leading academic accounting journals will be found in the companies they are employed in when they leave university. They, therefore, have ample opportunity to help the accountancy profession to bring about a significant change in its practices.

References

1 A. E. E. Noor, *Accountants — EDP and Management Science / Operational Research Specialists' Relationships: an empirical investigation with special reference to British industry*. PhD thesis, University of Sheffield, July, 1975 (unpublished).
2 R. Mattesich, 'The impact of EDP and management scheme upon accounting theory', in M. Backer (ed.), *Modern Accounting Theory* Prentice-Hall 1966.

Suggested further reading

R. A. Ackoff, *Scientific Method*, Wiley 1962.

S. Beer, 'Operational research and accounting', *Operational Research Quarterly*, March 1954.

R. V. Hartley, 'Operations research and its implications for the accounting profession', *The Accounting Review*, April 1968.

Y. Ijiri & R. K. Jaedicke, 'Mathematics and accounting', in M. Backer (ed.) *Modern Accounting Theory*, Prentice-Hall 1966.

J. L. Livingstone, *Management Planning and Control: Mathematical Models*, McGraw-Hill 1970.

R. Mattesich, *Accounting and Analytical Methods*, Irwin 1964.

R. C. Tomlinson, *Inaugural Address* as President of the OR Society, January 1974.

15

Accounting and organisational behaviour

ANTHONY G HOPWOOD

Fellow, Oxford Centre for Management Studies

Accounting systems play a crucial role in the functioning of today's large and complex organisations. By reporting on the economic success, or otherwise, of prior actions they can help to create an element of conscious continuity and engender a concern with learning and improvement. The decisions of managers and employees can be shaped by the information which they produce. And they provide means through which the diverse activities of different parts of the organisation can be more readily integrated and controlled. Accounting systems help to bring the actions, and more particularly, the economic consequences of the actions, of lower level managers and employees to the attention of organisational superiors, and the intentions of the superiors, in turn, are communicated throughout the organisation in the form of plans and budgets.

Although accounting is often seen as being only a means of attaining wider ends, the systems and the conceptual frameworks on which they are based can in these ways have a powerful influence on the delineation of the ends themselves. In helping to highlight the financial consequences of organisational functioning, accounting can orientate actions towards economic ends and the interests of those in society who might benefit from this.

Real though such a view of the organisational roles of accounting may be, it differs substantially from the predominant technical view that we still have of accounting. We concern ourselves with the different ways of accounting for costs and the relative advantages and disadvantages of the various approaches to the measurement of divisional performance in ways that invariably are divorced from the context of accounting in action. The accountant's interest in the management of investment still focusses on the technicalities of the final financial appraisal rather than on the ways in which accounting information influences the definition of problems by organisational participants, the derivation of viable alternatives and the informal ways in which projects are shaped and evaluated throughout their organisational history. Flexible and probabilistic approaches to both budgeting and investment appraisal are studied but usually in a way that removes them from any wider consideration of the role of planning processes in uncertain environments. Indeed the very difficulties of the accounting technology, and perhaps its own aesthetic attractiveness, tend to distract attention from the organisational roles and purposes that the technology can and does serve.

Such a technical orientation is a feature of both theoretical and practical discourse. Perhaps it is to be expected that in an academic environment problems are considered in ways that remove them from the specifics of organisational functioning. For the world of practice, however, our expectations might be different. But so many accounting systems are designed, changed and extended by specialists working in specialist departments and subject to specialist values and norms. Rather than being the result of ongoing managerial debate, the technical designs of many accounting systems are shaped in isolation from the world of organisational action. They might be subjected to very different criteria of evaluation than those prevailing in academic institutions, but the invisible walls of professional specialisation can be no less restricting than the more visible edifices that surround the ivory tower.

However, it is increasingly important that we should have a wider organisational view of the role of accounting. For whilst particular accounting techniques might remain problematic, increasing consideration is being given to the effect which the techniques, in combination, have on managerial consciousness and actions, and on the broader social as well as economic effectiveness of the organisation as a whole.

Does the emphasis of present accounting systems on retrospective reporting, it is now being asked, help to instil in managers and employees a concern with the short-term performance of the organisation to the detriment of its longer term viability? Can management accounting systems, being both influential and oriented towards reporting on the internal functioning of an organisation, help to weaken the significance of the very informational linkages to the wider environment that serve to provide the direction for longer term change and survival? And when that environment is uncertain and changing, how can accounting systems continue to provide organisational participants with the information they need? How much of the environmental uncertainty ought the systems to absorb, so protecting managers and employees from it, and how much ought they to convey to the managers and employees, so helping them to cope with it? And how can today's accounting systems adapt to the requirements of emerging forms of organisation that aim to facilitate the process of management in these more uncertain environments? While accounting systems have helped to reinforce the concerns of functional and divisional structures of management, facilitating, in the process, the operation of hierarchical pressures, can they service the more complex and often competing requirements of matrix and network organisations? In other words, can accounting systems be designed that consciously try to facilitate the exercise of local initiative and autonomy rather than subjecting them all too readily to hierarchical influence and control?

Such questions, and many others like them, are starting to become a more important part of management discourse. All of them have important implications for the design and operation of particular accounting techniques. But their consideration requires a view of accounting that goes beyond the mechanics of particular techniques or even their underlying economic or financial framework. It requires a way of looking at the role that accounting plays in organisational action and those human and social processes through which accounting systems influence managerial perceptions and decisions.

An emerging organisational perspective

The emerging interest in the behavioural and organisational aspects of accounting is itself a reflection of the need for a wider view of the accounting process. Not too surprisingly much of the initial work in the area concentrated on defining the extent of the problem. And the resulting documentation of the conflicts created by the use of accounting systems and the subsequent managerial manipulation and fiddling provided a vivid insight into human anxieties and ingenuity. Subsequent scholars tried to move beyond mere documentation, however. At first, given their commitment to the accounting mission and the inevitable desire for early results, the tendency was to look for ways in which existing accounting technologies could be made more acceptable and hence more influential. Participation, in the budgeting process especially, tended to become one rallying cry of the faithful. Others, in contrast, sought to demonstrate the motivational potentiality of budgets imposed from above.

Later it was realised, however, that the complexities of organisational life were inevitably incompatible with the discovery of easy and readily generalisable solutions. Influenced by related inquiries undertaken by those interested in organisational behaviour, accounting scholars are now starting to explore how the impact of accounting systems is moderated by both the process of decision-making in organisations and those features of the organisational mission, structure, technology and environment that serve to delineate the organisation itself.

What is starting to emerge from these enquiries is a view of accounting that questions the easy organisational processes assumed in so many discussions of accounting techniques. 'The provision of relevant information for decision-making', 'accounting for control' and 'accounting to motivate superior performance' may be easy enough phrases to use, but the underlying processes of decision-making, control and motivation are complex and the accounting techniques and the organisational processes which surround them cannot be seen as readily identifiable and separable parts of these processes. They represent just one of the ways in which organisational participants seek to manage the movement of the organisation in a more predictable manner through time and accordingly they need to be seen as integral parts of organisational functioning. Although our frameworks for doing this remain tentative, and also are clearly different from those enshrined in accounting textbooks, they do offer some potential for providing a basis for appreciating how ongoing organisations do design and use accounting systems and how, in turn, accounting systems might be designed to serve differing organisational needs.

Accounting and information processing in organisations

Organisations exist in environments rich in information. Changing markets and technologies and changing social, economic and political circumstances result in organisations being bombarded with information. And their survival and development depend not only on how they seek to manage the information which they receive from their environment but also, as is illustrated in figure 1, on how they manage the information which they both want and are required to provide to their environment and their own internal flows of information.

The management of information is an important activity for any organization and it is an activity characterised by both problems and choices. Not only does the processing of information have costs as well as benefits but also, by pursuing different information strategies, an organisation can consciously or unconsciously change the nature of its management process and its absolute and relative awareness of both the prevailing external circumstances and its own internal functioning.

Do, for instance, the information strategies emphasise the internal functioning of the organisation rather than creating a greater awareness of the external environment? And what aspects of the internal functioning do they stress? Do short-term consequences of decisions receive more attention than estimates of longer term impacts? Are

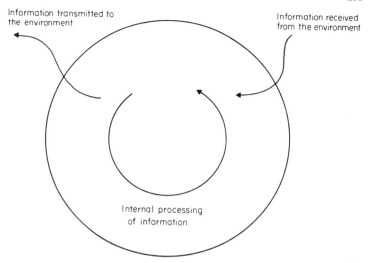

Information transmitted to the environment

Information received from the environment

Internal processing of information

Figure 1   The organization's informational context

economic consequences emphasised rather than operational or social consequences? And who gets to know of the economic consequences?

Such choices are significant because they can affect the pattern of organisational strategy and performance over time. In a study of insurance companies, for instance, the extent to which different companies strove to make visible the consequences of previous decisions was strongly related to differences in their financial performance.[1] And in a series of studies of hospitals the emphasis placed on making medical and economic consequences of decisions more visible, and on making the relative balance between the two more obvious, has been found to be related to the economic and medical performance of the hospitals.[2,3,4]

The problems of information processing in conditions of great uncertainty and rapid change are particularly severe. In order to respond and adapt to change, the organisation needs to assimilate and process a great deal of environmental information. To continue to function adequately, however, it needs to process the environmental information selectively and to be ever more sure of its own internal functioning. Its information strategy must become, in other words, a way in which it can both respond to and reduce the uncertainty, and obviously the choice of methods for achieving these differing ends and the balance between them can be crucial.

Consider, for example, an organisation facing an increasingly threatening economic environment. In such 'newly poor' conditions[5] it is common for organisations to strive for greater internal efficiency. Information systems which place greater emphasis on cost control, resource utilisation and the management of financial resources in particular are introduced.[6] Indeed, it was precisely under such conditions that the pioneering efforts in cost accounting took place.[7] But such strategies also need to be pursued with care, for the balance between internal and external visibility can, in the process, easily be shifted towards the former at a time when the organisation's longer term effectiveness may depend on a sensitive awareness and appreciation of external changes and possibilities. Efficient to the end, the organisation may still walk to its financial grave!

Similar choices are created by inflationary conditions. Changing prices, wage rates, costs and interest rates can, and certainly have in recent years, placed severe pressures on management accounting systems. The effectiveness of important mechanisms for creating internal visibility and regularity has thereby been challenged. But how should management accounting systems respond to such changes? Should, for instance, all the standards, budgets and plans be changed quickly and frequently? In this way, by readily reflecting the external changes, the accounting systems would protect managers and employees from a great deal of the environmental uncertainty. Budgets and plans would always be up to date. The internal integrity of the accounting systems would be preserved and budgets, for example, could still be used as instruments for management control. But at what cost? By allowing the mechanics of the management accounting system to absorb the uncertainty, might not this approach result in lower managerial and employee awareness of the total impact of inflation on the organization? And if this is the case, might not managers and employees be tempted merely to assimilate the changes rather than positively cope with them?

The way in which external uncertainty and inflation can influence the need for information processing suggests, moreover, that information needs are neither the same for all organisations nor static over time. They can and do vary across organisations, in different parts of the same organisation and over time. Organisations have, in other words, different information intensities. Those operating in highly uncertain environments, with complex technologies and management structures and a large number of interdependent sub-units, have a particularly high need for information processing.[8] With more certain environments, relatively simpler technologies and low internal interdependence, the need is much less.

Even if the need for information processing is high, however, organisations can still seek to reduce the need rather than strive to meet it directly. They can, for instance, create relatively autonomous sub-units which have a large number of internal informational linkages but a smaller flow of information to the rest of the organization. Many accounting profit and investment centres serve such a role. Organisations can also reduce their need for information processing by reducing their performance standards or expectations. On first sight such a strategy might appear undesirable. It is, however, a rather common one. But rather than consciously striving to lower their performance, organisations approach the problem by investing in costly surplus capacity, stocks and 'slack' resources. Production scheduling, for instance, requires less information processing when surplus productive capacity exists; similarly for manpower scheduling. And stocks of work-in-progress and finished goods can reduce the need for information exchanges between different production departments, for instance, and between the production and marketing functions.

Alternative strategies also exist where an organisation strives to satisfy a high need for information processing. Some of the alternatives involve the use of routine ways of processing information; others rely on non-routine approaches. Some are under the influence of the organisation's senior management; others reflect the

	ROUTINE	NON ROUTINE
Official information processing	Accounting systems Production control systems Materials managerial systems etc.	Ad-hoc requests Access to information Structural changes — task forces, liaison managers and matrix structures
Unofficial information processing	"Black books" "Just-in-case files"	"The grape vine"

Figure 2   Alternative approaches to information processing

unofficial attempts of other participants in the organisation to satisfy their own information needs either by the creation of their own routine 'black books' and 'just-in-case-files'[9] or by the use of more informal sources such as the 'grape vine'. Rather than pursuing a given information strategy, the organisation as a whole has some discretion in choosing between the broad alternatives illustrated in figure 2.[10]

Official routine information systems include most management accounting systems, production control systems and information systems for materials management. The senior management of an organization can, however, strive to satisfy a need for information by establishing non-routine ways of processing it. Investments can be made in the capability to satisfy ad-hoc requests for information, access into information sources and data-banks can be facilitated by both mechanical and organisational means and the organisation can also attempt to facilitate the informal exchange of information by changing the structure of management relationships. Committees and temporary task forces serve as means for processing information as do liaison managers, contact men and more comprehensive moves to establish a matrix of interlocking management relationships in the organisation.[8]

Interestingly, while routine approaches to official

information processing, including accounting systems, tend to result in hierarchical patterns of dissemination, the non-routine approaches tend to place greater emphasis on the horizontal dissemination of information. Such a difference is not, however, necessarily inherent in the nature of the alternative approaches. Rather, it again reflects the outcome of organisational choices. For even routine information systems can be and are now being designed to consciously encourage the exercise of self-control by organisational participants rather than merely facilitate the exercise of control by others. The unofficial 'black books' have, in other words, their official equivalents in information systems that have been designed to assist in the management of matrix organisations,[11] the planning and control functions of semi-autonomous working groups[12] and the operation of more participatively managed enterprises.[13,14] That routine information systems in many of today's organisations emphasise the vertical rather than the horizontal dissemination of information, reflects the broader organisational and social roles that such systems serve.

For at present the official routine accounting systems might play an equal if not greater role in trying to influence prevailing organisational consciousness than in providing the information that can be used for making particular decisions.[15,16] They might, in other words, strive to influence the criteria used in decision-making rather than the specific information inputs. However, that is not to say that such a role is unimportant. Far from it. Processes that help to establish consciousness are vitally important in all human societies. And means for helping to establish the dominance of economic interests are particularly important because in using technologies that neutralise and legitimise the social origins of the economic interests they can play a vital social role — a role, in fact, that all industrial societies have acknowledged by conferring professional status on accountants.

The role which accounting systems play in organisational functioning is thereby determined by a series of conscious or unconscious organisational and social choices. It reflects both the relative emphasis given to external and internal processing of information and the

choice of particular approaches to internal and external
information processing. These choices not only reflect the
availability of suitable information processing technologies and strategies but also the broader strategy of the
organisation, the desired nature of the management process
and those social and organisational factors which determine the distribution of power and influence in
organisations.

Organisations wishing to place a great deal of emphasis
on reducing the impact of external uncertainty need do little
to stimulate an awareness of environmental phenomena.[17]
They can place relatively greater emphasis on the
processing of internally generated information[18,19] and even
strive to protect the operation of their internal information
systems from environmental disturbances. Even then,
however, they have considerable discretion in selecting
which aspects of the internal functioning to highlight.
Should management accounting systems play a dominant
role in creating economic visibility? Or should equal or
greater consideration be given to creating operational or
social visibility?[20] Those organisations which, in contrast,
seek to respond, adapt or even change and exploit their
environment need to give relatively greater priority to the
establishment of information linkages with the external
environment.

The choice of a particular approach to information processing also reflects preferences as to the nature of the
management process.[21] Is, for instance, the emphasis to be
placed on standardisation, the specification of operating
procedures and associated mechanisms for ensuring
internal regularity?[22] And are the major means for
processing information to facilitate the exercise of either
vertical or specialist patterns of control?[23] Or should greater
consideration be given to more organic approaches to
information processing with multiple, overlapping and
even competing information channels?[24,25,26] And what are
the implications of this for the exercise and distribution of
power in the organisation?

Such issues are crucial for accounting. For rather than
seeing the accounting art as being the mere imposition of a
given technology, they provide a basis for seeing the design
of an accounting system as being part of an organisation's

approach to both information processing and the derivation of a desirable management process and strategy.
Accounting cannot, in other words, be seen in isolation. Its
organisational role and significance is the outcome of a
series of organisational choices and if the accounting perspective is to provide a sound organisational basis for
making such choices, it must be broadened beyond its
current technical orientation.

The use of accounting information

The mere existence of accounting information does not
ensure whether or how it is used. For the way in which
information is used by managers and employees is itself the
outcome of a personal and social process. The same
information can convey different meanings to different
persons dependent on their previous experiences, the
context in which they are working and their own
information processing abilities. Moreover, the effect of any
information on organisational functioning is dependent
not only upon the interpretation given to the information
but also upon those personal and organisational factors
that influence a person's propensity to act. Changed awareness can often be different from modified action. The social
nature of the organisation can also determine if and how
managers and employees use accounting information. For
the meaning given to information is associated with the
roles of both the sender and the receiver and the way in
which it relates to the ongoing social process.

Accordingly, different people can use the same
information in different ways with different implications
for organisational behaviour and performance. In a study of
the use of budgetary control information in managerial performance evaluation, for example, it was found that some
managers tended to use the accounting information rigidly,
taking it at its face value on a short-term basis, whilst others
used the information in a more flexible way, integrating it
with other formal and informal sources of information.[9,27,28,29] Other managers, on the other hand, tended not
to use the information for this purpose. They were the
rejectors rather than the believers and users of information.

The different ways in which the information was used

had very different consequences for the organisation. Whilst both the rigid and flexible users of the accounting information succeeded in instilling greater financial awareness in their subordinates than the rejectors of the information, the rigid use also resulted in very high personal anxiety and tension. And to reduce this the subordinates tried to manipulate the budget reports and place the blame for poor budget results on their colleagues. For a highly inter-dependent operation such behaviour could have costly consequences if the ensuing rivalries and conflicts impair the overall integration of the different operations.

However important the implications of differential use may be, changing the way accounting information is used is a difficult endeavour. The way in which information is used is a reflection of both more general approaches to management and the prevailing organisational climate.[9] Attempts to change patterns of both management and employee use of information must accordingly focus on the underlying features of organisational life that precede and motivate the designs of accounting systems, the process by which they are designed,[30,31] the managerial and organisational roles that the systems are perceived to serve and manager's interpretative skills. In the absence of such a fundamental examination of the accounting function, existing patterns of use may have to be regarded as a constraint on accounting system design.

Conclusion

An organisational view of accounting provides the possibility of moving beyond the constraining technical orientation to the subject that has dominated so much of professional and scholarly dialogue, to a view of accounting that emphasises the organisational and social roles that the technology serves and the human processes through which it becomes effective.

Perhaps it should be stated that the approach outlined in this chapter seeks to match the complexity of accounting design decisions in practice. Accounting systems are complex, multifaceted and often tailored to fit the differing requirements of different organisations. They do relate to other information processing strategies and they do vary as they serve different managerial purposes. In the ongoing organisational world, it should be remembered, important accounting and information choices are made that only are rarely, if ever, reflected in the traditional accounting textbooks.

It is important that we should try to understand the complexities of accounting in action. Not only will this provide us with a basis for improving existing practice but also, as new organisational, technological and social pressures impinge on accounting, it should provide us with some basis for responding in a considered manner.

References

1 S. W. Becker and D. Neuheuser, *The Efficient Organization*, Elsevier 1975.
2 G. Gordon, C. P. Tanon and E. V. Morse, 'Decision-making criteria and organization performance', in S. M. Shortell and M. Brown (eds) *Organizational Research in Hospitals*, Blue Cross Association 1976, pp. 62-71.
3 E. V. Morse, G. Gordon and M. Moch, 'Hospital costs and quality of care: an organisational perspective', *Milbank Memorial Fund Quarterly*, Summer 1974, pp. 315-346.
4 S. M. Shortell, S. W. Becker and D. Neuheuser, 'The effects of management practices on hospital efficiency and quality of care', in S. M. Shortell and M. Brown (eds) *Organizational Research in Hospitals*, Blue Cross Association 1976.
5 C. Olofsson and P. A. Svalander, *The Medical Services Change Over to a Poor Environment — 'New Poor' Behaviour*, Linköping University, n.d.
6 P. N. Khandwalla, 'The effects of different types of competition on the use of management controls', *Journal of Accounting Research*, Autumn 1972, pp. 275-285.
7 S. Pollard, *The Genesis of Modern Management*, Arnold 1965.
8 J. Galbraith, *Designing Complex Organizations*, Addison-Wesley 1973.
9 A. G. Hopwood, *An Accounting System and Managerial Behaviour*, Saxon House 1973.
10 A. G. Hopwood, *Accounting and Human Behaviour*, Accountancy Age Books 1974.
11 A. G. Hopwood, 'Designing information systems for matrix organizations', in K. Knight (ed.), *Matrix Management*, Gower Press 1977.
12 J. Wickings, 'Putting it together: the patient, the purse and the practice', *The Lancet*, 29 January 1977, pp. 239-240.
13 A. Magnusson, *Participation and the Company's Information and Decision Systems*, Working Paper 6022, Economic Research Institute, Stockholm School of Economics 1974.

14   E. Mumford and H. Sackman (eds), *Human Choice and Computers*, North-Holland 1975.

15   S. Jönsson and R. Lundin, *Role and Function of Myths for Planning — A Case of Local Government*, Working Paper 52, Department of Business Administration, University of Gothenburg 1975.

16   DR Scott, *The Cultural Significance of Accounts*, Reprinted by Scholars Bank Co. 1973.

17   J. G. March and H. A. Simon, *Organizations*, Wiley 1958.

18   G. H. Hofstede, 'Cultural determinants of the avoidance of uncertainty in organizations', paper presented to the workshop on *Accounting in a Changing Social and Political Environment*, Oxford 1977.

19   H. R. Van Gunsteren, *The Quest for Control: A Critique of the Rational-Central-Rule Approach in Public Affairs*, Wiley 1976.

20   A. G. Hopwood, *Towards Assessing the Economic Costs and Benefits of New Forms of Work Organization*, International Institute for Labour Studies, Geneva 1977.

21   C. Argyris, 'Organizational learning and management information systems', *Accounting, Organizations and Society*, vol. 2. No. 2 1977.

22   C. Ballé, *Computers and Structural Changes in French Business Firms*, Working Paper, Centre de Sociologie des Organisations, Centre National de la Recherche Scientifique, Paris 1977.

23   N. Bjørn-Andersen and P. N. Pedersen, *Computer Systems as Vehicles for Changes in The Management Structure*, Working Paper 77-3, Information Systems Research Group, Copenhagen School of Economics and Business Administration 1977.

24   T. Burns and G. M. Stalker, *The Management of Innovation*, Tavistock Publications 1961.

25   P. Grinyer and D. Norburn, 'Planning for existing markets: perceptions of executives and financial performance', *Journal of the Royal Statistical Society*, Series A, 1975, pp. 70-97.

26   B. Hedberg and S. Jönsson, 'Designing semi-confusing information systems for organizations in changing environments', paper presented at the workshop on *Designing Management Accounting Systems in Changing Environments*, San Francisco 1976.

27   C. Cammann, 'Effects of the use of control systems', *Accounting, Organizations and Society*, 1976, pp. 301-314.

28   M. Rahman and A. M. McCosh, 'The influence of organisational and personal factors on the use of accounting information: an empirical study', *Accounting, Organizations and Society*, 1976, pp. 339-356.

29   D. G. Searfoss, 'Some behavioural aspects of budgeting for control: an empirical study', *Accounting, Organizations and Society*, 1976, pp. 375-385.

30   R. N. Alloway, *Temporary Management Systems: Application of a Contingency Model to the Creation of Computer Based Information Systems*, Stockholm School of Economics 1976.

31   B. de Brabander and A. Edström, *A Theory of Success of Information Systems Development Projects*, Working Paper 76-45, European Institute for Advanced Studies in Management, Brussels 1976.

16
Accounting and computers

JOHN WHITMAN
Lecturer in Accounting, University of Manchester

With all the talk of how much of a time-saver the computer is — how it can perform in minutes what would take thousands of men months to do — did you ever stop to realise that it would take 50 people working day and night for 200 years to make the same mistakes that an electronic computer can make in only two seconds? — Henry Matusow[1]

Introduction

In 1964 Sir Leon Bagrit, chairman of Elliott-Automation Ltd., gave the Reith lectures on BBC radio. The title of the series was 'The Age of Automation' and much of the discussion concerned the implications for society of the new and rapidly developing computer technology. It seemed to many at that time that machines would before long take over almost all the routine work, leaving human beings with the problem of how to stop themselves from getting bored. It would be important to educate people in how to fill their time with interesting and rewarding activities. Sir Leon advised against over-optimism — '. . . when we talk about leisure a little caution may not be out of place. In spite of all the optimistic prophesies, we are not going to get this greatly increased leisure overnight . . . . a working week of fifteen hours may take fifty years to arrive.'[2]

In 1977 the danger of getting into a situation where we have so much spare time that we do not know how to spend it seems less imminent. Computers are still a mystery to most people, but we do have a better idea of what they can and cannot achieve. Today the main problem which these machines seem to pose for society is how to limit the extent to which our privacy is threatened. The creation of large 'data-banks' containing masses of information about each member of the population is technically feasible and in a sense has begun already. At present, records of income and tax payments, medical, educational and employment histories, credit ratings, motor vehicle licensing and even finger-prints are stored separately on different computers. The individual is less threatened than if all this information was brought together so that it could be accessed quickly by any official who felt a need to consult it. Nonetheless, a society in which each citizen's actions could be monitored and controlled by an all-powerful state does not now seem hopelessly far-fetched.

For the accountant the computer raises other issues, as well as these broad social considerations. The computer is both a threat and a challenge to his profession. Many of the tasks which in the 1950's would have been done by an accountant and his staff, are now done in the data-processing department. The new professions of programming, systems analysis and operational research are fulfilling functions which would traditionally have been the prerogative of the accountants. On the other hand, the computer does represent an enormous advance in the technology available to help the accountant in his basic task — the provision of information to management to aid decision-making. It will be interesting to see to what extent he responds to this challenge.

We shall consider in this chapter the sort of tasks which the computer performs in a modern commercial enterprise. We shall discuss the ways in which data-processing technology is changing, and try to assess the implications of these changes for the future. It is difficult to make predictions, but one thing is certain — computers are here to stay and the better we understand them the easier it will be to keep their use confined to applications of which we approve.

The development of the use of computers

There are three stages in the development of computer use within a business organisation — clerical tasks, decision-oriented applications and finally the 'integrated management information system'. The first computers in business were mainly introduced to take over clerical work. Wage calculations and the preparation of weekly or monthly wage payment slips can be done much more efficiently on a computer than by a wages clerk, because they involve the repetition of many routine calculations and the printing of a large number of documents, all in the same format. Similarly, maintaining customer accounts, updating the balances for new orders and receipts, and preparing monthly statements are standard computer applications. In these uses the computer justifies itself on the basis that the clerical costs of the organisation are reduced (although it is not certain that the loss of goodwill which arises, for instance, from the sending of bills of £1900 to people who owe only £1.90, does not in some cases outweigh the clerical cost savings). Even the Institute of Chartered Accountants suffered problems with its computer in the first year it introduced computerised subscription records. The institute had to write to all its members explaining that it did not know whether they had paid their subscription or not, but if they had not done so, would they please send the money as soon as possible. Such teething problems are generally quickly overcome, and it is unlikely that anybody would relish going back to manual accounting systems — pens, ink and ledgers — to cope with the voluminous book-keeping work which is today done by computers.

The second stage of computer use is more difficult to describe, because it covers a wide variety of applications which include some element of decision-making. Some business decisions can be programmed so that the computer can, as it were, take decisions itself, although it is more accurate to say that the computer is responding to a set of rules provided to it by a programmer. An example of this sort of decision would be the identification of customers who appear to be over-extending their credit period and the sending of reminders to them to encourage prompt payment. Another sort of decision that the computer can make relatively easily is the re-ordering of stock. In an installation where all the stock records are maintained electronically the computer can, according to some defined rules, identify those stocks that are running low and request that they be re-ordered.

A further development in the decision-making type of application is one in which the computer provides information that would be difficult to obtain quickly and cheaply in any other way. For example, in planning future operations an analysis of sales trends by region and by product may be very informative. 'A case may be quoted in which a large chain store, for example, discovered that: large salesmen tend to be more successful in selling large sized garments, black underwear sells better in ports than in inland towns, large numbers of white gloves are sold in Liverpool but only a meagre amount is sold in Birmingham.'[3]

As a result of the use of computers a whole range of mathematical techniques which would probably not otherwise have been utilised, have thrived. These techniques can give management recommended solutions to problems such as the minimum cost at which blends can be produced which contain satisfactory levels of certain essential qualities (linear programming), the minimum cost at which a series of demands for supplies can be met from a number of warehouses at different locations (the transportation problem), the minimum time in which a project made up of several interdependent activities can be completed (critical path analysis). These are all operational research techniques, and are sometimes referred to as decision models. They can provide solutions to well-defined problems, but we must remember the programmer's old adage. Garbage in, Garbage out (GIGO) applies equally well to these techniques — the solution produced will only be as good as the information on which it is based.

Another approach which uses the computer as an aid to decision-making relates to the building of financial simulation models. If we imagine a firm preparing a budget for the coming year's operation, we will see that a number of assumptions go into its formulation, e.g. assumptions concerning productivity levels and levels of demand for the products of the firm, possible levels of selling prices and costs, and possible levels of fixed costs. A single budget will be based on one possible level for all these variable elements, but because the computer will allow the planners to manipulate information rapidly, it is possible to prepare the budget on the computer and to make changes to the assumptions before a final plan is agreed. This process is useful in several ways. First, it performs the function of sensitivity analysis. It identifies which are the critical assumptions and which are unimportant. Second, it allows the planners to experiment to try to find a plan which best meets the objectives of the enterprise. Third, the process of arranging and rearranging the assumptions will provide useful insights into the problems of managing the enterprise. The survey by Wooller and Grinyer[4] of the use of financial simulation models in British companies indicates that this is a computer application that is spreading rapidly.

It would be wrong to conclude a discussion of decision-oriented computer applications without mentioning forecasting. Decision-making is about predicting the outcomes of different courses of action and choosing the one that seems to lead to the best result. Statistical techniques which analyse past data and identify trends are widely used and this seems to be a fruitful area for further computerisation.

Management information systems

The third stage we will discuss relates to the integrated management information system. Let us begin by briefly describing what on-line, real-time information systems actually are. As computers have got bigger, quicker and more reliable the amount of work that they can perform has increased enormously. Instead of merely supporting one input device, for example a punch-card reader, and one output device, say a line-printer, they can now accept data and programs to be run from several sources and execute the programs in such a way that any user at any individual input device could be justified in assuming that he was the only person with access to the machine. For instance, the computers in the University of Manchester Regional Computer Centre now process programs for universities all over England, from Norwich to Lancaster, and get results back to these universities in a very few minutes, and sometimes in a few seconds.

One example of an on-line system which has found favour is the airline booking system which allows office clerks to check the availability of a seat on any flight in which the customer may be interested, and, if a seat is free, to make the reservation straight away. Similarly, banks are introducing terminals which allow bank-clerks to check the current balance on each customer's account even though the information may be stored on a computer many miles away.

All real-time on-line systems have in common the facility to receive, process and retrieve information quickly, for a number of different users at the same time. Each user is able to get the results he requires without any significant waiting time.

There are many applications in which this facility to produce information speedily is invaluable; for example there is a data-base in the United States of America called Toxline which contains information about all known poisons, their symptoms and antidotes. With a computer terminal in the United Kingdom this information can be accessed sufficiently quickly and sufficiently cheaply to save lives.

Should we therefore design *management* information systems on the basis of real-time computer systems? An integrated real-time management information system is one in which a large data base which contains all the information that a manager might conceivably want is permanently available on-line to the computer. This allows the manager to keep an immediate track of current operation and allows him to access statistical packages with which to make forecasts, by retrieving the data which form the bases for these forecasts directly from the data-base. It allows him to feed these forecasts into decision models and simulation models to try to solve particular management problems and predict the consequences of certain courses of action. The distinguishing factor of this type of system is the speed with which such information can be accessed, and the great volume of data which must be stored on magnetic discs to enable this to happen. It is unlikely that there is any firm which operates a system having all these functions, but it is technically quite feasible. One advantage of such a system might be the saving in paper — all important reports could be stored on the data-base, available for display on a visual display screen.

In the heady, optimistic days of the 1960's there was much talk of such real-time on-line integrated management information systems. Since computers were making the processing of information cheaper every year it seemed to be a logical development that eventually all the information that any manager could conceivably want would be stored permanently on a computer, available for rapid access from a terminal at a manager's desk.

There were a few dissenting voices. J. Dearden, writing in the Harvard Business Review in 1966[5] said 'It is my personal opinion that, of all the ridiculous things that have been foisted on the long-suffering executive in the name of science and progress, the real-time management information system is the silliest.' His main argument was that there were few decisions that a manager had to make which required information so quickly.

As with all computer applications, we have to be careful to distinguish between what is technically feasible and what is economically feasible. There is no doubt that large computers can store and process vast amounts of information and that they can support a number of terminals situated, if necessary, all over the world, which allow any user of a terminal immediate access both to the information that is stored and also to the computing power of the machine. If it was thought to be worthwhile, a company could train all its major decision-makers in the building and manipulation of decision models and simulation models. What is difficult to know is whether the decisions that would be made by these executives would be any better as a result of using these models; and if the decisions proved to be better, would they be sufficiently good to justify the cost of the sophisticated equipment that would have to be provided?

For a while the logic of the developing computer technology was to centralise data-processing in an organisation into one large computer installation. In this way economies of scale can be achieved and central management can have quick, cheap and regular access to much detailed information about the entire organisation. Management writers began to talk of the decline of middle management; they thought that the control functions exercised by middle management would be superseded by the computer. Very efficient control systems could be developed which, by a process of exception reporting, would generate information to notify top management of problems as they arose. In the first flush of enthusiasm for a new technology writers (and managers) assumed that computers were going to solve many problems overnight.

One problem that early advocates of integrated systems did not consider was the problem of incorporating the human dimension into the design of information systems. Much research has been undertaken in recent years on the way that human beings process information. Much more is now understood about the limitations to human information processing, for example the dangers of swamping human decision-makers with too much information, and the importance of attitudes to risk. Therefore even if it proved to be theoretically possible to design an integrated information system which could do away with the need for middle management, it may lead to more problems than previously. People need to feel that they have some sort of influence on the running of the organisation for which they work, and it is inevitable that if the major decisions are made by remote executives whose only contact with subsidiaries is by means of a computer, people will feel somewhat alienated.

There is much evidence to show that the way in which budgets are prepared and the way in which people's performance is measured and evaluated has a large influence on the level of that performance. Participation in standard setting will generally lead to higher performance, and information systems that allow people regularly to review the extent to which they are reaching agreed standards will reinforce good performance. These sorts of consideration must be included in the design specifications of information systems.

Perhaps it is because of the problems that manufacturers have found in recent years that the most successful machines are not any longer the large, powerful computers which require a great deal of centralised information processing to justify their cost, but rather smaller machines that do not need the airconditioned environments or the attendant highly trained staff of operators, programmers, systems analysts and engineers. The trend seems to be towards networks of computers — distributed processing. Each unit of a large organisation can have its own small computer to do clerical work and to provide the facility to use decision-models and simulation models. These small computers can be linked together by telephone lines so that data can be sent cheaply and quickly between different parts of the organisation. This allows central management to collect information with no loss of autonomy by middle management.

The design of information systems requires a number of different skills. It requires the ability to understand an increasingly sophisticated data-processing technology. It requires an understanding of sophisticated management decision-models. It requires an understanding of the way in which human beings process information and the way they make decisions. It requires an understanding of the most relevant findings of the organisational theorists, as well as an understanding of the types of accounting reports that have been developed by the accountants. This is a lot to ask and it seems unlikely that any one person will possess all these requisite skills. The successful accountant in the company of the future will be the man with the humility to realise that whatever his specialism, he is unlikely to know all the answers. The ability to communicate his own knowledge and the ability to listen to and appreciate the ideas which other specialists can bring will be equally important. We must not be blinded by expensive machines into thinking that the way to better decision-making is simply via the provision of quicker and cheaper information.

Relationship with the development of accounting

We can detect, in the three stages of computer applications, a parallel with the development of the accounting profession. Until recently the accountant (and also the general public) had seen the accountant's role as that of a clerk, keeping track of what has happened in the past, ensuring the accuracy of his figures to the nearest penny, but giving little thought to the relevance of the information for future planning. Now the accountant has had to face up to the fact that the type of information which he has provided in the past may not always be relevant information. The emphasis has shifted from one of accurate record-keeping to one of identifying the information which decision-makers need. In the last resort, however, this can only be a partial answer. Ultimately, the information-providing services within an organisation must be seen as a total system.

As accounting has established itself as an intellectual discipline in its own right, there has developed a need for a good working definition of the subject. The most widely accepted definition is probably that of the American Accounting Association: 'The process of identifying, measuring and communicating economic information to permit informed judgments and decisions by users of the information'[6]. This is a useful definition because it places the emphasis firmly on the need to clarify the purposes for which accounting information is prepared. It is logically impossible to choose between different accounting methods unless one has a clear idea for what purposes accounting information will be used. There is, however, a danger in seeing accounting as consisting solely of the satisfaction of particular decision situations with specific information needs. We may fall into the trap of thinking that we can supply all the information needs of every member of society. We must not ignore the costs of collecting, processing, storing and retrieving information. The accountant cannot simply go to each decision-maker and say 'Tell me what decisions you make and what information you need to make those decisions and I shall supply you with all the information you want'. The accountant must realise that because of the costs of supplying information, he may not be able to let each decision-maker have all the information that he might ideally wish to have. The real problem is not solely to provide information for decision-making, but to design and operate information systems which help the organisation to achieve its objectives with the limited resources at its disposal. This may involve a recognition that some decisions will have to be made on the basis of imperfect information.

Conclusion

Computers force the accountant to rethink some of his attitudes. He has to recognise that in many companies the most interesting work in his area is being done by the systems analysts. They are trying to design integrated information systems, and although the accountant may be consulted, unless he is prepared to invest time to familiarise himself with computer technology, he may find that he is being left further behind. On the other hand the trend towards mini-computers, which do not require the cossetting needed by their elder brothers, is a sign that the computer industry has learnt from some of the mistakes of the past, and is encouraging the move towards the use of more accessible computers that can be used easily by the layman. The question for the accountant is whether he wishes to keep his traditional responsibility for his company's information systems, or whether he is prepared to see his position undermined by the other professions that have invaded his traditional territory.

We have talked about the tendency to be over-optimistic in the 1960's. There may be a tendency to be over-pessimistic in the 1970's. There is now evidence to show that society is beginning to take seriously the problems caused by technology, and to look hard for solutions. The short-term advantages and long-term disadvantages of nuclear energy are being weighed against each other; concerted pressure by consumer action groups has resulted in improvements in safety regulations and emission levels for motor-cars; politicians have at last begun to discuss the problems raised by the threat to privacy of the accumulation of large amounts of personal information. Perhaps accountants have less to fear from the advancement of computer technology than they anticipate.

References

1 H. M. Matusow, *The Best of Business*, Wolfe Publishing 1968.
2 L. Bagrit, *The Age of Automation*, Weidenfeld and Nicolson 1965.
3 K. London, *Introduction to Computers*, Faber and Faber 1968.
4 P. H. Grinyer and J. Wooller, *Corporate Models Today*, Institute of Chartered Accountants in England and Wales 1975.

5   J. Dearden, 'The myth of real-time management information'
    Harvard Business Review, Vol. 44, 1966.
6   American Accounting Association, *A Statement of Basic Accounting
    Theory*, 1966. '

17

Directions into the future: the prospects for research

BRYAN CARSBERG

Professor of Accounting, University of Manchester

The previous chapters in this book have described the current state of accounting and have revealed some of the historical processes which brought it about. We have seen that accounting involves the provision of a service which must be adapted to the needs of society. The adaptation of the service has been imperfect but the influence of changing patterns of social need is nevertheless clear. Moreover, the problems which seem important in accounting at the present time are those which reflect corresponding problems in society.

The purpose of this concluding chapter is to review the present state of knowledge in accounting and to discuss developments which may be expected during the next few years. We shall attempt to identify some areas in which research is most urgently required and to suggest methods for carrying out the research. Inevitably, we must be selective and our discussion must be at a general level, ignoring detailed problems of research design. However, it is hoped to convey some impression of the potential of research in accounting. The subject is now poorly developed. It has little in the way of established theoretical structure to guide researchers — little, that is, that would be accepted as sound theory in other subjects. Recently,

275

however, researchers have shown how theories of
accounting may be constructed and in particular how
scientific method may be applied to the subject. Their work
opens up the way for the development of accounting and the
potential benefits to society are very great.

The recognition that accounting is a service which
responds to the needs of society, indicates that any
prescription for current research activity must be founded
on some view of current social needs. We shall discuss some
aspects of the economic environment with that in mind.
First, however, it may be as well to define the subject matter
of accounting in a way that will circumscribe the scope of
our speculations.

The nature of accounting

The definition of subject boundaries must always be
arbitrary to some extent. Moreover, a precise specification is
of limited importance. It is important that researchers
should devote themselves to problems the solution of which
has a high value to society. It is less important to specify
whether they are engaged in accounting or some other
subject at the time.

An economist, attempting to define his subject, once took
refuge in the thought that 'economics is what economists
do'. The difficulty in defining accounting suggests a similar
ruse, and such a definition would at least capture the
pragmatic point that subjects are defined partly to comprise
the range of activities which can (or could at one time) con-
veniently be carried out by a single person.

However, it will be useful if we can be rather more
explicit. All accounting activities seem to involve the
collection and analysis of information which is intended to
be useful to people who have to take decisions. The information may be interesting to someone who does not contem-
plate any decision, but it would not be classified as
accounting unless it was prepared under the expectation
that it would influence some decision. However, many
kinds of information may guide decisions and yet not be
regarded as accounting — weather reports, for example.
One type of information normally classified as accounting
is information prepared in financial terms to guide

financial decisions; and yet to narrow the definition of the subject to the preparation and analysis of information expressed in money terms would be to narrow it excessively. Perhaps the nature of accounting information is conveyed most usefully if we regard it as information concerned with the use or distribution of resources — including money but including also quantities of other resources, labour, materials and so on — and dealing with outputs in money terms or in terms of other measures associated with personal satisfaction. Such a definition makes it difficult to distinguish accounting from some activities traditionally carried out by economists — but that is as it should be because accounting is essentially a branch of economics.

An accountant often has to deal with problems of communication because he prepares information for use by someone else. Communication is important to accounting and there is a need for research into methods of improving the efficiency of communication of accounting information. However, communication is not essential to accounting. Information is none the less accounting because it is prepared and used by the same person.

Accounting has many interfaces with other subjects. It is quite difficult to list activities which are frequently undertaken by accountants and which are clearly peculiar to accounting, not part of the domain of any other discipline. For example, the measurement of income is of central importance to the work of accountants. The computational technique used in the work, double-entry book-keeping, is perhaps peculiar to accounting, and yet the concepts of income measurement are of central importance to the study of economics as well as accounting. Auditing is another activity central to the work of accountants, and yet the auditor, attempting to satisfy himself that a set of accounts shows a true and fair view of the results of some business, applies a number of tests the legitimacy of which depends on the concepts of the design of systems and on the principles of statistical sampling.

We should not be concerned at the hybrid nature of accounting methods. Borderline disputes between subjects are normally sterile and the ability to draw on the concepts and techniques of many disciplines is a source of potential strength. The implementation of the research proposals outlined below will involve exploring the border country between accounting and many other subjects: economics, the applied mathematics used in operational research, the psychology of individual and group behaviour, law, statistics and others. Such imprecision of subject classification is characteristic of modern developments in social and business sciences. Indeed, it is perhaps true to say that a higher proportion than ever before of significant research of any kind is inter-disciplinary in nature. In the case of accounting, however, the nature of the subject seems to make it especially open to interdisciplinary development.

Accounting as a science

We noted above the important role that scientific method has in the development of research in accounting. We now examine this approach to research in greater detail. The term 'scientific method' may be understood in several senses including a quite general sense which covers all methods which contribute to the development of knowledge. However, we intend something much more specific. The essence of scientific method according to our use of the term is in its empirical content. The method involves the formulation of hypotheses to explain the relationships between variables which are being studied (for example, the positions of the Sun and planets in the Solar System) and subsequently the examination of evidence of values actually taken by the variables to discover whether the hypotheses are supported or refuted.

The state of mind involved in applications of scientific method may be contrasted with an authoritarian state of mind. The authoritarian may well argue that, for example, planets must revolve around the Sun (or indeed the Earth) in circular orbits because eminent men have believed a circle to be a perfect geometrical form. The empiricist, adopting scientific method, will carry out some observations to discover whether actual successive positions of the bodies are consistent with circular orbits. A good scientist knows that his findings will be more convincing the more he has tested them in unfavourable conditions without discrediting them. Consequently, he will conduct some of his observations in situations in which his hypotheses seem most likely to be refuted.

Accounting involves the collection and analysis of information which is useful to people who have to take decisions. An accountant therefore has to choose which classes of people he will try to help and with which kinds of decision. Any particular choice cannot be said to be valid or invalid in a scientific sense although the accountant may be discouraged from some choices by the harshest of all empirical mechanisms — if he chooses to assist decisions of slight importance, he is unlikely to be well rewarded for his efforts.

Scientific method is of primary importance, however, in considering whether a particular type of information, analysed in a particular way, is the most useful basis for a particular decision. In the past, accounting has tended to approach such questions in an authoritarian manner. It has tended to assume that information is useful simply because it has been prepared according to a set of rules which is in accord with long-observed conventions of the subject. The scientist would assert that we cannot be confident about the usefulness of some particular information until we have empirical evidence that people elect to use it even though other information is available. One possible approach to the identification of useful information would involve a researcher in selecting several types of information, according to *a priori* reasoning, as having relevance to a decision and then presenting actual information corresponding to those types to decision-takers. The choice of the best kinds of information would be estimated from observations of the behaviour of many decision-takers who had been faced with such a choice. The empirical test would not be a sufficient basis for choice. We should wish also to have a theoretical justification of the relevance of the information. It is, however, a necessary basis. One kind of information can be regarded as preferable to another kind, with high confidence, only if it has been observed to be preferred frequently in practice.

The accounting environment

We next turn from a discussion of research methods to a discussion of the forces which shape research needs.

The historical development of accounting represents a response to the development of society. The earliest

accounting activities probably involved the preparation of
plans for a group of people to erect a religious monument or
the planning of crop production and the division of the
yield. Such accounting activities probably took place 4000
years ago or even earlier. For most of the intervening period,
social and economic development has been slow, but each
step has been matched by some development in accounting
enabling the institutions of the time to operate effectively.
The Roman Empire was served by a system for controlling
the financing of a complex state including the payment of
the armies which maintained order in the provinces. Under
the manorial system in Britain people would assume
various obligations in return for the protection of a Lord of
the Manor. The observance of the obligations was super-
vised by various agents helped by an appropriate system of
accounting. The mediaeval trading companies were
amongst the first examples of large private enterprises.
Their needs provoked further developments in accounting
methods — indeed their needs were instrumental in the
development of the double-entry system of accounting, one
of the most significant technical developments in the
history of accounting and one which still dominates much
thinking in accounting at the present time. More recently,
the industrial revolution stimulated the development of
large-scale manufacturing enterprises, a development
which could be secured only by a separation of owners and
managers; for managers could not themselves provide
sufficient capital to finance activity on so large a scale. In
response to this situation, accounting came to focus on
reporting to absentee owners on the handling by managers
of the resources entrusted to them.

As the above discussion would lead us to expect, problems
which seem important in accounting at the present time do
so because of corresponding problems in society. We need to
study the provision of accounting information for trade
unions because of the power which trade unions have today
to influence the progress of our economy, and the
desirability of ensuring that they use the power responsibly.
We need to study means of providing information to ensure that business organisations are behaving in a manner
consistent with national interests, because society has
developed to a point at which we can no longer regard as an

adequate safeguard, the checks and balances of a free market economy. We need to study the international harmonisation of accounting practices because of the growing importance of international cooperation as evidenced in the European Economic Community and because of the growing number of companies whose operations cross national boundaries. Attention has been focused on the adjustment of accounts for inflation because we have recently observed, in a particularly dramatic way, the power of inflation to distort economic relationships and the interpretation of accounting reports. We wish to promote the standardisation of accounting practice because we have recently seen cases in which undesirable consequences have been associated with variety in practice.

The relationship between accounting methods and the needs of society seems clearest if we study a long period of time in broad outline. We then see that accounting methods normally respond to social demands after some time lag. On a shorter time scale, however, the match is less close. Sometimes accounting practice seems to fall behind social needs or even to change in the wrong direction. There are also occasions on which research moves ahead of practice as a result of experimentation with techniques developed in other disciplines. The results of such research may be incorporated into the main stream of accounting development but only if they can be shown to meet important social needs. Recent examples of such developments have been provided by some academic researchers who have developed large-scale mathematical models as aids to decision taking; others have studied the effect of accounting systems on the behaviour of employees to provide a basis for conclusions on the merits of the motivational effects of the systems. Such studies are beginning to exercise an influence on accounting practice, but their potential is not yet fully established.

One aspect of the environment which is important for the development of accounting practice and for the planning of accounting research concerns the division of economic activity between small privately owned organisations, large privately owned organisations and governments. In order to identify the relevance of this line of thought, let us consider what type of business organisation would involve the fewest difficulties for accountants and others concerned with financial decisions. The form of organisation in question would be one which involved the selling of all outputs and the buying and hiring of all resources in perfectly competitive markets. Perfect markets involve free competition between large numbers of individuals or firms; they have the consequence that the good or service concerned is bought and sold at a price which is constant at any time for all participants in the market, and the price cannot be influenced by the activities of any participant because each has too small an impact on his own. Private or government monopolies in the sale of goods are ruled out, as are trade union monopolies on the supply of labour. No firm would systematically make a profit in excess of a normal rate of interest on its capital employed — any such profit would be eroded by competition leading to price reductions. The congenial simplicity of the environment may be enhanced if we also assume that all effects of production would be appropriately priced — there would be no social costs of business activity, no one, for example, behaving in such an anti-social way as to pollute the environment without bearing a cost appropriate to the dis-utility he had caused.

In such a world of perfect markets, accounting would be a simple matter. Little analysis would be needed to guide decisions. Since firms would have to accept prevailing market prices, their decisions would merely involve estimating the chances of being able to produce an output at a cost which did not exceed price. Problems of control would also be relatively easy to manage. It would be necessary to monitor standards of performance and to keep track of assets and liabilities but the complexity of such tasks would be limited because of the normally quite small size of firms.

The situation described in the last two paragraphs could not exist in practice for most goods and services. It is generally admitted that governments must provide some services — such as defence — because it is not practicable for each individual citizen to purchase some quantity of the service appropriate to his personal tastes. In addition, the economies of large-scale production are bound to lead to the situation in which a few large firms dominate the production of certain products; and some of the effects of firms' activities will not be priced according to market mechanisms — there will be social costs (such as pollution) and perhaps social benefits.

These inevitable departures from the idealised environment of perfectly competitive markets generate more complex problems for accountants — and other people. It is more difficult to exercise financial control over a large organisation than a small one: the financial plans are more complex and it is more difficult to see that they are carried out. Large organisations also have to consider financial analyses of more complex decisions. They do not take the prices of their products as fixed in the market: they have power to fix prices for themselves and they need accounting information to guide their decisions. They also need accounting analyses of the worthwhileness of complex investment projects.

It is also important to appreciate that large organisations are more likely than small ones to meet difficulties in communicating financial information to people outside the organisation. A small business may be owned by one or a few people who can discover much of the information in a flexible manner by direct experience or by personal contact; it may have only a few employees who can satisfy their information needs by similarly informal methods. A large business, however, has to rely on finding acceptable standard forms for communications between managers, owners (shareholders), employees and others; and it lacks a simple means for discovering the needs of all the groups concerned.

The existence of significant social costs and benefits also generates additional problems for accountants — problems which they have not yet confronted in a systematic way. Nationalised industries and other government organisations will probably wish to treat social costs in much the same way as private costs — as something which must be covered by the benefits resulting from their operations; this implies the need to measure the social costs, a process which makes considerable demands on ingenuity. In private firms there may be a similar need for a different reason: governments may wish to hold firms to account for social costs they incur in order to control their incidence and that is possible only if the costs have been measured.

The dominant position of large scale business and of government activity has grown considerably in recent years and that growth has been partly inevitable. The economic advantage of large units is clear in some industries and some social changes, widely accepted as desirable, could be achieved only by government. However, there remains a substantial element of real choice. It is not inevitable that large firms and government should have grown exactly to the extent they have. In order to judge whether the present balance is a good one, we need to know more about the relative advantages and disadvantages of size. We need to improve our capacities to undertake cost benefit analyses, research studies to which many specialists have a contribution to make: economists, behavioural scientists, political scientists and others.

The accountant also has an important contribution to make to the required research. He has available techniques which will enable him to analyse and evaluate the difficulties in securing effective financial control over large organisations. If there exist two small organisations which trade with each other, their wish to seek their own advantage, subject to constraints imposed by the market, will enforce on them some discipline which will promote minimum standards of efficiency. If the two organisations merge, so that their previous transactions with each other now become internal, the motivational pressures change and it may become possible for the large organisation to survive with lower standards of efficiency. In such a situation, the accountant may try to develop new systems which simulate some aspects of the previous situation and hence retain some of its advantages. The accountant can contribute to our knowledge of the advantages and disadvantages of large firms by developing systems appropriate to the larger organisations, and by evaluating advantages and disadvantages of small and large firms — differential costs of control, differential levels of efficiency taking account of motivational factors and so on. Some research on such topics has already been undertaken but much remains to be done.

Another impact of the dominance of business activity by large organisations is worth noting at this point. If a firm is one of the several small units operating in a market, it will base its decisions on estimates of the market price for the resources it needs and on estimates of demand conditions for its products; it has in effect to optimise its position in relation to given market conditions. If firms are individually large, however, they are more likely to be operating in conditions such that they influence the market substantially by their own actions or such that a market can hardly be said to exist at all; in these circumstances decisions are likely to depend on negotiations with other large organisations. One firm may negotiate a bulk supply contract with another firm; it may negotiate with a trade union over conditions of employment and indeed about methods of operation; it may negotiate with the government over some special assistance and so on.

The widespread importance of processes of negotiation has implications for accounting. Accounting information is required to support negotiating procedures by giving estimates of the probable consequences, from the viewpoints of both parties to the negotiation of various possible settlements. It is necessary to identify potential conflicts of interest, 'fall-back' positions and so on; such questions have not been the concern of traditional accounting information, directed towards advising people who have to undertake arms-length transactions in open markets.

The information needs of external users

We now turn to a more specific consideration of the research needs in particular topics in accounting. It is convenient to subdivide the discussion into two sections, one dealing with accounting for external users of information, the other with accounting for internal users. The division is intended to separate a study of the detailed systems required by managers to guide decisions and control within the firm from a study of the aggregated information required by groups who are associated with an organisation. Shareholders comprise the most frequently studied group of external users. Employees will also be regarded as a group of external users because they require information to guide decisions on their relationship with an organisation even though they also work in the organisation.

There now exists a well-defined framework for studying

the information needs of various external users. The framework has appeared in the literature only recently, however, and much work remains to be undertaken on the development of its implications. The framework may be summarised as follows:

1   The first step is to identify the users of accounting information.

2   Next, it is necessary to study the behaviour of each group of users in order to understand the nature of the decisions for which accounting information is required, the goals which the users are trying to achieve in their decisions and the capabilities of the users for analysing information.

3   Thirdly, one has to identify the various types of accounting statement that might be provided to the user in order to help him most effectively with his decisions.

4   Finally, it is necessary to choose the optimal type of accounting statement.

Let us consider the research implications of these four steps. Step 1, the identification of users, seems relatively simple. It is necessary simply to develop a list of groups of users agreed by consensus to have some kind of entitlement to receive information. This description suggests that the first stage of the process is unscientific but it is hard to see how it could be otherwise. We might prefer to leave a decision on who should receive accounting information to normal market processes. Groups would then receive information if they were prepared to pay for it (or impose its receipt as a condition in some wider contract) and they would receive as much information as they were willing to pay for. However, such a process could not work, partly because information could not be preserved for the exclusive use of those who had paid for it, partly because some users are not organised into groups and partly because of difficulties in establishing a pricing policy given that all accounting information would be produced from a common system at a common cost. Consequently, we need some general rules about the conditions under which information will be disseminated.

In practice, it is not difficult to derive an agreed list of users. Most people would agree that the list should include at least shareholders, potential investors, creditors, employees, customers and the representatives of society at large; and it is not important to agree a priority ranking. We could conduct empirical research to attempt to make sure that no important users had been overlooked but it is not very likely that we should identify any users whose interest had not been noted in the literature.

Empirical research is much more important in the second stage of our decision framework dealing with a study of the decision process. We need to know what kinds of decision are taken by the users of accounting information. To a certain extent, this also is obvious. Shareholders take decisions on how to vote at company meetings and on whether to buy or sell shares; employees take decisions on what demands to make in negotiations over pay claims, conditions of employment and so on. There may be other types of use which are less obvious, however. It is not clear how many customers examine the accounts of a business before buying its product on the grounds that they wish to be satisfied about its prospects for continuing in business and being able to satisfy their service requirements; but it would be desirable to have such information before deciding whether to devote resources to the development of accounting reports that are useful for customers.

However, the main reason for undertaking empirical studies of the ways in which accounting reports are used at the present time is in the need to obtain insights into the objectives which the decision-takers are seeking. We cannot judge what information would be useful until we understand these objectives. Such studies may require the researcher to ask people about their objectives and about their thought processes when they are taking decisions; they may also involve observations of actual decision processes. The empirical work may be guided by normative models of economics and other subjects. Normative models indicate that decision takers try to predict the future costs and benefits associated with each feasible decision and select the course which gives greatest satisfaction — not perhaps a very surprising conclusion; more substantially, however, they may also give indications of how the costs and benefits should be evaluated. Without supplementation from empirical surveys, however, the normative models may be misleading. They do not, for example, indicate to what extent the limited ability of decision-takers to undertake complex analysis or process a large amount of information may effectively redirect objectives to some simple proxy for what is fundamentally desired. Nor do they indicate what non-cash effects (such as association with a company with a desirable product line) are considered to be important and how they are compared to cash effects.

The remainder of the process of identifying optimal accounting information consists of an examination of alternative forms of accounting report and a selection of the one or ones which best satisfy the needs of users. No doubt there remains scope for creative imagination in the search for new methods of accounting not previously described. There is also a great deal of work to be done in testing the usefulness of methods which have already been used in practice or described in the literature. It is important to understand that methods used in practice are based on long-standing convention and have not passed rigorous tests of usefulness; nor have they shown their superiority in competition with methods which have been proposed as alternatives.

So we come to the most difficult research problem. How should we select the best accounting method? We have indicated that individuals have to form expectations of future events as a basis for decisions. It follows that an accounting report, if it is to be useful, must assist the making of predictions of the future. We should test a proposed method of accounting by investigating its usefulness in making predictions: we should apply the predictive value criterion. Some insights into the predictive value of accounting information may be obtained 'in the laboratory'. We may experiment with predictions using simulated data and we may also ask people to make predictions using real data to guide fictitious decisions. However, the usefulness of an accounting method for prediction may not be tested fully in this way. The ability of a skilled research worker to use accounting information to make effective predictions does not demonstrate that the same information would have general usefulness. Use of a particular type of information could be justified only by showing that, in actual practice, it enabled the more accurate prediction of events regarded as important. Consequently, the choice of a method of accounting depends ultimately on the experimental use and study of alternative types of information.

The above description is silent about the cost of producing accounting information. However, cost must be taken into account. Clearly, we should not be willing to bear a very large cost to provide information which had only a small chance of improving the predictions of relevant events. The allowance in our analysis for the cost of producing information is complicated because, as we have already noted, the costs cannot normally be charged to those who benefit. We may avoid this difficulty by taking an aggregate view of the social effect. We conclude that the provision of accounting information should be expanded only so long as incremental benefits are greater than incremental costs. The implementation of this rule raises some difficult theoretical and practical research questions concerned with the measurement of benefits and costs.

We conclude this section by amplifying one or two points touched on above. Mention has been made of the possibility that decision-takers may wish to predict costs and benefits which do not arise in cash terms. For example, shareholders and employees may both wish to take account of the social acceptability of a firm's product before deciding whether to accept association with the firm. The measurement of such non-cash factors presents many interesting research problems, and those problems are particularly important in the preparation of reports to enable representatives of society (parliament) to control the activities of firms. Such reports would involve the classical problems of cost-benefit analysis as developed in the study of economics. Measures are required for reporting on the costs and benefits imposed or conferred by the activities of a firm on society at large, rather than on its shareholders or employees alone.

Finally, in dealing with research prospects in external reporting, we may note that separate research may be required to develop optimal forms of accounting for different types of organisation. The above discussion may relate most easily to privately owned businesses. However it may also be applied to questions concerning the ways in which public sector organisations should give account — local authorities to their ratepayers and central government to its taxpayers; similarly special considerations may arise in the ways in which other organisations give account: charities to benefactors, friendly societies to their members and so on.

Management information

In some respects, research into management information systems is further developed than research into reporting to external users. The problems of communication are perhaps less of an obstacle in the case of management information: the users of the information are also the people who organise its provision.

Like external reporting, studies of management information requirements rest on a well-developed theoretical structure. The structure recognises two inter-linked processes as forming a series of activities which must be carried out by managers: decision and control. The decision phase of managers' activities involves specifying the objectives of the organisation and identifying the range of alternative courses of action which may be contemplated — what products should be manufactured, in what quantities and using what resources; what prices should be charged for the products; what investments should be under-taken and how they should be financed; and so on. It is then necessary to establish a relationship between the different courses of action which may be selected and the objectives in a way which will make it possible to estimate the optimal set of decisions. This part of the process is often known as model-building — the relationship being the model — particularly where operational research techniques such as linear programming are used in the analysis.

Once good decisions have been taken, it remains necessary to ensure that they are converted into good results. The control part of the management information system deals with this problem. Essentially, the control task is to monitor actual results and compare them with expected results. Differences represent danger signals which should be investigated and may indicate the need for corrective action. It is desirable to monitor not only the results of the organisation concerned, but also various aspects of the external environment which may predict future divergences between actual results and plans and hence represent an early warning system.

The decision phase and the control phase of the information system together represent an integrated feedback cycle. The decision leads to control processes which enable the organisation to learn about its performance and feedback the knowledge into improved decisions and so on.

Recent academic research on management information systems has concentrated on two fronts: model-building, using techniques developed in operational research, and applications of behavioural science.

In a modern large industrial organisation many of the activities are interdependent — it is often misleading to consider, say, the optimal output of one product as an independent decision. The optimal output of one product often depends on the output levels of other products because they are produced by the same limited stock of plant and machinery, drawing on the same limited pool of skilled labour. Consequently, decisions concerning the prices and outputs of different products and levels of investment in plant and machinery have to be settled as an interconnected set. That is a complex analytical problem which cannot be easily solved using routine arithmetical calculations. It may be handled by developing large-scale mathematical models of the processes of an organisation, models which can be analysed using the techniques of simulation or linear programming.

Several such models have been described in the literature and, indeed, numerous articles have been written dealing with esoteric mathematical points which arise in their analysis. Little progress has been made, however, in the practical applications of the main decision models. One or two isolated applications have shown that the methods can be made feasible but these have related to specialised firms. Much work is needed to show how the data requirements of large models can be met in practice. More fundamentally, perhaps, work is needed to show how the models can fit into the process of decision and control in a way which enables managers to relate to the models successfully whilst maintaining effective control of operations. No calculations can deal with all possible results of decisions. Managers are accustomed to receive calculations as a guide to decisions, but they normally have to make subjective modifications to the indications given by the calculations to take account of factors not dealt with — strategic factors, for example. Operational research models will work only if they give managers scope to make such modifications.

Even if a carefully designed system for decision and control can be made to work, the effects of its operation may be unexpected. There are two main reasons for this. First, individuals' capacities for processing information may be limited or biassed, and that may cause an unexpected reaction to information provided to them. The second reason concerns the motivations of the managers who use accounting information. Individuals have personal objectives. If we wish them to contribute to the attainment of group (firm) objectives, we must make that end compatible with their personal objectives — we must give the individuals adequate motivation. A system for decision and control may appear to be effective on the drawing-board, yet if it fails to give adequate rewards or satisfaction to employees its actual effect may be to reduce the achievement of the firm's goals. For example, a sales manager who is paid a commission may conspire to hold down prices in order to increase sales revenue even though the information system indicates that higher prices would be likely to yield increased profits. At an extreme an information system may put pressure on employees so that they are motivated to frustrate its operation by feeding it false information or they may even simply refuse to operate it.

Our understanding of such behavioural factors is developing but remains in need of much more research. Further understanding depends mainly on studies of the actual effects of operating different kinds of system. The development of managerial information systems, including managerial accounting, is not urgently in need of further work on the specification of models. The need is for empirical work to identify the characteristics of systems which are successful in practice.

Conclusion

In this chapter, I have commented on what seem to me to be amongst the most important research issues in accounting.

The coverage is inevitably selective. I have ignored such fields as auditing and taxation where the specialist can doubtless perceive equally exciting challenges. My intention, however, has not been to present a comprehensive coverage but rather to illustrate the nature of the research which now seems to be needed and to suggest a framework for that research.

The reader of this chapter may feel that I have described a situation in which research needs are very great and that, in doing so, I have revealed a subject which is in an early state of its theoretical development. I would not dissent from that view. Accounting is an old-established subject. It has, perhaps, satisfied adequately the demands made upon it at many stages in history. During the last two or three hundred years, however, the demands have accelerated and practice has lagged behind. The reasons are not clear. Perhaps the development would have been more rapid if the subject had become established in universities at an earlier time. Whatever the reasons, the way now seems clear for rapid advances. The recognition, acknowledged above, that those advances depend on the application of scientific method seems the surest basis for confidence that they will take place.